# PATRIOT OF PERSIA

Christopher de Bellaigue was born in London in 1971, and was educated at Cambridge University where he read Iranian and Indian Studies. Between 1996 and 2007, he lived and worked as a journalist in South Asia and the Middle East, writing for *The Economist,* the *Financial Times,* the *Independent* and the *New York Review of Books.* His first book, *In the Rose Garden of the Martyrs,* was shortlisted for the Royal Society of Literature's Ondaatje Prize, and his second, *Rebel Land,* short-listed for the 2010 Orwell Prize, was described by the *New York Times* as a 'rare and remarkable feat'. He and his Iranian wife, the artist Bita Ghezelayagh, returned from Tehran to the UK in 2007 so that de Bellaigue could take up a fellow-ship at St Antony's College, Oxford. They now divide their time between London and Tehran.

ALSO BY CHRISTOPHER DE BELLAIGUE

*In the Rose Garden of the Martyrs*
*The Struggle for Iran*
*Rebel Land*

CHRISTOPHER DE BELLAIGUE

# Patriot of Persia

## Muhammad Mossadegh and a Very British Coup

VINTAGE BOOKS
London

Published by Vintage 2013

2 4 6 8 10 9 7 5 3 1

Copyright © Christopher de Bellaigue 2012

Christopher de Bellaigue has asserted his right under the Copyright,
Designs and Patents Act 1988 to be identified as the author of this work

First published in Great Britain in 2012 by
The Bodley Head

Vintage
Random House, 20 Vauxhall Bridge Road,
London SW1V 2SA

www.vintage-books.co.uk

Addresses for companies within The Random House Group Limited
can be found at: www.randomhouse.co.uk/offices.htm

The Random House Group Limited Reg. No. 954009

A CIP catalogue record for this book
is available from the British Library

ISBN 9780099540489

The Random House Group Limited supports The Forest Stewardship
Council® (FSC®), the leading international forest certification organisation.
Our books carrying the FSC label are printed on FSC® certified paper.
FSC is the only forest certification scheme supported by the leading
environmental organisations, including Greenpeace. Our
paper procurement policy can be found at:
www.randomhouse.co.uk/environment

Typeset by Palimpsest Book Production Limited, Falkirk, Stirlingshire
Printed and bound in Great Britain by Clays Ltd, St Ives PLC

به خردی به خوی کیان اخت شد

ازین روی نامش کیان دخت شد

# Author's note

Persia is the old European name for Iran. Iran is an even older, indigenous name. In the 1930s Reza Shah told foreigners to stop using the name Persia, but some ignored him. Later on his son Muhammad-Reza Shah revoked the ban. It is now customary for Iranians and foreigners alike to refer to the country as Iran, although some Iranians living outside the country introduce themselves as Persian. I use both terms interchangeably.

# Contents

# Acknowledgements

It would not have occurred to me to write this book without the experience of living and working in Iran, an inspiration, in different ways, for so much that I write. To several scholars of Iran, most notably the late Iraj Afshar, Kaveh Bayat, Ali Dehbashi, Mansoureh Ettehadieh, John Gurney, Homa Katouzian, Paul Luft, Abbas Milani, Mustafa Nouri, Kamal Parsi-Pour, Morteza Rassoolipour, Yann Richard and Kamran Safamanesh, I am grateful for inspiration and practical help, while others, including my parents-in-law Abtin Ghezelayagh and Manijeh Amini, Muhammad-Hossein Zeynali and Mahmoud Emami-Naini, were also forthcoming with encouragement and support.

I enjoyed important institutional backing. In 2007–2008 I was the beneficiary of the fellowship that was endowed by that fine historian, Sir Alistair Horne, at St Antony's College, Oxford, where I also received much kindness from Margaret Macmillan, Avi Shlaim and Timothy Garton-Ash. The British Academy gave me a generous grant. I used superb resources: in Tehran, the Institute for Iranian Contemporary Historical Studies (where I am particularly grateful to Akbar Mashouf, Ahmad Fazeli and Ghollamreza Sharifi-Ashtiyani) and the Library of the Majles, and, in Britain, the library of the Middle East Institute at St Antony's, the British Library, the National Archives, the library of the School of Oriental and African Studies and, most pleasurably, the London Library.

From the Mossadegh family, Hedayat Matine-Daftary and Majid Bayat gave generously of their time – to recall, advise and, not infrequently, correct. Farhad Diba was forthcoming with counsel and suggestions. John Gurney, Homa Katouzian and Hedayat Matine-Daftary were kind enough to offer comments on the finished manuscript. My father Eric de Bellaigue, performed his usual task of suggesting stylistic improvements. My agent, Peter Straus, ably assisted by Jenny Hewson, my publishers, Will Sulkin at The Bodley Head and Terry Karten at HarperCollins, Kay Peddle of The Bodley Head, who prepared the book for publication, and Clara Womersley, my publicist, were something of a dream team for a writer. My homeland dream team, Bita, Jahan and Kiana, endured, grew and came out smiling.

# Prologue

## *Father of the Nation*

I have an Iranian friend who is too young to remember Mossadegh, but her parents were in public life and were close to him. When my friend was a small child and Mossadegh was living out his last years under house arrest, he sent her sweets. Her mother picked the wrappers from the floor, flattened them, and put them somewhere safe. Now my friend is a middle-aged woman with two strapping sons, but she has kept the sweet wrappers. They are like a sign, planted in the soft soil of her childhood, showing what she owes to whom.

When Mossadegh was prime minister in the early 1950s, and the world was coming down around his ears, a grizzled villager called Ayub found himself in the great man's presence. Mossadegh was lying on his famous iron bed, which had been moved to the balcony on account of the heat. Ayub felt awkward and embarrassed until suddenly the prime minister seized him with his surprisingly strong arms and embraced him. Ayub had never met Mossadegh before. His eyes filled with tears and he was unable to speak for emotion. Iran was not a place where prime ministers embraced peasants.

A lot of sentimentality surrounds Muhammad Mossadegh, and at first sight there is something startling about this. Mossadegh was a peculiar man. He was quite bald and had a long, drooping, rather bent nose, and thin, sensual lips, and he fainted and howled in public. He was a shameless hypochondriac and quite often threatened to die. He seemed always to have been ancient – from around the age of forty, when the last of his hair abstracted itself from his head, he looked a decade older than he really was. He ran Iran, which is a big and complicated country, wearing a pair of pyjamas.

In many western countries, eccentrics are barred from high office by the innate caution of the party machine. There was no party machine in Iran in the 1950s; politics was about personalities and Mossadegh was the biggest of them all. Far from disbar him from the public's affection, advanced age meant respect and a licence to behave oddly. Mossadegh used these advantages to bamboozle his enemies and captivate his friends. Winston Churchill considered 'Mussy Duck', as he called him, to be a lunatic. To millions of his compatriots, Mossadegh personified their country more completely than anyone else. Quite simply, he was Iran.

He started life conventionally enough, a product of the Persian upper class, in the last decades of the nineteenth century. In the 1920s and 1930s he achieved fame with a struggle against royal despotism which almost cost him his life. Mossadegh became notorious around the world in 1951, when he dared to nationalise Britain's biggest overseas asset, the Anglo-Iranian Oil Company. He went on to lead the most enlightened government his country has ever known. The British wanted revenge and they enlisted the help of the United States on the grounds that Mossadegh was a communist stooge. On August 19, 1953, he was overthrown by a conspiracy hatched by the American and British secret services in favour of the Shah. He was banished to his estate and became a non-person under the Shah's new dictatorship. The father of the nation had been cast aside, but he was impossible to forget.

'Father of the Nation' – many Middle Eastern rulers have claimed this title for themselves. It exempts them from popular scrutiny, indulges their every beastly act. 'Don't give me grief for knocking my people about,' the dictator chides, 'for one occasionally has to be cruel to be kind.' Mossadegh was remarkable in his region in that he did not feel the need to be cruel. He was not a soldier, deriving prestige from the pips on his shoulders and the shine on his shoes. He did not borrow his authority, like a mullah, from God. It was all his own.

He was more than a politician, and less than one. As a reader of his public, he was unrivalled. But he spent his life fleeing from office and his refusal to compromise his principles for the political good was pure obstinacy and pride. He was an old-fashioned hero and this explains another, rather surprising element in his renown. Mossadegh did not end up a political winner. The 1953 coup was a catastrophe which slammed him to the floor, and from which Iran never fully recovered. But Iranians are kind towards heroes who fall. It depends on the manner of the fall, because a valiant defeat against overwhelming odds at the hands of a malignant evil is regarded as victory on a higher, metaphysical plane. The epics are full of such heroes, and the story of Islam would not be complete without them.

Mossadegh was instrumental in his own downfall. His judgement failed him at the zenith of events, for it is a captain's job to steer his ship into calmer waters and Mossadegh was driven on by his obsession, into the teeth of the storm. The Shah lived to tell the tale, and he had pretensions to captaincy of his own. With America's help he built a magnificent ship which turned out to be made of paper and was swamped by the first wave.

Years later, the United States would recognise publicly that, in toppling Mossadegh, they had made a terrible mistake, for in the process they stifled values that were in sympathy with their own. In 2000, Madeleine Albright, President Clinton's secretary of state, acknowledged that in 1953 the United States played a 'significant role in orchestrating the overthrow of Iran's popular prime minister, Muhammad Mossadegh', and that this had clearly been 'a setback for Iran's political development'.

Mossadegh was the first liberal leader of the modern Middle East. He was a rationalist who hated obscurantism and believed in the primacy of the law. His understanding of freedom was exceptional in Iran and the wider region. Indeed, the West would have liked him more if he had been less committed to freedom. He would not back down from his demand for economic independence from Britain. He would not lock up communists to please Washington.

The plot to oust him was benighted. In the long run, it did great harm to western interests. It was the start of a US policy in support of shoddy Middle Eastern despots, which suffered its first defeat in 1979, when Ayatollah Khomeini's Islamic revolutionaries over-threw the Shah, and unravelled further with the Arab Spring of 2011. The undeclared logic of this policy was thus: 'Middle Easterners cannot be trusted with independence and freedom; pro-American strongmen offer the best hope of stability.' Saddam Hussein was such a strongman. So was Hosni Mubarak. The rogues' gallery is long and well lit.

In his bellicose way, President George W. Bush tried to challenge this policy. More subtly, President Barack Obama did too. But it is the people of the Middle East, indifferent to the occupant of the White House, who will eventually shrug it off.

I first understood the importance of Mossadegh after I went to live in Iran in 2000. A political thaw was underway in the Islamic Republic, and while the ruling hardliners had little good to say about a secular, nationalist prime minister from the 1950s, he was a poster boy for many younger Iranians. A considerable number of books and articles were being published in Persian about him and his era. His hangdog face seemed to be everywhere. And yet he was spoken of with regret and even guilt, as well as reverence. Could more have been done to save him when the coup-makers closed in on August 19, 1953? Were the people, ultimately, complicit in his overthrow? Most important of all, why did his vision for Iran not materialise?

I was one of a tiny number of westerners in Tehran during the unrest which followed the contested election of Mahmud Ahmadinejad, in 2009, and never in that torrid, terrible summer, as thousands of people did battle with their inestimably better-equipped adversaries, and were eventually crushed, was Mossadegh far from my mind. I researched this book as the capital smouldered and crackled – going to the historical institutes and taking notes, poring over newspaper archives – and the more I researched the past, the more I realised that events in the streets were a new battle in an old war. Democracy and authoritarianism faced each other. Nationalism and religion were the bugle calls. Mossadegh would have been at home.

In Iran, it is not always wise to acknowledge links between the present and the past. During one confrontation between protesters and the security forces, I found myself trapped in the house of Iraj Afshar, an eminent historian. We sat on his terrace and I asked him what he made of the events unfolding outside his gate. He smiled and invited me to admire his tomato plants.

Afshar was one of several distinguished historians who encouraged me to recount for a western audience this extraordinary life. I was also drawn by the continuities that Afshar did not acknowledge – the relevance of Mossadegh's ideals to the aspirations of millions of others in the Middle East, and the warning that his story serves to any adventurer occupying the White House or Downing Street. As the region inches along its path to change, and the West asks itself how to react, our decision-makers must look at 1953 and vow: never again!

Mossadegh has not been neglected by historians writing in English. He has been the subject of fine political biographies. American scholars such as Mark Gasiorowski of Louisiana State University have painstakingly investigated the West's machinations against him. But nowhere have the man and his fullness been brought out, and this is partly due to the wall that modern politics has interposed between Iran and the West. The standard popular account of the coup was penned by the journalist Stephen Kinzer, who does not read Persian. This is a bit like writing about Pearl Harbor knowing only Japanese.

As an Englishman who is married to an Iranian and spends part of the year in Tehran, I learned long ago to suspend all patriotic urges when writing about Iran. Approaching Mossadegh has necessitated even more rigour because of his famous loathing of Britain, and his desire to end British meddling. In Mossadegh's time, millions of Iranians attributed to the British an almost boundless capacity for mischief. Although Mossadegh's hatred of Britain clouded his judgement, I regret to say that it rested on sure foundations. Mossadegh saw the hidden hand of the British everywhere because that is where it was.

From an American perspective, the tragedy of Mossadegh is that the United States allowed itself to become Britain's accomplice and trigger-man. American agents overthrew him according to a British plan. Until then, Iranian nationalists such as Mossadegh had regarded the US as a force for good in the world. This view clouded as evidence for US involvement in the coup emerged, and by the time of the 1979 revolution it had been blocked out entirely. Nowadays, America and Britain are vilified in equal measure.

Mossadegh would have been highly amused by the idea of an Englishman writing his biography. I do not wish to invite sympathy, for my experiences in Iran have been mostly happy; however, living in a country where Anglophobia runs deep, I have sometimes felt as though I was bearing the cross of my forefathers' misdemeanours. I have been forced onto the defensive, and on occasion felt positively browbeaten. Only once did I knowingly exploit the fear and loathing that Britain inspires, and now, in the interests of transparency, I must declare myself.

I have an old leather briefcase which I once took for repair to a dealer in leather goods near the British Embassy. When I went to pick it up, the same man said that I would have to pay double the quote he had given me. I objected but he stood firm. He would return my case only if I paid the higher price. Furious, I leaned across the counter and looked into his eyes. Then, pointing to the Union Jack fluttering a little way up the road, I said in as menacing a voice as I could muster, 'It seems you have forgotten which embassy stands there at the top of your street.'

It took a second or two for the man to register the threat. Then the colour drained from his cheeks. 'All right!' he said. 'All right! Give me whatever you want! Just take your briefcase and go!'

# I

# The Unchanging East

Muhammad Mossadegh was born in 1882, in the *belle époque*, one of the most dramatic eras of transformation the world has ever known. Huge numbers of people were moving from the countryside to the towns, and once-unimaginable strides were made in technology, medicine, education and hygiene. The bourgeoisie and the working class became dominant; the old aristocracies declined and the last vestiges of serfdom disappeared. These were the triumphs of modern thought, which would blow away the cobwebs of backwardness and superstition, and while they were concentrated in Europe and the United States, they had meaning for every nation. The world watched the western laboratory, with its physicists, tycoons and arms manufacturers, and waited to see if it would prosper or explode.

To begin with, witnesses of epochal change may be content to watch; then comes the impulse to take part. At the end of the nineteenth century, inquisitive people across the globe experienced such an impulse, and the result was a wave of emulative political and cultural movements, imported from the West but coloured by home-grown traditions, whose goal was the spread of human dignity, freedom and prosperity. Soon, these movements came up against strong barriers. They either jarred with local customs or with the interests of the European powers from which they derived inspiration – or both. This is when the trouble began.

Christian Europe had pulled ahead of the Muslim Middle East after the Renaissance and the Enlightenment transformed attitudes towards knowledge and power. With that came a fantasy of ownership – the idea that progress was Europe's to bestow, and not the common destiny of mankind. The lines were calcified by imperialism and nationalism, outstanding features of the *belle époque*. Notions of racial and cultural superiority were not often challenged, even though they inhibited the exchange of ideas.

Back in the 1830s the British statesman Thomas Babington Macaulay had asserted the superiority of 'a single shelf of a good European library' over 'the whole native literature of India and Arabia . . . it is, I believe, no exaggeration to say, that all the historical information which has been collected from all the books written in the Sanskrit language is less valuable than what may be found in the most paltry abridgements used at preparatory schools in England.' (Macaulay, it is almost superfluous to say, was not a reader of Indian languages or Arabic.) Well over a century later, Britain's home secretary Herbert Morrison likened independence for the country's African colonies to 'giving a child of ten a latch-key, a bank account and a shotgun.' Between these dates, in English, French, German, Spanish, Portuguese and Dutch, innumerable similar statements were uttered and defended, ingested and refined. What, if not the superiority of Europe over the rest of the world, could account for the God-given gift of empire? Some of the subject races – the imperialists were forever creating divisions, and then subdivisions – were susceptible to improvement. Others were not.

Ideas of inherent superiority were much weaker in the Muslim Middle East. There, the global exchange of ideas had for centuries found expression in multi-ethnic blocs such as the Ottoman Empire, which stretched from Arabia into south and eastern Europe, and where the only true barrier between people was neither race nor geography, but religion. So, it was strange for the inhabitants of the Muslim lands to be told, as they now were, that their culture and way of life were anachronisms needing to be modernised or thrown away. In the dark ages – as Eurocentric a designation as you could find; they were not dark in the Middle East – Muslim sages had advanced the learning of the ancients while Europe stagnated. Their rulers had built the world's biggest and most developed cities, and their traders had traded at its furthest known extremities. Before that, the lands where Islam now flourished – Egypt; Mesopotamia; Persia – had been the cradles of civilisation itself.

Persia, heir to the great world empires that Herodotus had interpreted in terms of slightly appalled fascination, its poetic and artistic legacy picturesquely degraded, staggered on somewhere between the Ottoman Empire and British India. To the Europeans of the late nineteenth century, it was an object of curiosity and puzzlement, but rarely of pressing concern.

Persia's ancient world empires had been very great. Five centuries before the birth of Christ, the Achaemenids ruled from the Nile to the Indus, and the later Parthian and Sassanian kingdoms would be Rome's great rivals in the East. The Sassanians were finally subdued with the Arab invasions of the seventh century and the arrival of Islam. After that, the Persian-speaking area found its genius in a malleable, humorous, eminently exportable culture, a synthesis of Islam and older Iranian traditions that became the dominant cultural form over much of the Muslim world. The innovations of its poets, builders, scientists and craftsmen found expression as far afield as Central Asia, India and the Ottoman lands. Persian became an international language of culture; one of its best-loved exponents, the mystical poet Jalal ud-Din Rumi, was a Central Asian who spent most of his life in Turkey.

There was an imperial flourish in the seventeenth century, when the country's Safavid shahs expanded the borders and promoted trade and partnership with the Europeans, and their wealth and splendour became axioms used by Shakespeare and Racine. But the Safavids degenerated into parricide and fanaticism and fell to yet another external assault. Persia was a failed state until the last years of the eighteenth century, when the eunuch Agha Muhammad Khan of the Qajar tribe united the country once more.

Agha Muhammad Khan's nephew perpetuated the Qajar line, and the Qajars survived and multiplied, albeit not very gloriously. They managed to dominate most of the Persian plateau, corresponding roughly to the borders of modern Iran, but lost possessions in Khorasan (to the Afghans, backed by the British), and in the Caucasus (to a resurgent Russia). The Qajar shahs lorded it over a shrivelling empire and dreamed of regaining lost land and prestige. By the time of Mossadegh's birth, the longest-serving of the Qajar monarchs, the shrewd, libidinous Nasser ud-Din, used venerable titles – 'Centre of the Universe', 'Shadow of God' – which seemed to mock his peripheral position in world affairs.

Feebleness and irrelevance did not guarantee a quiet life at the end of the nineteenth century, for while Persia continued to seem forbiddingly large and inaccessible, the rest of the world had become dramatically smaller. Explorers and cartographers had shed light in the most obscure, uninhabited corners. A global economy, financed by global capital, was joining producers to consumers in evermore complex webs of mastery and subservience. The primacy of Europe's big powers in virtually every sphere was being entrenched by treaty and force of arms. Between 1876 and 1915 a quarter of the surface of the world changed ownership, with half a dozen European states taking the lion's share.

There were three main reasons why Persia was not formally included in this epic transfer. The first was that it was too poor to justify the expense of annexation. The second was that the two imperial powers which showed most interest in Persian affairs, Russia and Britain, were constrained by mutual wariness from trying to swallow the country whole. Finally, the Persians nimbly played off the powers against each other, extracting concessions while keeping both at arm's length.

The powers' interest in Persia had begun as a side-effect of the Great Game they were playing for India and its riches. If the Russians were to realise their long-standing dream of seizing the subcontinent, they would have to subdue or cross Persia. The British were equally determined to make sure that Persia, and particularly its eastern reaches, bordering India, never fell into Russian hands.

Over the course of the nineteenth century, the Great Game became an elaborate stalemate played out over thousands of miles. From the north, imperial Russia spread its influence. From the Persian Gulf in the south, a British lake serving India, the British did the same. Maintaining substantial delegations in Tehran, the Persian capital, the powers exercised immense influence over the country's affairs.

The result of all the attention was developmental stasis. The 'neighbours to the north and the south', as Russia and Britain were known, were a force for stability and continuity, preventing the country from breaking into fragments, but the powers regarded initiatives aimed at internal reform as likely to reduce their influence, so tended to block them. In Nasser ud-Din Shah, guarding his archaic prerogatives, they found a natural ally. The powers manipulated, flattered and threatened the Shah. They guided his policies and appointments. Their companies bid for internal monopolies and their banks extended loans which further increased Persia's foreign dependence. A pseudo-empire falling uneasily into the overlapping embrace of two real empires, the 'independent' Persia of the public declarations was a sham.

The country lagged even by the rock-bottom standards of the immediate neighbourhood. At a time when Ottoman Turkey, the 'sick man of Europe', was several decades into major administrative, military and economic reforms, Persia was ruled by an absolute monarch and its structure and methods of administration were mostly medieval. Senior offices were put up for sale, reading and writing were elite entertainments, and religious heterodoxy was punishable by death. More than 80 per cent of the population lived in the countryside and huge tracts were the personal fiefs of absentee landlords. There was virtually no modern transport system. By the eve of the First World War, railways had been built across Egypt, Turkey and Syria, and British India boasted more than 50,000 miles of track. Persia, by contrast, had only enough serviceable line to get the gentlefolk of Tehran to their favourite shrine, Shah Abdolazim, eight miles distant.

Some foreign visitors depicted Persia's backwardness as one of the unchanging features of the East. Nasser ud-Din's French doctor wrote of a country so 'unchangeable in habits', the Shah's way of life 'scarcely differs from those of his ancestors, nor, perhaps, from those his great-grandsons will lead.'[1] A youthful Gertrude Bell, who would go on to found the modern state of Iraq, described a country that had been mortified by its own history. 'Mother of human energies, strewn with the ruins of a Titanic past, Persia has slipped out of the vivid world, and the simplicity of her landscape is the fine simplicity of death . . . the East looks to itself; it knows nothing of the greater world of which you are a citizen, asks nothing of you and of your civilisation.'[2]

Romantic outsiders are apt to see continuity, even immobility. They do not see where the object of their attentions has come from, nor imagine where it will go. They recoil from the idea that their observations will soon be out of date. So it was with many of the foreigners who came to Persia in the latter stages of the nineteenth century, saw the camel caravans and the poverty amid the ruins of expired empires, and went home again.

What would raise the country from its own sickbed and allow it to realise the promise of its glorious past? In fact, the country boasted many of the attributes needed for a new kind of country-building – the kind that had transformed the European map. A 'Europe of nations' had come into being, as the old empires and confederations broke up or were reconstituted, and new states were born. Persia, no less than Greece or Serbia or Germany, occupied a coherent geography. The majority of its people were united in their devotion to Shiism, Islam's second sect, and spoke Persian, an Indo-European tongue quite different from the other main regional languages, Arabic and Turkish. More than the Arabs, spread over a vast and variegated surface, more than the Ottoman Turks, a minority within their own empire, the Persians seemed suited to one of the principal pursuits of the *belle époque*: the building of a secure, centralised nation state.

Nationalism, the essence of the new nation states, had spilled outside Europe's borders and entered the world of Islam, diluting that sense, as an Arab historian later put it, of 'belonging to an enduring and unshaken world created by the final revelation of God through the Prophet Muhammad'.[3] Ottoman officials and intellectuals had decided that their Turkishness was worth as much as their Muslim identity, if not more. Egypt's Assembly of Delegates, which first met in 1866, fired the opening salvo in a long national struggle for freedom from foreign interests. Further east, Indian Muslims were founder members of the Congress Party, which would eventually propel the country to independence.

Was Persia, then, immobile? Not quite. At the end of the nineteenth century change was happening in Persia, whatever the clichés about the slothful East, and the only question open to the people was whether to accept and ride the wave, or allow it to bludgeon the country and break its back.

Starting in the first quarter of the century, Persia had carried out a few western-style reforms. The earliest were military, but the army remained ill-disciplined and inefficient. The need for deeper change grew more pressing, and its advocates more assertive, as the century wore on. Nasser ud-Din was personally attracted to the West, and made three prohibitively expensive trips there, picking up the latest gadgets and impressing his hosts with his charm and curiosity, as well as the strangeness of his retinue.* But the Shah's interest in power turned out to be stronger than his interest in western-style reform. At different times in his reign Nasser ud-Din promoted reforming, independent-minded ministers, only to dispense with them under pressure from vested interests or when they threatened his own position.

Again, the gap showed between the mystique of the monarchy and its practical limitations. Nasser ud-Din was theoretically omnipotent but he could not prevent knowledge that would be prejudicial to him from entering the country. The Shah enjoyed reading about other rulers, particularly French ones with convoluted love-lives. But a growing number of his educated subjects devoured subversive newspapers and satires that had been published abroad. Members of a small, new, educated class travelled outside the country, with

---

* In Paris, the Shah was solaced by a Georgian slave-girl purchased in Istanbul, who took her seat at the Paris Opera dressed as a man and chaperoned by a eunuch. While travelling through the French countryside on the same trip, the equipage was thrown into confusion after the Shah's beloved 'fetish' (as the foreigners called him), the poisonous adolescent Aziz ul-Sultan, activated the emergency alarm.

a sobering effect on their sense of Iran's position in the world. Poverty and political repression at home led to the establishment of expatriate communities in Istanbul and elsewhere, whose members were exposed to revolutionary ideologies.

Back home, secret societies mushroomed. A sect of millenarians called the Bahais, loathed as heretics by the orthodox, sputtered on in spite of pogroms. The mystic orders fomented anti-clericalism and a charismatic divine called Jamal ud-Din al-Afghani raised the flag of Islamic resurgence. The Shah went in fear for his own life, deputing spies to report even on his own harem, while commerce with the Russian Caucasus exposed the country's Azeri minority, in the north-west, to social democracy and atheism. The country-side dozed while the cities and towns leaped with dissatisfaction: with the Shah's despotism; with the Bahais; with the influence of the powers; with the injustice permitting a tiny, landed elite – the country's top 'one thousand families', as they came to be known – to lord it over some nine million souls.

Patriotic opposition and Russian unease had led to the cancellation of a commercial concession that the Shah had granted to a British citizen, Baron Julius de Reuter, in 1872, which would have ceded control of almost all future economic activity to foreigners. But Nasser ud-Din still needed cash, and in 1890 he granted the British Tobacco Corporation a monopoly over the cultivation and sale of tobacco, thereby sparking Iran's first major nationalist movement. The nationwide boycott of tobacco even spread to the seraglio, where the Shah's wives laid down their pipes in defiance. Eventually the Shah cancelled the concession – but at a cost. In an arrangement that exemplified the country's growing bondage, Nasser ud-Din paid compensation to the British Tobacco Corporation by indebting himself to a second British concern, the Imperial Bank of Persia.

Tehran was the country's most dynamic city and political bell-wether. Never beautiful, always a work in progress, the capital had suffered the lack of a rich, visionary builder-king, though it had progressed from the agglutination of villages, enclosed by Safavid-era walls, that Agha Muhammad Khan had unified in the 1780s. A century on, it was Iran's biggest city, its population in excess of 150,000. It was adorned with spindly public and royal buildings and home to an extensive Court on the site of the old fort, half a dozen European legations and communities of Jews, Armenians and Zoroastrians. Behind, rose the stately Alborz mountains, watering the city and also the hunting lodges and walled arcadia to which the capital's elite, imitating the Shah and his retinue, retired for the summer to carouse and hunt.

The nature of social intercourse was somnolent and conspiratorial. Men conducted their affairs on daybeds in the garden or courtyard of their high-walled houses; the business was sealed with lunch and the opium pipe. Here, in the homes of the elite, politics were founded less on ideology than alliances and preferment, for Qajar Iran was far from being a meritocracy. Women spent much time secluded in their apartments. Islamic law conferred on them few rights, and yet they enjoyed, in some cases, considerable power. Over the course of his long reign Nasser ud-Din came variously under the sway of his mother and his favourite wife or concubine. And then, of course, there was the strange power wielded by his 'fetish'.

For the capital's 500-odd foreigners, the city was not without charm. A European lady out shopping for chintz might spot the Shah driving sedately through the streets in his glass coach preceded by liveried runners, before she attended a performance of Molière's *Tartuffe* by an Armenian troupe. But the capital had another, darker side. Violence was ever-present. At a word from a tub-thumping preacher, aghast at some perceived slight to Islam or a shortage of water or grain, mobs would rampage through the city before dispersing once more, their anger sated and their arms full of loot.

Many rich and well-connected Tehranis lived in the neighbourhood of Sangelaj, to the west of the citadel and the bazaar, in spacious mansions of brick and adobe, with women's quarters (to which no unrelated male was admitted), stables, private bathhouses and legions of servants. The neighbourhood was grand, but around it lay the Tehran of the very poor, with snake-charmers and blacked-up entertainers and amputees begging on the corners. One of the streets bordering Sangelaj was so full of ruffians, the police refused to enter it.

The capital embodied Persia's twin impulses. It was home to the country's most powerful clerics, commanding huge endowments and thousands of followers. Down the year clattered the processions and holidays of Shia Islam, climaxing in the month of Moharram, when the streets teemed with flagellants mourning the Imam Hossein, the Prophet Muhammad's grandson, whose martyrdom at the hands of the caliph was deprecated as if it had happened yesterday, rather than in 680, and pious notables filled the bellies of the poor from cauldrons at the side of the road. Open squares and halls were the scene for Shia passion plays, accompanied by extravagant shows of grief and lamentation.

At the same time, there were other, contradictory signals. The number of traditional schools with a core curriculum of Arabic and religious instruction was in decline, as secular colleges, some of them staffed by foreigners, taught maths, science and French to boys and a few upper-class girls. Daring mothers engaged piano tutors for their daughters. Iranians had overcome their old mistrust of western medicine, and there were modern hospitals overseen by Europeans. To the old occupations of corpse-washer, tobacco-salesman, apothecary and minstrel had been added new ones: telegraph operator, postman, portrait photographer.

Increasingly, Persia clothed itself from Europe. The old male costume of flowing robes and bright colours was under threat from frock coats and wing collars. The *kolah*, a tall black version of the Central Asian astrakhan hat, had been abbreviated and flattened to the point where it resembled a pill-box. Among upper-class women, foreign fashions were causing a *succès de scandale*, with traditionalists outraged by a new short kind of chador worn with a separate veil of leather and horsehair which left part of the wearer's face scandalously uncovered. There was an infatuation for western miracles like salad and soup, chairs and tables, and knives and forks. In the Tehran bazaar, wrote Ella Sykes, who had come to Persia to keep house for her brother Percy, a British diplomat and army officer, 'European goods of the shoddy order vastly preponderate over the Eastern products . . . while Tehran supplies every kind of inferior crockery and cutlery, with masses of the cut-glass candelabra and lustres so dear to the Persian soul.' Invited to a hen party in the seraglio, she was dismayed by her stout, jewel-laden fellow-guests and their curious adornments, from *kohl* moustaches and heavy rouge to short trousers and coarse white stockings – an ensemble inspired, apparently rather dimly, by the ballet in Paris.

Modernity could not be repulsed and on May 1, 1896 it thundered through the Qajar ramparts. On that day Nasser ud-Din Shah was assassinated while leaving a shrine where he had given thanks for the fiftieth year of his reign. The Shah's assassin was a follower of the pan-Islamist Jamal ud-Din al-Afghani, but his action spoke for a multitude of currents, secular and Islamist, democrat and revolutionary.

'When a king has ruled for fifty years,' the assassin told his interrogators, 'and still receives false reports and does not ascertain the truth, and when after so many years of ruling the fruit of his tree are such good-for-nothing aristocratic bastards and thugs, plaguing the lives of Muslims at large, then such a tree ought to be cut down so it won't yield such fruits again. When a fish rots, it rots from its head.'[4]

# 2

# A Silver Spoon

Mossadegh came, as his political rivals would remind him, from a princely background, and his manner, even when he was propounding revolutionary ideas from a hospital bed, bore the signs of his caste. His mother, Najm al-Saltaneh, the person he loved more than anyone else in his life, was a great-granddaughter of Fath-Ali Shah, a first cousin of Nasser ud-Din, and a sister-in-law to the Crown Prince, Muzaffar ud-Din. She was very grand and she devoted her long and eventful life to trying to keep things that way.

Iran had not had an enduring aristocracy along European lines. The trouble with the Duc de Luynes, the Comte Aimery de la Rochefoucauld observed in the 1890s, was that his family had been 'mere nobodies' in the year 1000. The Qajars had been minor tribal chieftains as recently as the mid-eighteenth century, and might easily sink back again. The precariousness of the succession was compounded by the majestic libido of Fath-Ali Shah. In between sitting for portraits, enjoying the chase and losing territory in ill-judged wars, Fath-Ali sired a mammoth progeny, extending to well over 100 children and innumerable grandchildren, who all but bankrupted the state with their demands for pensions and positions.

Even if there was no succession crisis – and the British and Russians generally came together to ensure there was not – the death of a Qajar monarch produced angst and upheaval. The dead Shah's wives, particularly the childless ones, were expelled from the seraglio and his cronies replaced. The new courtiers and hangers-on piled in from the north-western city of Tabriz, capital of the province of Azerbaijan and traditional seat of the Crown Prince, and offended the old guard with the brashness of their manners and their rush for the capital's biggest houses.

Petite and pale-skinned, Najm al-Saltaneh was a fighter and a survivor. Born subservient, a woman in a man's age, restricted for the most part to the society of immediate family, fellow women and eunuchs, she exploited the few opportunities that were open to her and ended up wielding much influence over princes and ministers. Poorly educated but highly intelligent, Najm al-Saltaneh wrote better Persian than most women of her station, and the letters she composed to her brother, Prince Abdolhossein Mirza Farmanfarma, exhibit warmth and spontaneity alongside the usual pieties. Among her intimates, she was known for the foulness of her language, the prerogative – then, as now – of all upper-class Tehrani women.[1]

Thrice married, each time to rich, older men, she thrice bore widowhood and the attendant financial uncertainty. She took a pragmatic approach to this world and the next. On the one hand she proclaimed her indifference to material possessions and her belief in destiny, organising religious ceremonies and making the perilous pilgrimage to Mecca and other shrine cities. On the other, she campaigned tirelessly for her family's welfare, overseeing property and plotting matrimonial alliances.

Najm al-Saltaneh's first husband had died in 1880, indebted after a ruinous provincial governorship. The new widow was only twenty-seven, with two daughters to raise. There was no social or religious bar to a second alliance, and her elevated origins and relative youth drew suitors. Two years later, she married Mossadegh's father, Mirza Hedayatullah Vazir-Daftar.

Vazir-Daftar was forty years her senior, and had several children from previous marriages. He was, in the old Iranian parlance, a man of the pen, not of the sword – an administrator, not a ruler. But he had been minister of finance and the class he represented had penetrated society's upper ranks. He had won office under relatively progressive statesmen, but he took his place in the reformist camp partly because his main rival (who happened to be his first cousin), was in the opposing, reactionary party. Vazir-Daftar's outlook was mildly conservative. He blamed Iran's short-comings not on the unfitness of its institutions but the ineptitude of their occupants.

Vazir-Daftar's huge extended family had made its money and reputation by controlling the country's revenue administration. The duties of a provincial revenue official included preparing assess-ments, signing off accounts and clearing drafts on the provincial revenue. Officials were paid on a commission basis and there was no audit.[2] Besides the inevitable abuses, the system was a bastion of the hereditary principle. More often than not, the title of revenue officer was passed from father to son, often at a very young age – along with account books written in baffling legalese. Later on, having inherited his father's office, Mossadegh would admit the futility of trying to defend his fellow revenue officers from accusa-tions of venality. For all practical purposes, he wrote, the office of revenue official was 'synonymous with "thief".'[3]

The pattern of preferment in the revenue administration was complex, and the competition keen, even within one family. Having shown early promise as an official, Vazir-Daftar's own father had blown his brains out after his honour was impugned in a dispute. Vazir-Daftar was married off to the daughter of his uncle, an even grander revenue officer, but would remember this as a humiliation, remarking that his uncle had given away his daughter as if 'tossing a concubine to a slave'.[4] There were other marriages, and legions of children. Vazir-Daftar's last union, to Najm al-Saltaneh, had little to show for it save Mossadegh and his sister Ameneh, and a revealing vignette in Mossadegh's memoir, in which he describes his father, at a time when he was managing the national tax administration, having been embarrassed by the gift of a crystal chandelier and a music box with dancing marionettes. The gifts had been made by a revenue officer who now sought Vazir-Daftar's approval for his own corrupt practices. Vazir-Daftar wanted to return the gifts but Najm al-Saltaneh put her foot down, exclaiming, 'You, who don't accept anything from anyone – you want me to send back this gift which they brought for me?' To this, Mossadegh's father had no answer, and once his wife had left the room he muttered, 'Let God ordain a happy conclusion to this affair.'[5]

The anecdote shows two distinct moral exemplars acting on the young Mossadegh. On one side stood luxury-loving Najm al-Saltaneh, tearing a strip off her husband for not accepting the perks that came with his job, and capable of overriding his wishes. On the other stood strait-laced Vazir-Daftar, 'forever invoking God', and exceptional among revenue officers in that he could not be bought. It is unlikely that Mossadegh saw enough of his father to develop an intimate relationship with him. Sons were expected to stand with their heads bowed in their fathers' presence, and to speak only if spoken to.

Mossadegh's love for Najm al-Saltaneh would naturally outweigh his feelings for his father, but it was Vazir-Daftar's morality that he would adopt – even at the risk of his mother's displeasure. Years later, when serving as deputy finance minister, Mossadegh would dispatch a collector to demand tax arrears from his mother. Arriving home for lunch, Mossadegh came across the collector shame-facedly discharging his duty, and the old lady subjected her son to such a tornado of invective as only a Persian matriarch can muster.

Pale, as Persians of breeding were meant to be, wide-mouthed, a grave, economical little figure, the child-Mossadegh in the photographs is in fact a child in dimensions only. In a group portrait with his father and some other men, he sports a *kolah*, a white collarless shirt and a double-breasted coat, and occupies the most prominent position in the group after the rather wary-looking Vazir-Daftar. Echoing his father, who sits at a small table, his cane across his lap, Mossadegh rests his elbow on the same table – every inch the mandarin in waiting. In another photograph, wearing the same get-up, he sits alongside two other grandees, his hands joined in his lap, his expression of serenity compromised only by the fact that his feet do not reach the ground.

It is hard to imagine this child scampering about or stealing fruit or getting up to no good and being thrashed in the large house he shared with his parents. It is much easier to imagine him as he is portrayed here, and in other photographs, awaiting the burdens and privileges of his station.

If Najm al-Saltaneh had married Vazir-Daftar for his money, the plan did not work. By the time he was carried away by the cholera epidemic of 1892, Vazir-Daftar had confided his worldly possessions to his eldest son by his first marriage.[6] This arrangement so displeased Najm al-Saltaneh that, rather than carry on living in her late husband's house, she married a third time, to the private secretary to her brother-in-law, Crown Prince Muzaffar ud-Din, and took young Muhammad and his sister to Tabriz. Vazir-Daftar's many heirs contested his estate, and family resentments deepened.[7] In later life, Mossadegh would describe the practice of siring children from different wives as a recipe for fraternal strife.

Even for Iran in the Qajar era, when childhood could be short for pauper and noble alike, Mossadegh was required to behave like an adult at a very young age. At nine, he was deemed mature enough to pay a courtesy call to a grandee. Two years on, following his father's death, he began assuming some of the duties associated with being head of the family. Najm al-Saltaneh was to boast of his poise, the neatness of his bookkeeping and his conscientious management of her various properties.

The death of his father can only have strengthened the bond between Mossadegh and his mother. As Najm al-Saltaneh's elder son (she had one more son by her third husband), and the heir to his father's position, Mossadegh was spoiled with love and burdened with expectation. He also received attention from his mother's beloved younger brother, Prince Farmanfarma. The prince was a legendary figure: diminutive, regal and too ambitious for his own good. Through a convolution of betrothals, he was the uncle by marriage, son-in-law and second cousin of Crown Prince Muzaffar ud-Din. Farmanfarma shared his sister's love of family, but his attitude to religion was expedient. He drank and womanised in the Qajar way, taking numerous temporary wives, as Shia Islam permits, but he also knew the value of pious gestures. He became a friend of the British diplomat Percy Sykes, though the latter never fully trusted him. Few did. Farmanfarma hungered for power at the centre, but he was often sent off to pacify faraway provinces, partly because he was an effective military administrator, partly because his rivals wanted him out of the way.

In a photograph from Mossadegh's teens, the dashing, still-youthful Farmanfarma, who is dressed like a Cossack officer – he owned a large collection of military uniforms, and picked up honorary commissions like any European grand duke – rests his hand affectionately on his nephew's shoulder. Mossadegh stares impassively from the folds of his camel's wool gown – his *aba*.

Not surprisingly, given the chronic morbidity of her husbands, Najm al-Saltaneh reserved her most constant affections for her brother. The tone of her correspondence with Farmanfarma – affectionate, emotionally untrammelled, occasionally shrewish – hints also at her relations with her elder son as he got older and she came to depend on him. Even allowing for the suffocating attentions that many Iranian mothers lavish on their first-born sons, Najm al-Saltaneh's references to Mossadegh glow with pride. In one letter she recorded that he had 'grown up beautifully. It's a miracle; fatherless children aren't supposed to grow up this well.'[8]

Najm al-Saltaneh had strong ideas about how a great man should behave. A few years later, when Mossadegh was starting his political career, he was the object of virulent press attacks and retired to bed, claiming to be suffering from a fever. Najm al-Saltaneh visited the invalid, but instead of comforting him, she started swearing and beating him with her cane. 'Get up!' she cried. 'You think you can cross the sea without getting your feet wet?' Mossadegh's recovery was immediate.[9]

With the assassination of Nasser ud-Din Shah and the accession of the mild, sickly Muzaffar ud-Din, Najm al-Saltaneh reached the summit of her vicarious power. She was sister-in-law of the Shah, her husband was his private secretary, and Farmanfarma captured the prestigious war ministry. Nasser ud-Din Shah had already awarded Muhammad the title Mossadegh al-Saltaneh, or 'Verifier of the Sultanate'.* Now, aged just fifteen, backed by his mother's

* Most Iranian public figures had longwinded titles not only as a means of

clique, he was appointed chief revenue officer for the vast territories of Khorasan and Baluchistan, in eastern Iran, an office he
discharged from an imposing building in central Tehran.

Mossadegh later claimed that he had easily learned the art of
revenue accounting from the clerks he had inherited from his
predecessor, and he won extravagant praise from one contemporary
chronicler, who commented that he had come on 'a century in a
single night', and noted his 'wisdom, learning and intelligence'.[10]
But Mossadegh's record was not, in fact, spotless, and evidence has
come to light suggesting that he transgressed in such basic matters
as the disbursement of salaries, and approved unauthorised expen-
ditures.[11]

A corrective to the ascetic self-image he cultivated in later life,
our picture of Mossadegh from this early period is one of grateful
accumulation. Between the ages of fifteen and twenty-five he
acquired several properties around the country, and the revenues
they brought him would allow him to educate himself abroad.[12]
Mossadegh was quite the young man about town. He was sighted
with his mother at theatrical performances and tea parties, and
Muzaffar ud-Din Shah visited one of his estates to see the irrigation
system he had installed. It is more than likely that Mossadegh
attended the lavish lunches that Farmanfarma gave at his palatial
colonnaded house, which lay in a huge compound, full of smaller
houses occupied by various wives and other relations, and which
one of Farmanfarma's sons called a 'fairyland of pools and garden
hideaways'.[13] A formal portrait photograph taken around this time
shows Mossadegh seated in braided jacket of some ostentation, a
traditional agate-encrusted ring on his little finger. He sports a
fashionable sliver-moustache and an equable, self-satisfied gaze.

Given his background, it is not surprising that he grew up with

---

identification (there were no European-style surnames), but also to emphasise their
indispensability to the Crown. Examples include Ayn al-Dowleh, 'eye of the state',
or Amin al-Sultan, the 'trusted of the King'. Titles were conferred by the Shah, and
were generally reconferred after the death of the bearer, though not necessarily to
his son. As a consequence, they are a false friend to the historian, who risks confusing
the actions of one Ayn al-Dowleh with those of another.

a sense of destiny – even greatness. The granadee who had received Mossadegh when the boy was nine had taken the opportunity to consult his anthology of Hafez, whose supple and esoteric verses adapt themselves to auguries. More than half a century later, Mossadegh would recall the lines that were chanced upon, which touched on the romance of Leyla and her besotted lover Majnun, pointing to a career of ardour, privation and achievement.

> O my heart, it is better to be ruined by a rosy wine;
> It is better to achieve grace without gold or treasure.
> Where they give ministries to the poor, I expect you to be
>     highest of all.
> On the road to Leyla's house, which is fraught with mortal
>     risk, the first condition is that you be Majnun.'[14]

Najm al-Saltaneh was in pursuit of a more literal Leyla. Showing typical opportunism, she had pressed for Mossadegh's engagement to her niece, the daughter of Muzaffar ud-Din Shah. With Mossadegh in his sixteenth year, it was time to close the deal, but this was to reckon without the recklessness of Farmanfarma. Scandal broke with allegations that he was plotting to depose the Shah. The prince denied it all, but to no avail. He fell, and the family fell with him.

Farmanfarma was lucky to get away with his life. He was given three years' exile. Najm al-Saltaneh's husband was stripped of his position as the Shah's private secretary, and her sister, the Shah's wife, was cooped up in the harem. To complete the humiliation, at the beginning of 1898 Mossadegh lost his fiancée to the son of the prime minister. Najm al-Saltaneh, who had also fallen out with her sister in a dispute over property, was overcome with rage and grief, and swallowed opium – 'though not', a contemporary observed cattily, 'enough to kill her'. A cruel, 'very amusing' ditty was composed around the incident.[15]

Mossadegh seems to have reacted phlegmatically. He had shown no interest in contracting a temporary marriage, a common device for sating youthful appetites. Rather than a matter of the heart, he

regarded marriage as an inescapable rite for someone of his background, believing (as his mother reported) that 'if a man is some-
body, and he has money, then people will give him their daughter.
If not, they will not.'[16]

A few years later, in 1903, after Farmanfarma had been rehabili-
tated, Najm al-Saltaneh aimed again – with more success. This time
her target was Zahra Zia al-Saltaneh, the daughter of a senior
divine. 'Even if you didn't give my son the Shah's daughter,' Najm
al-Saltaneh sniped at her sister, 'he shall have the daughter of the
Shah of religion.' And so he did.

Zahra was a noted beauty: tall, slim and fair. At nineteen, she
was older and more mature than most brides of the day. Mossadegh
had only the reports of his mother to go on; he would not see her
face until they were man and wife.

An account of the wedding ceremony, based on Zahra's recollections, has been relayed by the couple's eldest grandson,
Abdolmajid Bayat.[17] Musicians played while the guests, segregated
according to sex, ate from tables loaded with sweets and fruit. A
mullah recited prayers and Qoranic verses. To make married life
sweet, one of the guests rubbed two sticks of candy over a length
of cloth that was held over the bride's head. Another ran a needle
and thread through the same cloth to shut the mouth of her new
mother-in-law – a forlorn hope, in the case of Najm al-Saltaneh!
Before them lay the traditional embroidered coverlet and an assortment of fruit and other adornments, symbols of wealth and fecun-
dity.

At length, after being pressed several times – the bride must not
appear forward – Zahra consented to be Mossadegh's wife. The
newly-weds were congratulated and family members poured
sugared almonds and gold and silver pieces over their heads, which
the children present picked up as keep-sakes.

Only after the ceremony, when they were alone, did Zahra reveal
her face to her husband. It was not a success. Zahra had been
heavily made up according to custom, with woad mascara, rouge,
and kohl outlines to accentuate her almond-shaped eyes. She must
have looked rather dramatic, and Mossadegh was unhappy. 'Madam!'

he demanded. 'What is this get-up? Go immediately and wash your face.'[18]

The marriage of Mossadegh and Zahra Zia al-Saltaneh owed less to Leyla and Majnun than to ordinary calculations of preferment and propriety. Marriage was a way of allying families, producing heirs and pleasing God. The chances of a loving partnership were slim, not only because the parties had no say in the choice of spouse, but also because men and women, even after marriage, continued to live largely separate lives.

After the wedding, Bayat writes, installed in her husband's home, Zahra 'reigned over the women in the private apartments. She had her coach and team and a eunuch to wait on her. For his part, Mossadegh spent most of his time in his own quarters; he had his own stable, his own servants.' Zahra's life was far from taxing. She 'made herself up, received visitors, heard the latest titbits from the city, consumed sweets and smoked the water-pipe. She said her prayers, enjoyed hearing religious recitals; her life progressed without the slightest collision, without the slightest demand from society.'[19]

Mossadegh was clearly not indifferent to Zahra's beauty, and there was an early flurry of children, but there was precious little common ground between the two. Zahra was traditional and pious; Mossadegh was neither. She had none of her husband's (or mother-in-law's) interest in the affairs of the nation. She preferred flowers.

For all that, in spite of these beginnings, the partnership would prosper over sixty-four years. Although they would spend many years living apart, a bond of affection and trust would form between Mossadegh and Zahra, with much waspish humour. And when, on the day of the coup, the mob approached to destroy her house and kill her husband, it was with the greatest difficulty that Zahra was persuaded to abandon him and flee to safety. 'If they want to kill him,' she protested, 'they should kill me too.'[20]

In 1906, following Russia, and anticipating Turkey, Persia had a constitutional revolution. It was not driven by formal political parties, but a shifting alliance between young radicals and secularists on the one hand and an array of more conservative forces on the other: sections of the Islamic scholars (the ulema), the merchants (the bazaaris) and provincial notables. The revolution would not achieve its goals but it would redefine the country – and Mossadegh with it. Henceforth, to be a 'constitutionalist' would mean something specific: to follow a dream which flared and guttered over the next few years and to take strength from those who manned the barricades. In time, Mossadegh would be recognised as constitutionalism's champion.

The Persian constitutionalists were fired by the ideals of the French Revolution: to truss up the monarch using the law, control his spending and prevent absolutism. In France, constitutionalism had led to regicide and a republic, but not in Persia, where many people regarded the monarchy as a bulwark against godless communism. Constitutionalism in Persia was forced to make room for different views, from the radical to the religiously conservative. Inevitably, there was a parting of the ways.

By 1905, Muzaffar ud-Din had turned out to be almost as bad a Shah as his father had feared. (He was known in diplomatic circles as 'Mauvaise Affaire ud-Din'.) He devoted his energies to appeasing the army, whose pay was as much as two years in arrears, and raising secret loans to finance foreign trips which had been recommended by his doctors. Persia prostituted itself for the sovereign's kidneys, and popular resentment against Europe increased. The country experienced another surge of nationalist feeling. A vital condition for the making of a modern nation was being met.

Much ire was directed against the Belgian civil servants who had been engaged to reform the country's customs administration. Revenues duly rose but were used to fund Muzaffar ud-Din's jaunts to Europe, where he purchased every new curiosity he was offered. Russia's support for the Belgian customs administrators called into question their loyalty to the Persian state, and Persian merchants grumbled that new tariffs favoured their Russian counterparts. The Belgians were not popular in the revenue department that employed Mossadegh. With the creation of a unified exchequer staffed by civil servants, they started taking over its functions. Evidence for personal conflict comes in the form of a letter from this time, signed by several public figures, bluntly warning the Belgians not to confiscate land owned by Mossadegh al-Saltaneh.[21] The Belgians' unpopularity was compounded by their hauteur, and their top official was eventually sent home after a photograph circulated showing him dressed up as a mullah.

The Belgian experience showed the dangers inherent in foreign-led reforms. Some of the Belgians' rationalising measures were eminently sensible, but they were carried out by the wrong people and for the wrong reasons. Over the coming decades, the country would engage Swedes to set up a gendarmerie, Russians and Englishmen to start armies, and Americans to run the economy. With the exception of the admirable American Morgan Schuster, who ran the country's finances between 1909 and 1911, and was forced out by Russia (with British connivance), Persian patriots regarded these foreign missions with suspicion. They contributed to a near-universal conviction that the country's woes were the fault of outsiders.

Different groups spent the first years of the century manoeuvring against a backdrop of deepening crisis. While Muzaffar ud-Din Shah took the waters at Baden-Baden, Persian towns erupted in riots – against the new tariffs, against the Bahais, against tyrannical provincial governors and the price of bread. When the Shah was at home, Tehran seethed with plots and he was constantly rumoured to be dead. Women threw themselves at his carriage; illegal pamphlets inveighing against 'parasitical' mullahs were smuggled in from socialist cells abroad. Islam was in danger and a mob took an hour to obliterate a bank that the Russians had foolishly built over a cemetery. 'I knew then', remarked one awe-struck observer, 'that the spiritual power of the people is a superior force of God.'

The revolution started in earnest at the end of 1905, when some sugar merchants were bastinadoed for raising prices. The bazaar closed and the shrine at Shah Abdolazim was occupied by radical mullahs and their supporters, issuing demands for a new body – a 'house of justice', whose functions no one could quite define.

The dispute dragged on until the British intervened in the

summer of 1906. Distinguishing themselves adroitly from the Russians, who were identified with society's ultra-conservative elements, the British minister turned over the grounds of the Tehran legation to thousands of constitutionalists and helped them articulate their demands. On August 5, an ailing Muzaffar ud-Din signed the law that would establish the first parliament, or *majles*, in an old palace in Baharestan Square, in the eastern part of central Tehran.

The foundations had been laid for a constitutional monarchy, and Mossadegh was prominent enough to have played a shining young man's role. But it would be hard to imagine a young man more closely associated with Persia's ruling establishment than Mossadegh al-Saltaneh. He passed close to events, rather than plunged in.

For all that, his opinions were starting to emerge, and they were cautiously reformist. He was aware that the days of unaccountable revenue officers passing on their posts like heirlooms were coming to an end, but he could not support the culling of the elite by abusive radicals who might drag the country towards a republic. He supported the idea of a constitutional monarchy but doubted that the movement sat on sure foundations. Many of those who criticised the old order, he complained, had spent 'a little time abroad, watching the approach of the constitution from afar', and had returned to Iran equipped with only a 'superficial' knowledge of events, while others 'hadn't even heard of constitutionalism, and didn't know the difference between absolutism and constitutionalism'.[22]

Shortly before the first constitution, Mossadegh had taken a step back from public life. The reformists were rounding on the revenue department as a haven for idle reactionaries, so he quitted and took the opportunity to improve himself. The Qoranic Arabic and Islamic jurisprudence he had learned as a child had been supplanted in the new syllabuses by French, modern political philosophy and the law. He engaged private tutors. 'Nothing', he would recall, 'was important to me save increasing my knowledge, even slightly, every day.'[23]

Iran's first parliament opened in October 1906, as soon as the

Tehran seats were filled. Elections had taken place on a restricted franchise – women, the poor and other undesirables were denied the vote – but members of the new chamber were trenchant in their defence of what they considered to be the national interest. They rejected a new Anglo-Russian loan, threw out the Belgian customs chief and fostered a press, critical and satirical. This last innovation was a particular irritation to Muzaffar ud-Din's successor as Shah, his son Muhammad-Ali.

Muhammad-Ali came to the throne on his father's death in January 1907. The American financial adviser Morgan Schuster described him as 'perhaps the most perverted, cowardly, and vice-sodden monster that had disgraced the throne of Persia in many generations. He hated and despised his subjects from the beginning of his career, and from having a notorious scoundrel for his Russian tutor, he easily became the avowed tool and satrap of the Russian government.'[24] The new Shah and his Russian backers immediately declared war on the majles.

Mossadegh was a member of one of the myriad associations which had been set up in support of constitutionalism, but the radical constitutionalists distrusted him because of his uncle. Prince Farmanfarma was Muhammad-Ali Shah's brother-in-law and the radicals saw him for the self-serving grandee that he was – and Mossadegh, his nephew and close adviser, in a similar light. So, when it came to filling the empty seats in the majles, and Mossadegh was elected from the central province of Isfahan, the deputies were only too happy to reject him on the grounds that he was not yet thirty, the minimum age for a deputy.

The battle between the constitutionalists and their opponents was conducted without pity. Revolutionaries assassinated the prime minister and a bomb was thrown at the Shah's car, while the radical press heaped odium on the Crown. Having supported the constitution, the conservative mullahs came to see it as a vehicle for secularism and awarded themselves a veto over legislation. Then, in 1907, the British and Russians came to an infamous arrangement whereby they divided Iran into zones of influence. Armed conflict became inevitable between the constitutionalists and the Shah's

Russian-led force of Cossacks. No longer would the British play the benign role of counterweight.

On the morning of June 23, 1908, the parliament in Baharestan Square and an adjacent mosque, bristling with armed deputies and their supporters, were besieged by the Russian Colonel Liakhoff, his two thousand men, and their cannon. A tense stand-off followed, but the Cossacks were not interested in negotiating. Shots rang out, the constitutionalists replied, and the battle for Iran began.

At first the constitutionalists surprised the Cossacks with the vigour of their response, but Liakhoff brought up more cannon and the bombardment took its toll. Inside the parliament building, two senior constitutionalist divines lost their nerve and fled. Younger militants fought on, but it was in vain. And so, in the words of E. G. Browne, the Constitutionalists' most fervent supporter in Britain, 'the buildings that had for the best part of two years been the centre of the Nation's hopes, and the focus of the new spirit which had stirred the dry bones of a seemingly dead people to new life . . . were reduced to ruins, and the defenders either slain, taken captive, or put to flight.'[25]

Mossadegh had been on his way to Baharestan Square to take part in the defence when he heard the sound of firing and cannons. 'I was unable to go on,' he would recall, 'and returned home.'[26] Another constitutionalist, more impulsive and hot-headed, would surely have forced his way through the chaos, but Mossadegh would never show much relish for physical violence.

He went to ground during the retribution that followed, when some of the radical constitutionalists were executed or fled. Later, he reluctantly answered the Shah's summons to join a sham assembly designed to mask parliament's annihilation. Najm al-Saltaneh had arranged for his inclusion and one may easily imagine the alarm she felt at his progressive politics. Although she believed that the ruling class should help and if necessary suffer for the people, the levelling of society that is implicit in parliamentary democracy was not something she could welcome. Besides, for her, as for her brother, politics was not about being right. It was about winning.

Mossadegh's inclusion in a discredited assembly must have placed him in an acute dilemma. On the one hand, he could not associate himself with a despot like Muhammad-Ali Shah. On the other, he was tied by his mother to the ruling house and shared the traditional Persian fear of chaos. He had not been married long and had three young children. The solution he found was solitary exile aimed at self-improvement. Najm al-Saltaneh encouraged him; she saw the wisdom in an expedient absence from a sticky field.

Thus, in early 1909, accompanied by his younger half-brother Abolhassan, whom he was to place in a French boarding school, Mossadegh set out for Europe to acquire an education.

# 3

## *Fokoli*

Mossadegh was twenty-six when he arrived in Paris and although he had occupied high office, started a family and lived through revolution and upheaval, he was a stranger to the banal tribulations of modern life.

He was a prince twice over when he left Iran, in the sense that he lived in regal serenity, isolated from petty domestic details, and because every first-born Iranian male, down to the poorest, is made to feel like a prince by his mother. Mossadegh's knowledge was deep but rather arcane. He knew about crop-sharing, foreign concessions and Islamic jurisprudence, but less about posting a letter or riding an underground railway, let alone boiling an egg or unblocking a sink. He was a learned, rather serious-minded ingénu.

In Paris he became a student at the elite École Libre des Sciences Politiques, running down his quarterly remittance from home, swotting at all hours to make up for his rudimentary French and moving from one set of modest digs to another. The host country was afflicted by strikes and political instability, but Mossadegh had turned to France for help in interpreting his own nation and those at a comparable stage of development. He read about Turkey, Algeria and Russia – sitting cross-legged, '*à la turque*,' when he tired of chairs. At the beginning of 1910, he witnessed the silent, lapping Paris that came into being after the great flood, when the city was overwhelmed by the Seine and became Venice for a single uncanny week. And he had a love affair, probably unconsummated – he took that secret to his grave, as did she – with an adoring emancipated young woman. He, whose traditional Islamic culture proscribed all contact between unrelated men and women! He, who had not seen his bride's face before they exchanged vows!

It was well known that there was a danger in all this. To study abroad was to expand one's horizons and there was a strong possibility that the exile would lose his moral, Muslim compass. To study in Paris, the world capital of sin, was especially risky. Paris was home to the so-called *fokolis* – from the French *faux col*, or detachable collar – a derogatory catch-all for Persian students who went to Europe claiming to seek an education, but brought back a fancy wardrobe and a case of the clap.

Little could be more damaging for a young exile than for scandalous reports of licence and free-thinking to filter back home. Mossadegh's French sojourn coincided with the publication of an article in Tehran about the 'depraved of Paris', but the young Persian's instinct was not to revel but to study, to the point that he neglected to visit the city's main attractions.[1] Indeed, it was his very seriousness, his combination of shyness and inscrutability, and the austerity of his lifestyle, which captured the heart of twenty-one-year-old Renée Vieillard.

She was the daughter of a French colonial pioneer who had returned to France in 1892. A budding feminist, enthralled by the Muslim world, Renée took courses at the country's top school of oriental languages, and knew many of the Middle Easterners who had converged on Paris to study and to plot the destiny of their nations. For these exiles, the French Revolution was an inspiration, and Auguste Comte, whose positivist philosophy presented science as an heir to religion, was a modern guide. Their home countries were thrillingly on the move. In Turkey, the Committee for Union and Progress had deposed the 'red sultan', Abdulhamit II. In British-run Egypt, nationalists were demanding self-government. In Persia, the constitutionalist opponents of Muhammad-Ali Shah were once more in the ascendant.

Renée Vieillard relished this cultural and political ferment. Alongside her studies, she edited feminist and orientalist journals, argued for building a mosque in Paris – the plan would be realised after the First World War – and led discussions of women's rights in the Muslim world. Mossadegh must have been astonished and flattered by this energetic young woman from France's anti-clerical tradition, six years his junior and plainly besotted. She found in him a welcome contrast to some of the more ostentatious overseas students – the Egyptians were the worst, apparently – and later claimed to have had presentiments of his greatness. A stock romantic device was employed. She would help him with his studies and coach him in French. She wanted no payment.

'Brown-haired and thin,' she would recall, 'with the eyes of a gazelle, always calm and reserved, he did not mix with his classmates. Once classes were over, he would return to his room in the very modest guest house in the rue Gay-Lussac where he lived . . . how to explain this sense of deference which I felt for this man who was so different from those around him!' And so, 'the young Iranian and the young Frenchwoman . . . influenced each other reciprocally by these exchanges, without any discordant note entering our relations. Ours was an exalting spiritual communion.'[2]

Renée Vieillard had to overcome Mossadegh's reticence before he consented to speak to her on the record about events in Persia. The interview she conducted with 'A Persian Constitutionalist, Mossadegh al-Saltaneh', in August 1909, came at a hopeful time. Muhammad-Ali Shah had been overthrown a few weeks before, and parliamentary democracy would soon resume. She published the interview in the Parisian newspaper Les Nouvelles, under the pseudonym A. de Rochebrune. It is likely that Mossadegh insisted she use an alias of indeterminate sex in order to avoid embarrassing questions back home. He was aware of the effect that an interview in the foreign press could have on his reputation in Persia.

A. de Rochebrune found the young Mossadegh al-Saltaneh to be 'very educated, boasting a very enlightened patriotism', and not hesitating to 'sacrifice all for the cause of liberty'. Mossadegh waxed lyrical about 'the achievement of all the people of Persia', but he did not neglect to puff up his uncle Farmanfarma, whom he depicted as a top constitutionalist. When the subject turned to Persian women, Mossadegh was careful to define their role within Islam, but also asserted that 'our women are not inert dolls, capricious and vain little creatures,' but 'queen of the household'. He tactfully praised France's role as a trailblazer for nations such as Iran. Renée concluded her article by suggesting that, for the countries of the East, France was 'an elder sister', and that 'in the Orient, there are races that continue the task started by the French revolution of 1789'.[3]

Renée Vieillard was barely out of her teens for the few months that she was close to Mossadegh, but she would cherish the episode for the rest of her life. She cited Mossadegh's doctoral thesis in a book which she wrote many years later about the Prophet Muhammad, and there would be more letters after Mossadegh became prime minister. Later still, she would develop close relations with several younger members of his family. In truth, her effect on the studies of the young émigré seems to have been beneficial, for in his first exams in Europe he scored a creditable 16/20 in his main subject, general finance.

That Renée Vieillard meant something to Mossadegh is not in doubt. He spent many intimate moments with her and confided to her the strength of his feelings for his mother – giving her a rather preposterous picture of Najm al-Saltaneh as a 'passionate social reformer'. Five years later, when she was in Egypt, Mossadegh sent Renée a copy of his recently completed doctoral thesis, which he had just published.

Mossadegh's position at home meant that the friendship could not last, and he did not publicly acknowledge Renée except to refer in his memoir to a certain 'very intelligent' person who helped him with his studies during his first summer in Paris.[4] Subsequent researchers, trying to track down the newspaper interview in the national archive in Paris, found that the only issue of Les Nouvelles to have gone missing was the one with the interview in it, raising the tantalising possibility that Mossadegh himself destroyed it. The copy of the interview that is now in the public domain was found in an archive of press clippings in the Tehran University library.[5]

Mossadegh was not the first Muslim man to be drawn to the seductive autonomy which flourished in Europe, and which, in Iran, was stifled through family supervision and the seclusion of the sexes. He was part of a generation of Iranian men who were inspired by Europe but who expected their wives to remain Iranian. It is hard not to feel for the wives. In his interview in *Les Nouvelles*, Mossadegh gave an unintentional insight into his own marriage at this stage when he described Iranian women as 'more mother than wife'.

It is impossible to know whether some upheaval in Mossadegh's relationship with Renée Vieillard contributed to the dramatic deterioration in health that he experienced towards the end of 1909, and which has generally been imputed to overwork, exacerbated by the damp winter. The symptoms, including stomach ulcers which forced him to lie down during lectures, sleeplessness and extreme nervous tension, would recur throughout his life. A reputable physiologist ordered complete rest, and was ignored.

Mossadegh's work ethic was already formidable, and eventually he had a complete collapse, stopped attending classes and engaged a full-time nurse – a welcome maternal figure called Marie-Thérèse, of whom he became very fond. There was a spell in a sanatorium and Marie-Thérèse, having lent him money for his passage, accompanied him to Iran to recuperate.\* The invalid was so weak that, when the party changed trains at the Russian border, he had to be carried from one to the other in a wheelbarrow.

It says much for the dominance that Najm al-Saltaneh exerted over her son, even now that he was married, that she took charge of his convalescence after he arrived back in Tehran, weak and emaciated, one summer's day in 1910. She was furious with him because he had not been in touch since January's great flood, news of which had reached Tehran, and he replied with the classic filial evasion that he had not wanted to worry her. There was immediate strife when he insisted on observing his French doctor's orders that he drink only small quantities of water. Tehran is boiling hot in summer, and within a short time Mossadegh had dehydrated himself to the extent that his tongue had stuck to the roof of his mouth and he could barely speak. Still, he refused to bow to his mother's entreaties until she learned what the weather was like in Paris. When she heard that it was cold

---

\* Marie-Thérèse settled in Tehran where she became a governess. To Mossadegh's distress, she died just three years later, after falling into an open manhole.

and wet, she swore roundly at him and ordered two watermelons to be brought, which he gratefully gobbled up.

Mossadegh went to convalesce at the property of a friend, Eqbal al-Mamalek, in the cool hills north of Tehran. Eqbal enquired what he had learned of French cooking and, not wanting to reveal his ignorance, Mossadegh claimed to have mastered the French dessert *crème renversée*. In fact, Mossadegh had seen Marie-Thérèse make *crème renversée*, but remembered little. He ordered eggs and milk to be procured and mixed with sugar, but the proportions were wrong and the woodstove too cold. After a day and a half's puffing and prodding, the ingredients were quite raw. 'If you know as much about finances as you do about cooking,' Eqbal sighed, 'one can only weep for this country.'[6]

It is not impossible that news of Mossadegh's friendship with a European woman had reached home. Certainly, his subsequent, hyper-cautious conduct while abroad, and his fear of adverse reports reaching Tehran, suggest a determination to avoid further entanglements. Whatever the reason, when Mossadegh embarked on the second leg of his European education, in the autumn of 1910, he was on a very tight leash indeed. The party that set out for Switzerland in that month comprised, besides Mossadegh himself, Zahra and their three children, two female companions for Zahra, a brace of young male cousins also seeking European knowledge, and the indefatigable Najm al-Saltaneh, hoping for relief from her cataracts.

The group must have looked very fine. Mossadegh was quite used to the western uniform of starched collar, frock coat and pinstriped trousers. For the women, on the other hand, entering non-Muslim lands for the first time, sartorial choices were a minefield. The chador, the black length of cloth that pious Iranian women of all classes wear when out of doors, was ill-suited to Europe, but it would be unthinkable to go about bare-headed. Najm al-Saltaneh donned a woollen headdress favoured by Russian peasant women. Zahra and her companions devised an arresting ensemble composed of long European dresses, gloves and veiled, large-brimmed hats. Later on, the Swiss would not conceal their perturbation at the refusal of one of Zahra's companions to remove her gloves to learn the violin.

Their destination of choice was Fribourg, but they were not made welcome by the fervent Catholics of that pastoral canton, so they moved to Neuchâtel, at the north-east corner of the lake of the same name: industrious, bourgeois and Protestant. At first they were refused lodging on account of being Muslim, but Mossadegh managed to rent a four-bedroom flat in a secluded spot overlooking the famous vines. A few months later, after an inconclusive visit to a Paris eye specialist, Najm al-Saltaneh would return to Persia. She had spent much of her sojourn in prayer, and declared herself well satisfied with her first and only experience of Europe.

It would be hard to imagine a university town further from the continent's gnashing ideologies than Neuchâtel. The place was silent after 9 p.m. and had neither theatre nor bar. But Mossadegh, it was already clear, had a nervous disposition, and he thrived, albeit slowly, in a place with few external stimuli. Over the next four years, he made the classic journey of emancipation of a pampered Middle Easterner in a rigorous western environment. When he arrived in Neuchâtel he was still a grandee defined by birth, and by the time he left he had become a doctor of law earning distinction by his own hard work. In Neuchâtel, his meticulous, fussy, lawyerly side found full expression, and of course he improved his French, the international language of the age.

The Mossadeghs kept themselves to themselves. Their daughter and elder son, Zia Ashraf and Ahmad, were sent off to board with a well-to-do local family, the Pernouds, to improve their French. They attended a local school and came home at weekends. Mossadegh's third child, a boy called Ghollamhossein, was too young to be sent away. Zahra returned to Tehran for the birth of her fourth child, also a boy, but the infant died of measles shortly after she brought him back to Neuchâtel. By this time Zahra's companions had also returned to Tehran. A pious Muslim woman mourning her child in an alien environment, she found life in exile a trial.[7]

They were the only Persians in the place and Mossadegh was

determined to give a good account of himself. He dressed dapperly, paid his bills on time and won the gratitude of some local boys when he defended them in court after they were collared for stealing fruit. He was less understanding when his own children transgressed. Once, returning home for lunch, a delicious Persian aubergine stew made with tart, unripe grapes, he was appalled to learn that Ghollamhossein and Ahmad had stolen the grapes from a neighbour's vines. 'I'll murder the pair of you!' Mossadegh shouted, and leaped at the boys, who fled. 'Don't be scared,' Ghollamhossein consoled his weeping brother. 'He can't kill us. They'd put him in jail!'[8]

Years later, as prime minister, Mossadegh would recall the manner in which he quite undeservedly got his motorcycle licence in Neuchâtel, chuckling at the unworldliness of the Swiss – and at his own physical clumsiness. Rather than ride with the candidate, the invigilator had sent him down to Lake Neuchâtel and back. Mossadegh rode confidently as far as the lake, where, unable to stop, he cannoned into a fruit stall and turned it over. 'Cochon! Cochon!' screeched the stall-holder. Mossadegh compensated her, righted his vehicle and drove back to the invigilator. 'Mr Mossadegh,' he said, 'you have taken a long time. You must have driven very carefully. I congratulate you. Here is your driving licence.'[9]

There is no sense from Mossadegh's stay in Switzerland of an impressionable young man devouring the culture around him. He did not expect to become like the Swiss, and was not surprised when they behaved differently from him. On the one occasion when he forgot to bring money to a restaurant where he had eaten dozens of times and was well known, the restaurateur took his watch as collateral. In Iran, the man's behaviour would have been considered extremely hostile. In this instance, Mossadegh derived satisfaction from finding a key to the Swiss character, which, he believed, was to behave in the same way with a customer of long standing as with a perfect stranger.

The essays he wrote for his degree necessitated a study of Swiss law and the other European codes, but his overriding interest lay in the Muslim Middle East. For his doctoral thesis, on the last will and testament in Islam, he studied Ottoman and Egyptian legal theory and spent three months in Tehran consulting senior doctors of Islamic law. In the published thesis, he came down on the side of clerical modernisers when he argued that Islamic laws were historical phenomena and subject to revision as society changed. He also attacked the 'imposition' of European laws and institutions on Iran, arguing that 'the direct result of imitating Europe will be the spoliation of a country like Iran, for everything should be in proportion with the need'.[10]

Switzerland offered peace of mind enough for him to contemplate returning there whenever (as would happen often) he despaired of Iran's future. But he never wavered in his own identity, telling the children, 'We are Iranian, and we are going to stay a short period in Europe and then go back to our country.' If he had Swiss nationality, however, it would allow him to practise there, and he was close to that goal when he, Ghollamhossein and the pregnant Zahra returned to Tehran for what was planned as a short trip in the summer of 1914. They arrived in Tehran on the eve of World War One, and were prevented from returning. The elder children, Ahmad and Zia Ashraf, were still in neutral Switzerland with the Pernouds. They would remain there until the end of hostilities.

The Persia to which Mossadegh returned in 1914 was no longer young from the elixir of constitutionalism. In his absence the country had been exhausted by internal strife and the abysmal interventions of the powers. The optimism generated by Muhammad-Ali Shah's abdication in favour of his eleven-year-old son, Ahmad, had evaporated as a result of divisions between radical and moderate constitutionalists. A conservative ayatollah was publicly hanged; a deputy told the mullahs to withdraw from politics. Appalled, the clerical mainstream turned its back on constitutionalism, which many now associated with atheism and immorality.

In foreign affairs, too, there had been reverses. Russia, encroaching on various pretexts, had stealthily colonised much of the north of the country, while in the south-west the British nurtured the new asset that would transform Persia from a pawn in the Great Game to a prize of capital importance: oil.

# 4

# *Razing Caesarea*

For centuries there had been oil seepages onto the bleached hills of western Persia. The oozings were used for caulking boats on the great rivers of Mesopotamia – the Tigris and Euphrates – and, before Islam, for feeding the fire temples. Oil rights had been part of the ill-fated Reuter concession of 1872, but exploration only started in earnest after 1901, when a fresh concession was awarded to a British entrepreneur, William Knox D'Arcy.

D'Arcy had made his fortune mining in Australia, but Persian black gold proved more elusive, and conditions for his engineers – drilling in one of Persia's hottest, least accessible places, surrounded by villainous tribesmen – were almost unbearable. After three years of fruitless exploration, D'Arcy was running out of funds. In the nick of time, geopolitics intervened, for the British government feared that the Russians might try to hijack the concession, allowing them to break out of their corral in the north and loom threateningly over the Persian Gulf. The government drummed up a 'syndicate of patriots' to take over D'Arcy's venture, but even after oil was struck, the Anglo-Persian Oil Company, as it was now called, remained vulnerable to absorption by one of the more established oil companies.

Again, imperial strategy overrode the market. At the time of Anglo-Persian's troubled birth, the Royal Navy was engaged in an arms race with a new pretender, imperial Germany. The First Lord of the Admiralty was a youthful Winston Churchill, and he hoped to make a quantum leap. In 1912, Churchill decided that in future all battleships should be built to run not on coal, the standard fuel for such vessels, but oil. Oil-powered ships travelled faster than coal-fired ones, and could refuel while at sea. They could also carry bigger guns. But there was a powerful argument against making the switch. Britain had an abundance of coal; oil, on the other hand, would have to be imported, putting the country at the mercy of distant suppliers. 'To commit the Navy irrevocably to oil', as Churchill put it, 'was indeed to "take arms against a sea of troubles".' And yet, if that could be achieved, the navy would gain a new potency. 'Mastery itself was the prize of the venture.'[1]

Once Churchill had taken his decision, it was vital to ensure that the Royal Navy would have as dependable a supply of oil as possible. If Anglo-Persian was to be swallowed up, why should the British government not do the swallowing? On June 17, 1914, after listening to the First Lord at the dispatch box, the House of Commons overwhelmingly authorised the government to buy just over half of Anglo-Persian's shares. A second, secret contract gave the Admiralty a twenty-year supply of fuel oil, on generous terms. Churchill was well satisfied. Anglo-Persian was saved for the nation, and the navy had a guaranteed supply of oil. No one asked the Persians what they thought. The following month the First World War broke out and the question became academic. Production from the Persian fields soared, and British naval superiority was maintained for the duration of the war.

Persia was a non-belligerent on the edge of events, but the Great War was a catastrophe for the country which would affect national politics for years. Most Persians fervently supported Germany and its ally, the Ottoman Turks. The Turks were Muslims and a popular rumour had it that the German Kaiser had converted. ('Haj Wilhelm' was the unlikely nickname given to this Prussian Protestant.) The traditional powers in the region, Russia and Britain, were now in alliance, and in November 1915 a Russian force advanced to within a day's march of Tehran, prompting pro-German deputies to go into exile – first to the west of the country, and later, scattered by the Allies, to Ottoman territory and Berlin. The north and the west of Persia remained a battlefield, with the Ottomans fighting the Russians and British, while German agents infiltrated the south. Crucially for the British, their oil interests in the south-west were protected by their tribal allies there.

In the capital, ministers trembled in fear of assassins, who were influenced by revolutionary currents in Russia and targeted enemies of the people at their desks or in the bazaar. On one occasion, the prime minister permitted himself a night's sleep only after clambering onto his unlit roof and pulling up the ladder he had used to get there. By the end of the war, Persia was in the grip of famine, and while the more fertile provinces were awash with wheat and rice, the medieval transport system was unequal to the burden of distribution and people dropped from starvation in the streets.

Politics disintegrated. No fewer than eight prime ministers (including Prince Farmanfarma) formed sixteen different cabinets during the war years. Their royal master was the uninspiring Ahmad Shah, a peevish and obese adolescent whom the Russians and British manipulated unrelievedly, and whose first significant action following the end of hostilities was to put his fortune in the Paris stock exchange.

The war prevented Mossadegh from returning to Switzerland, taking up citizenship and practising the law. He was in demand to give classes at Tehran's new School of Law and Political Science, but soon enough he was drawn back into politics. He accepted a position on a budgetary oversight body that had been set up to weaken the Belgians' grip on the economy, he was a prominent member of a nationalist group, and he cultivated friends in the rabble-rousing patriotic press. He did not join his fellow patriots when they went into voluntary exile in fear of a Russian takeover, though he maintained clandestine contact with them after their departure. He shared the exiles' nationalist sentiments, but not their pro-German bent. Besides, he was suffering from acute stomach pains and fever that later developed into appendicitis. It was probably not a coincidence that these symptoms appeared as the Russians advanced on Tehran and Ahmad Shah toyed briefly with the idea of flight. Mossadegh's insides would often react to the national angst.

He refused to join Farmanfarma's short-lived government, which he judged to be an instrument of the powers. His instinct was right but the decision offended both his uncle and Najm al-Saltaneh. In 1917, his mother prevailed upon him to serve as deputy finance minister under another, more distant cousin, Qavam al-Saltaneh – the first chapter in what would be a long and ultimately venomous political relationship. By now, the Belgians had been relieved of control over the economy, and the finance ministry was a target for modernisers.

Mossadegh had already declared his reformist tendencies with a paper denouncing the capitulation agreements by which Muslim states such as Iran had conceded legal jurisdiction over their Christian residents to separate, Christian authorities.[2] Discrete legal systems were enshrined in Islamic law, but Mossadegh raised an overriding concern. 'Islam is in danger,' he wrote, 'and we see that it is getting weaker by the day. If we respected Islam's rules and observed the wishes of the law-giver [God], the Muslim states would not now be in this condition, and the Christian states would not have subjugated them . . . in order for a country to be independent, it is necessary that it have jurisdiction over all its residents.' His recommendation that the law be changed to 'suit the needs of the times' was the clarion call of the Muslim moderniser – behind which conservatives detected a secularist agenda.[3]

Qavam also claimed to be a moderniser, though in truth the new finance minister was driven more by ambition than ideology. Literary, ruthless and urbane, Qavam had been Muzaffar ud-Din Shah's private secretary at the granting of the first majles, inscribing the historic rescript in his own, elegant hand. He and Mossadegh had known each other since childhood and shared the same social background. Their common tenancy of the finance ministry brought together the only Persian statesmen who would defy and outlast the monarchical despotism which lay in store.

From the start, they were at loggerheads. Mossadegh had an elevated estimation of his own abilities and behaved as if he were the minister, demanding extra powers and working long into the night. The lordly Qavam, by contrast, bided the summer in a pleasant house in the foothills, and his office, piled with urgent chits gathering dust, was a monument to bureaucratic inertia. Qavam did not appreciate the deputy minister's encroachment onto his territory, nor his tendency to direct petitioners to his summer residence, and he volleyed back the official correspondence he received using a fleet of hired Victorias. Tensions rose and Mossadegh resigned, but there was a clamour for him to return and eventually it was Qavam who left his post. Emboldened by his success, Mossadegh set about cleaning out the ministry: an Augean stable tainted by avarice and long service under the Belgians.

It says much for the fleeting nature of public office in Persia in the first half of the twentieth century that Mossadegh's fourteen-month stint as deputy finance minister would be, after the premiership, the longest tenure of his career. Equally significant was his ability to re-engage obsessively with Iran so soon after deciding to make his home in Switzerland. But Switzerland had never been a serious rival for his affections. Neuchâtel was blessed relief from the torrid emotions that Iran never failed to inspire – an escape from home, not a home. Only in Tehran could he flourish and grow, and now, in his mid-thirties, his distinctive political persona began to emerge – one of ostentatious, combative morality. Here was Mossadegh's demagogic gene.

Mossadegh began a pursuit of top ministry officials on charges of corruption and other irregularities, and it turned into a poisonous affair which brought the press to paroxysms, toppled a government and aroused the Shah's displeasure. According to Mossadegh, these bureaucrats' decision to annul a concession that had been awarded to an Armenian businessman was an act of 'treachery' that had cost the country dearly in lost revenues. Mossadegh accused the grandees of making unauthorised withdrawals from government coffers, and in the process was subjected to criticism of an intensity he had never experienced. In a public statement of considerable sanctimony, he claimed to be soldiering on in office against his will. In truth, he derived a true contrarian's enjoyment from the struggle.

One day, while he sat at his desk, he heard a newspaper-vendor in the street outside shout, 'Deputy minister accused of reneging on Islam!' The newspaper's claim, resting on a mistranslation of a line in his doctoral thesis (in French), was easily disproved, but even so an allegation of apostasy might provoke religious fanatics to assassinate him. Seyyed Zia ud-Din Tabatabai, an anti-establishment newspaper editor who would become one of Mossadegh's most persistent enemies, was especially vitriolic. His newspaper accused Mossadegh of selling government land he was tenanting, and of underpaying taxes on his own estates.[4] 'So unabashed a shortfall!' the paper shrieked. 'So naked an infraction!'[5]

After several months, the case ended inconclusively. The court suspended the four defendants from their posts, but the suspensions were quashed in cabinet and Mossadegh himself, somewhat paradoxically, had his wages docked for exceeding his powers.[6] One of the judges conceded that the outcome had been a whitewash, and that Mossadegh had been punished for daring to 'catch thieves'. Much of the newspaper-reading public agreed.

A defeat on paper, but a moral victory, the episode helped form Mossadegh's intensely polarising reputation. To one hostile observer, his pursuit of the bureaucrats was evidence for his 'lust for renown'. He was the kind of man who would 'raze Caesarea for the sake of a handkerchief'.[7]

Mossadegh was building a public image but he wanted it to be based on integrity and patriotism, and this set him apart from the self-serving politicians around him. As long as men like Qavam held office, they would not want for a constituency; power, in Persia as elsewhere, makes its own friends. But Mossadegh's desire to be on the side of right chimed with his qualities as a public figure, and his personal prestige would never be higher than when politically he was most wretched. This was connected to the ideal, rooted in the national psyche and in the history of Shia Islam, of virtue and self-sacrifice in leadership. At the height of the campaign to defame him, his mother Najm al-Saltaneh, that prayerful woman of the world, coined a phrase that would become his political motto. Noting his despondency, she said, 'a person's weight in society is proportional to the adversities he faces on behalf of the people'.[8]

At the end of the war, Persia was on its knees. The October Revolution had paved the way for Russia's withdrawal from a forward position in the country's affairs, raising Bolshevik prestige in Iran but permitting Britain to exploit the absence of its old rival. The sense of crisis, never far away, was sharpened by burgeoning secessionist movements, while the Cossack Brigade collapsed in the absence of firm Russian direction, alarming Mossadegh, who ran across a group of unruly Cossacks, roaring drunk, as he returned home one evening.

In April 1919 Mossadegh set out for Switzerland to be reunited with his elder children, Zia Ashraf and Ahmad. The great peace conference to divide the spoils of the First World War was underway at Versailles. The British ensured that Persia's delegation was not admitted to the conference, and that its desiderata were not discussed. The agent of Iran's frustration was George Nathaniel Curzon, who had been Viceroy of India from 1898 to 1905 and who was now Britain's acting foreign secretary. He was secretly pursuing a separate, bilateral deal with a triumvirate of powerful Anglophiles in Tehran, and intended the Anglo–Persian Agreement to be one of the crowning achievements of his career.

Curzon had travelled all over Persia in the 1880s as a brilliant, bossy, prolix Oxford graduate and rising public figure, and had not wavered in his belief that the two countries were natural partners in a 'friendly alliance' to defend India against Russia. Persian patriots had noted appreciatively Curzon's denunciations of the 1907 Anglo–Russian Convention – though Curzon had been moved more by the convention's small print than any distaste for the principle of an imperial carve-up. Now, at the close of the First World War, with the Russians absorbed in revolution and civil war and Britain establishing a new mandate in Mesopotamia, his dream of a chain of vassal states guarding the overland route to India finally seemed feasible.

Curzon expected to become prime minister. His tendency in this, his grandest phase, was to regard not only the British Empire, but the whole world, as an annex to his Derbyshire estate. For the Persians, he planned an onslaught of charity and benevolence. He exhibited that peculiarly English trait of wishing, as the comic character Haji Baba of Isfahan puts it, to 'do us good against our inclination'. Curzon understood the imperial challenge that Bolshevism would mount after its brief retreat into virtuous monasticism, as well as the importance of Britain's interests in the Persian oilfields. He believed that no sensible Persian could desire anything but the agreement he was offering, under which the British would have a free hand to modernise all areas of public administration and the armed forces, and Persia would get armaments and a big loan in return. Indeed, had the Persians been seeking profitable integration into the British Empire, Curzon's terms might have been attractive. But the mood in Persia was not submissive. It was prickly and nationalistic. The government of India and some of Curzon's subordinates in the Foreign Office advised him of this. He dismissed them as fools.

The Anglo–Persian Agreement was negotiated in secrecy by Sir Percy Cox, the British minister in Tehran, and three Persian nobles: the prime minister, Vusuq ul-Dawleh (who was Qavam's half-brother), Farmanfarma's son Prince Firooz, who was named as foreign minister during the negotiations, and the finance minister, Sarem ul-Dawleh – with the Shah, hearing the jingle of English coin, in rapacious attendance. Against Curzon's better judgement, the British gave the triumvirate an advance on the prospective loan worth £130,000 – 'palm oil', as Cox put it, for buying off anticipated opposition – and promises of asylum should the need arise. The Shah was already receiving a subsidy in return for supporting Vusuq and his government.

In Curzon's words, 'no more disinterested and single-minded attempt was ever made by a Western Power to re-establish the existence and secure the prosperity of an Eastern country'. But most educated Persians were appalled when the agreement was made public in August 1919. The barely-concealed protectorate status that Curzon was offering compared unfavourably with the Bolsheviks' promise of a new bilateral relationship based on equality, and their unilateral renunciation of all Tsarist privileges harmful to Persian sovereignty. But it was the secret nature of the negotiations, and rumours of a 'British bribe', that were the treaty's undoing.

Mossadegh read the news over breakfast in Switzerland. 'He grew agitated,' his elder son Ahmad recalled. 'He wept. We couldn't go near him. That evening several of my father's Iranian acquaintances came to see him and they occupied themselves with lamentation and weeping until the middle of the night. And this went on for several days.'[9]

Mossadegh's shame must have been compounded by the knowledge that his first cousin Prince Firooz had been one of the treaty's architects, and a beneficiary of the 'British bribe'. Brilliant, snobbish and ambitious, Firooz incarnated all that Persian reformers found objectionable about the Qajar upper class from which Mossadegh would gradually withdraw. As a student in Paris, Firooz had occupied a suite at the Lutetia, the art-deco hotel where James Joyce wrote part of *Ulysses*, and had attended fancy-dress parties with Cocteau. He had also been married to Mossadegh's only sister, Ameneh, but the marriage had ended in divorce, and Mossadegh seems to have blamed Firooz.[10] The two men were opposites even in superficial ways. Firooz owned one of the first Rolls-Royces in Tehran and left unpaid tailors' bills wherever he went. He did not shrink from political assassination.[11] He was feted by Curzon. It is hard to imagine Mossadegh relishing his association with such a man.

After recovering from the shock of the treaty, Mossadegh got to work to galvanise Iranian opinion in Europe, taking a leading role in a new 'Committee of National Resistance' that was set up by Persian émigrés and firing off letters to the League of Nations. He travelled to Berne for the sole purpose of having a rubber stamp made for the committee, and convinced himself that a flirtatious advance by an attractive young woman was a British trap to besmirch him. One can well imagine his ecstasy of embarrassment as he declined her invitation to meet for a smoke: 'I am sorry, *madame*, I am ill. I am very busy. I am tired. Forgive me. I don't have the time.'

The strength of opposition to the treaty came as an unwelcome surprise for Curzon, Cox and the triumvirs. Vusuq used bribery and intimidation to silence his critics, while Curzon hoped that the majles would pass the treaty into law. But the impetus now lay with its opponents. The nationalists were heartened by international criticism – Woodrow Wilson's administration in the United States was particularly disapproving – while Curzon's warm feelings for the Persians evaporated. 'These people have got to be taught –' he wrote, 'at whatever cost *to them* – that they cannot get on without us. I don't at all mind their noses being rubbed in the dust.'[12]

The Persians refused to be taught, and the Bolsheviks, having seized the advantage in their civil war, now made a sensational return to Persian affairs. A Russian landing on the Caspian coast in May 1920, and the ignominious British withdrawal that followed, were blows to Curzon and his protégé Vusuq. By the time the government fell in July, the Anglo–Persian Agreement was a dead letter, though it was some time before Britain's foreign secretary was reconciled to its demise.*

How had Curzon and the triumvirs misread Persian public opinion so badly? Vusuq was not the only Persian statesman to suggest that his country was unready for the burden of modern government. He was not alone in proposing an authoritarian administration bolstered by foreign expertise. But he and Curzon had underestimated the strength of patriotic feeling, and their secretive methods suggested that they had something to hide. In the words of one British official in Tehran, the average Persian's thinking ran as follows:

'We know that you British are asking to lend us money; you have done so before. We know that you are willing to lend us advisers; we have had foreign advisers before. But why do you find it necessary to pay these Ministers to make this Agreement? Evidently you want something for your money which does not appear in the Agreement, which you wish to conceal. We believe that you want to seize Persia as you have seized Egypt and Mesopotamia and that Vusuq ul-Dawleh has sold his country to you.'[13]

---

* Curzon lost his job with the change of government in Britain in 1924, and died the following year.

Still-born it was; but the treaty would have a lasting effect on Persian perceptions of Great Britain. Dispelled for ever were memories of the British as supporters of the early constitutionalists. In their place came an inflexible belief in Britain's duplicity and the morally corrosive effect of its representatives. In time, Persians' fear and hatred of the British would assume proportions rarely seen in the formal empire. British influence was so compelling an idea, everyone ended up being drawn to its flame. If a politician fell, it was that he had displeased the British. Careers would stand or fall, and policies be implemented or put into abeyance, not simply in response to the British position, but on the strength of the Persians' intuition of what that position might be. If the British had no position, that itself became a position. Paid-up Anglophiles went to such lengths to disprove their sympathies that conversely a strident critic of Britain might be accused of throwing up a smokescreen to hide his real sympathies and genuine patriots might make concessions to British interests in order to hide the depth of their antipathy.

Chronic insecurity, mingled with fatalism, tainted public life as Persia tried to become modern, but this on its own does not explain the theories and delusions that arose with respect to the British. The most important source was the conduct of the British themselves. Reading the words of the diplomats and leader writers, with their lucid emphasis on British benevolence, it is easy to miss this. Infusing British policy, the stink in the corner of the room, was a profound contempt for Persia and its people.

It was relatively new. It had not existed in Safavid times, when English traders and ambassadors marvelled at the country's prosperity and even took service in the Shah's Court. It began to be felt in the nineteenth century, as the empire took over much of the globe – and it persists, *sotto voce*, even today. Sir Mortimer Durand, the British minister in Tehran in the 1890s, has been described as possessing a 'good deal of contempt for the Persians'. The writer Harold Nicolson, who served in Persia in the 1920s and considered himself a friend of the country, called the Persians 'the most contemptible race on earth', and their finest minds 'no better than an English schoolboy'. In the Second World War, Winston

Churchill worried lest the British minister in Tehran, Sir Reader Bullard, allow his contempt for the Persians, 'however natural', to impair his judgement. There were exceptions – British decision-makers who preferred honest Persian patriots to the schmaltzing of a Firooz – but the supremacists ruled the roost.

Policy was the casualty. The pathetic and unworthy Persians could not be trusted to take the right decisions. Britain's diplomats diligently undermined their own public support for Persia's independence. Thus, in 1920, we find Herman Norman, the minister in Tehran, writing that he had installed the current Persian government and would endeavour to keep it in power.[14] The British prided themselves on their clean hands, but usually the only people prepared to be their local allies were the venal and the unpatriotic. When the results were unsatisfactory, the British denounced the Persian political class as venal and unpatriotic. 'We cannot,' Curzon wrote, 'support these corrupt and rapacious oriental officials if we earnestly desire to improve the general condition of the country and of the administration.' [15] But Curzon did not have any better idea.

They railed against the illogicality of it all, but the British were complicit in the blackening of their own reputation. If the English language had a word for well-founded paranoia, it might be applied to Persian feelings towards the British for much of the twentieth century.

Iran's history would have been poorer if Mossadegh had been born with commercial nous. So incensed was he by the Anglo–Persian Agreement, he resolved to make his home in Switzerland once and for all, and to go into trade. Borrowing heavily from his mother, he went to Basle and bought a cornucopia of health and vanity products, which he dispatched to Tehran. But Mossadegh's shipment went astray and two years passed before it eventually reached its destination. The thermometers were in smithereens, the washing powder was damp, and the scented soap had become viscous and slimy. Zahra said, 'Muhammad, that's enough trade.' Najm al-Saltaneh was less forgiving. Mossadegh was forced to sell a property in order to pay her back.[16]

By that time, he had returned to Persia, heartened by the demise of the Anglo–Persian Agreement and resolved to repatriate the teenagers Zia Ashraf and Ahmad, whose long exile had caused them to forget their Persian. In June 1920 he had received a telegram in Neuchâtel from his old friend Moshir ul-Dawleh, a liberal politician of great integrity, who had become prime minister and wanted Mossadegh to take the justice portfolio. Moshir had accepted the premiership on the condition that the Anglo–Persian Agreement was formally placed in abeyance. Mossadegh dropped his plans to emigrate.

As a government minister, Mossadegh was entitled to privileged travel arrangements, and he and the children received visas to return home by the quickest route – on a P&O liner, the *Delta*, sailing from Marseille to Bombay, from where they would board another vessel bound for the Persian Gulf. After dinner one night on the way to Bombay, he was engaged in conversation by an Englishman of imposing appearance, tall and spare, blond and blue-eyed. This was Sir Percy Cox, who was now on his way to Iraq to run the British mandate there. Cox had spent his early career as unofficial ruler of the Persian Gulf from the Iranian port of Bushehr, where he carried the deceptively modest title of 'political resident'. He viewed with scepticism the polite fiction of Persian sovereignty over a region that had effectively submitted to British rule. One of Cox's most significant acts while at Bushehr had been to negotiate on behalf of the Anglo-Persian Oil Company a lease on coastal land suitable for refineries and depots. He had reached agreement not with the Tehran government, but with the local Arab ruler.

During his conversation on board with Cox, Mossadegh mentioned that he hoped to disembark at the Iraqi port of Basra and take the train to Baghdad, from where he would cross the Persian border and make for Tehran. The following day, Cox received news that the Basra–Baghdad railway had been sabotaged, so Mossadegh would have to find an alternative route. It evidently amused the Englishman to hear Mossadegh reply that he would disembark at Bushehr, 'one of our own ports'. Cox enquired innocently: 'Bushehr is a Persian port?' Mossadegh never forgot the slight.[17]

In Bombay, Mossadegh and the children stayed in the neo-Gothic Taj Mahal Palace, the city's grandest hotel, receiving visits from Iranian nationalists who were in exile in India. He avoided Vusuq ul-Dawleh, who had left Persia after being ejected from power and was in the same establishment. Mossadegh cabled for a loan from Farmanfarma, which he used to buy a car and engage an Indian chauffeur. Since 1916, Farmanfarma had been governor of the southern province of Fars, and Mossadegh expected to enjoy his uncle's hospitality on the road from Bushehr to Tehran.

For Mossadegh, perhaps the most challenging aspect of the trip home was dealing with his adolescent daughter. Feeling herself to be Swiss, missing the Pernouds terribly, fifteen-year-old Zia Ashraf had not concealed her reluctance to return to Iran, and she defied her father's wish that she wear the hejab – the Muslim head-covering – during the passage from Marseille. There was a row and at Bombay Mossadegh instructed her to keep her distance from him in public. Mossadegh took no issue with Zia Ashraf's emancipation but, as usual, fretted for his reputation.[18] He had even booked the family's tickets on the *Delta* under an assumed name, for it would not do for it to be known that he, that stern critic of the Anglo–Persian accord, was travelling on a British ship![19]

The Mossadeghs' passage ended at Bushehr, from where they drove north to Shiraz. The hometown of the medieval poets Hafez and Saadi, graced by elegant palaces and fragrant rose-bowers, Shiraz was Persia's most romantic city. It stands amid good farmland close to the ruins of Darius the Great's seat at Persepolis, and was renowned at the time for the excellence of its wine. Fars, the province of which Shiraz was the capital, was strategically very important. Populated by recalcitrant tribes, bordering the oil-producing region and the Gulf ports, it had been the scene of much German intrigue during the First World War and had been brought to heel by a British-led levee, the South Persia Rifles, which Persian nationalists regarded as a barely-concealed occupation force.

Even by its own standards, the region was agitated in the autumn of 1920. Influenza and cholera had ravaged the population and the crops were destroyed by drought and locusts. The tribesmen were moving from their upland summer quarters towards the provincial capital, from which unruly movement of people and animals the sedentary population recoiled in fear. There had been shock too at the recent robbery, on the Shiraz–Bushehr road, of Persia's envoy to the League of Nations, Prince Arfa ul-Dawleh. Worse still, the province had an absentee governor. Threatened with an insurrection against his misrule, Farmanfarma had retreated from Shiraz and would soon return to Tehran.

The British had pushed for Farmanfarma's appointment in 1916, when German agents had been rampant over the south. The prince cooperated with his old friend Percy Sykes, the founder of the South Persia Rifles, in pacifying the region, but his lodestar, as ever, was self-interest. Finding himself answerable to the Persian government, the British and the tribes, Farmanfarma took money from all and satisfied none. He played the tribes off against each other and received a huge sum in return for conferring the vacant leadership of an important tribe on an undeserving candidate. The salaries of local functionaries had fallen into arrears. When nationalist voices were raised against his governorship, he had them suppressed.

The quintessential Anglophile had become a liability to his British paymasters. Irked by his incessant demands for money, wary of his ambitions to become the uncrowned king of southern Persia, they cut off Farmanfarma's monthly subsidy and rejected his demand for control over the South Persia Rifles. He only desired this, wrote Herman Norman, the British minister in Tehran, 'for the purpose of extorting money from the people'.[20]

To the great and the good of Shiraz, the arrival of Farmanfarma's very different nephew, a man of the world with no prior connections to the province, was a godsend. They immediately pressed the prime minister to release Mossadegh from the justice ministry and appoint him governor in place of his uncle. Mossadegh was amenable and asked for time to negotiate conditions.

Normally, this would have involved discussion of the stipends and subsidies that Mossadegh would be paid – and so it did, only he astonished everyone by rejecting the offers he received as being too generous. When the local grandees proposed to give him substantial monthly retainers, he not only declined but demanded that the grandees stop extorting money from their own people. Mossadegh cabled to Tehran that he would stay in office as long as these notables kept their promise.

Accepted custom and a bond of affection constrained Mossadegh from criticising Farmanfarma openly, and yet he was clearly appalled by his uncle's conduct. Once united in cautious espousal of reform, the two were now divided under the polarising pressure of the Anglo–Persian Agreement. Mossadegh was among the notables who saw off the prince when he left for Tehran. He also placed Ahmad and Zia Ashraf in their great-uncle's charge. But once the uncle was out of sight, the nephew started ringing the changes.

During his tenure in Fars, Mossadegh accepted a fraction of the emoluments that Farmanfarma had enjoyed. He returned gifts and directed disputants to the courts, rather than adjudicate personally in the old Qajar way. He cut the provincial budget and his own entertainments allowance. Most pointed of all, he criticised the policy of divide and rule that had been pursued by 'representatives of the state', and their 'profiting from war and dispute and plunder and pillage'.[21]

For all that, there was a certain hauteur in Mossadegh al-Saltaneh's bowing to serve the people. He did not recoil from the notion of a governing class, though his gubernatorial style was to be widely accessible and not to stand on ceremony. 'No society', he wrote years later, 'can achieve anything without a competent, self-sacrificing leader, and the definition of a trusted leader is that person whose every word is accepted and followed by the people.'[22] His understanding of democracy would always be coloured by traditional ideas of Muslim leadership, whereby the community chooses a man of outstanding virtue – and follows him wherever he takes them.

In some ways, the divide between uncle and nephew was generational. Farmanfarma approached things imperially. His every action seemed to emphasise the greatness of his birth and appetites. His personal army and his tribe of wives, concubines and children;

his much-cherished British gong, the Order of St Michael and St George; his love of wine and the chase and his gleaming Hupmobile motor car – public life for Farmanfarma was more durbar than drudgery.

For Mossadegh, by contrast, the game was not about power, but ideals. He was part of that generation of western-educated Asians who returned home, primly moustachioed, to sell freedom to their compatriots. Beholden to the same mistress, *la patrie*, these Turks, Arabs, Persians and Indians went on to lead the anti-colonial movements that transformed the map of the world. Though they would diverge, and native cloth would replace the starched collars, their political inspiration was shared and European.

Mossadegh's achievements in Fars were impressive. He brokered peace between the tribes and improved law and order to the extent that Prince Arfa's possessions were returned and the Tehran–Shiraz road was made safe even for the treasury bullion coach. He outlawed the bastinado, paid overdue salaries and opened schools. A Shiraz newspaper called him a symbol of 'unity, consensus and stability'.[23]

The photographs from this time show him dapper in frock coat and wing collar, his receding hairline hidden by the customary *kolah*, thin, worrying hands emerging from oversize cuffs; or wearing an overcoat in among the chiefs, most of whom wear the more traditional *aba*. The contrast with Farmanfarma, lop-shouldered and walrus-moustached, taking the salute at a tattoo of the South Persia Rifles, must have struck everyone. Mossadegh was not the kind to attend a tattoo of the South Persia Rifles.

He inclined to melodrama. When he learned that his deputy had been abusing his position, he threw the town into a panic by preparing to leave for Tehran. The townspeople besieged him and extracted from the deputy-governor a pledge of improved conduct. It was not Mossadegh's style to bluff on a question of honour, and he would certainly have quit if he had not been satisfied. He took a fatalistic, almost careless view of power, but believed instinctively in his own moral impetus. Early in his governorship he responded to some act of presumption on the part of the British consul by saying that he might as well resign if the Englishman intended to behave in this way. The consul beat a hasty retreat.

For the first time, Mossadegh was subjected to British scrutiny. Assessing the implications of his appointment, Herman Norman had written that the new man enjoyed little influence or popularity, an unobjectionable statement at the start of Mossadegh's tenure, but hardly perceptive. G. P. Churchill of the Foreign Office's Eastern Department was as vague as he was ominous, describing Mossadegh as 'very ambitious' and not possessed of a 'good reputation', before concluding, somewhat farcically, that he constituted a 'grave risk'.[24] To what, it is hard to say, though Mossadegh was already known for his patriotism and honesty, qualities that acted like grit in the colonial machine.

The bumptious British consul was soon replaced by a more ambivalent imperialist. W. L. Meade was an Irish patriot and a highly sympathetic character. The new consul supported Mossadegh's efforts to make friends with the tribes, and Mossadegh respected the Irishman's sense of honour and patriotism. The two men, in Mossadegh's words, worked 'like brothers', and Meade's communications to Mossadegh were couched in terms of such fraternal solicitude that one might easily forget he was a servant of the British Crown.

They had a shared admiration for the Irish nationalist Terence MacSwiney, who starved himself to death in October 1920 in protest at his internment by the British. MacSwiney's famous maxim, 'Victory is won not by those who can inflict the most, but by those who can endure the most,' was not dissimilar to Najm al-Saltaneh's comment about the leader who suffers for his people. Mossadegh would go on hunger strike several times in the course of his life – though his appetite invariably got the better of him.

If there had been more men like Meade in the imperial machine, Mossadegh's relations with the British might not have soured so dramatically. But Meade was an exception who ended up disliking policy in Persia, and he was regarded without favour in Whitehall, where his nationalist proclivities may have been noted. A few years later, on his return from Persia, Meade had a meeting with Curzon's principal private secretary, Laurence Oliphant, in the course of which he praised Mossadegh's honesty and competence. Oliphant responded without enthusiasm to Meade's local insights and commentary on policy, minuting that they were 'of a destructive rather than constructive nature'. It was a classic encounter between a local expert, sympathetic to the aspirations of honest Persian patriots, and a Curzonite who approved of honest Persian patriots only if they did as they were told. Meade 'has just retired from the political service,' a relieved Oliphant ended his memorandum, 'and will not be returning to the East.'[25]

While Mossadegh restored order in Fars, the situation in other parts of the country continued to worsen. Revolts in the north made a mockery of the government; famine and pestilence raged and no caravan seemed safe from highwaymen. British officers and diplomats in Persia were resigned to the failure of the Anglo–Persian accord, and considered alternative means of keeping Persia stable and immune from Bolshevism. They had taken control of the Cossack Brigade, whose personnel were by now mainly Persian, and were encouraging a group of ambitious civilians to plan a pro-British government fortified by the Cossacks. This government would not resurrect the Anglo–Persian Agreement. It would inaugurate a strong, militarised Persia.

The man the British identified to lead the endeavour was Seyyed Zia ud-Din Tabatabai, the newspaper editor who had already crossed swords with Mossadegh when the latter was deputy finance minister. Small, delicately formed and highly ambitious, Zia was the son of an anti-constitutionalist preacher who had embraced constitutionalism at a providential moment. He wore a small turban or a sheepskin hat – reminder of his humble origins and loathing for the *kolah*-doffing elite – above pale, sensual features and a neat beard. Zia's Anglophile enthusiasms were not in doubt. He had received a share of the 'British bribe' and defended the Anglo–Persian Agreement. Now he wanted to lead a national revival, with the Cossacks as his shock troops and the British in support.

On February 21, 1921, the plan was put into action. The Cossacks marched on Tehran, brushing aside sporadic resistance. A terrified

Ahmad Shah received Zia and installed him as prime minister, though he demurred when Zia (following Mussolini's example) demanded to be named 'Dictator'. Even more significant, Ahmad confirmed Colonel Reza Khan, who had led the Cossack assault, as the force's permanent commander.

Zia's willingness to challenge vested interests won him early support. A member of a new class of bright Persian professionals, he poured venom on the blue-blooded 'scions of the royal apartments'. His first, scorching proclamation, plastered on walls throughout the capital, promised revenge on the elite with their inherited privileges. Some eighty members of the ruling class were arrested, including Farmanfarma and Firooz.

Mossadegh would surely have met the same fate had he been in Tehran. Instead he became one of a few provincial governors who refused to recognise the new regime – Qavam was another – provoking from Zia a blunt threat against his life. Mossadegh was encouraged in his defiance by the British consul, Meade, who differed from his superiors in Tehran in that he regarded Zia with great suspicion, but their shared hope that Ahmad Shah would summon the courage to get rid of his new prime minister proved unrealistic. Encouraged by Norman and reassured by Zia's protestations of loyalty, Ahmad had uneasily blessed the putsch; he accepted the resignation letter which Mossadegh reluctantly sent him, and ordered him back to Tehran.

On his way to the capital, Mossadegh got wind that Zia intended to arrest him, so he slipped into the rugged mountainous summer quarters of the Bakhtiari tribe, to the south-west of the central city of Isfahan. Although some of the Bakhtiari chieftains were famous Anglophiles, and had enriched themselves guarding Britain's oil installations further south, others had supported the Axis powers during the First World War. They would welcome Mossadegh, one of them promised, as warmly as they had welcomed the most daring of the German agents.

While enjoying Bakhtiari hospitality, Mossadegh learned that Zia himself had been overthrown, barely three months after taking power. The prime minister had alarmed the Shah with his loathing for the Qajar elite. But Zia's departure did not signify the advent of a rigorous, independent-minded Shah. Ahmad would now be manipulated by his war minister, the same Colonel Reza Khan who had led the Cossacks into Tehran.

# 5

## *Eclipse of the Qajars*

Six-foot-three of glowering, muscle-bound ambition, Reza Khan crushed the shell of Qajar power. He wrote no foreign language, and barely his own; his culture was cards and wenching, though later he acquired the genteel vices of opium and extortion. Following the inverted social logic of the English upper class, Sir Percy Loraine, the new British minister in Tehran, approved of Reza's disdain for aristocratic Persian flimflam, his calling a spade a spade. Loraine liked Reza, indulged his lapses in etiquette, and expected him to 'do with Persian hands that which the British had wished to do with British hands, i.e. create a strong army, restore order and consolidate a strong and independent Persia'. Loraine and his Soviet counterpart both considered Reza a friend of their respective countries. It was a remarkable feat for a man who had learned geopolitics in the barrack room.

Iran seethed as he started his ascent. Banditry and insurgency threatened the whole flimsy structure. It was one of those times when the Persian longing for a strongman capable of dragging the country back from the precipice seems like the summit of logic and good sense.

Reza posed as a loyal servant of Ahmad Shah, but Ahmad's instinct for self-preservation told him to beware. In the last years of his rule the Shah's love of travelling became a mania. He ended up reigning from Deauville and Monte Carlo, playing the money markets and communicating via telegraph with a series of short-lived governments, and with his brother, the Crown Prince. In Tehran the minister of war bided his time. He shared the pit with a succession of prime ministers, and pole-axed every one. His power base was the European-style army which he built and then used to put down regional seditions. Patriotic Iranians gave him the longest of leashes; he needed to be indulged in order to be enjoyed.

Reza fooled almost everyone, or perhaps they wanted to be fooled. 'It is in the power of Reza Khan', Loraine wrote in May 1923, 'to become PM, to close the majles or rule as a dictator, even to overthrow the Qajar dynasty; any of these courses would diminish the difficulties which beset his path, but the fact that he has abstained from all of them pretty well disposes of any idea that he is solely actuated by personal ambition.'[1] Within three years, Reza would have realised all but one of Loraine's hypotheses, and the only one he neglected to essay, the closing of the majles, he would achieve in all but name, by rigging elections and crushing dissent. But Reza guarded himself with inscrutability. One moment, he was a paragon of loyalty to the Shah; the next, a coarse and seedy sergeant major on the make; and then again, Persia's saviour.

Mossadegh too had become impossible to ignore. He had shed his youthful caution and his political objectives were becoming clear: unconditional independence from the powers, democracy and a solvent, frugal state. His honesty and forthrightness were in demand to shore up those rickety governments which came and went after Zia's departure. Between October 1921 and October 1923, Mossadegh served at different times as finance minister, foreign minister and governor of the province of Azerbaijan. But each time he was installed, those same qualities came to be seen as liabilities. He attacked prerogatives, corruption and the powers. He seemed to believe that every battle was worth fighting.

Early on he looked Reza Khan in the eye and refused to endorse a bond issue aimed at raising funds for the army. The reason was that an endorsement would also be needed from the government's British financial adviser, and Mossadegh did not believe that the government should have such an adviser. He stirred up a whirlwind in his short time as finance minister (under Qavam again, who had been named prime minister), booting time-servers into retirement, slashing salaries and cutting the privy purse for well-born friends and cousins. He brought out the first properly organised budget in Iranian history – typically, it was balanced – and demanded that a deputy who had allegedly dispensed favours to win office lose his immunity from prosecution. It was the first time the majles had heard such a request, and the deputies were outraged.

He was cold-shouldered by men he had known for years, and the Shah's brother was aghast when Mossadegh froze his stipend. Summoned to answer his critics in parliament, he had his first public fainting fit.[2]

Mossadegh reasoned that he should have 'wide authority in all areas to end without delay any state of affairs not to his liking'. To be fettered by rules and bureaucrats was to allow his mission to be imperilled. It irritated him that others could not see this as clearly as he could. He shared this impatience with Reza Khan. What separated him from Reza was that he would not arrange for his opponents to be defamed in the newspapers, or taken in on trumped-up charges, or killed. If he was defeated, he would throw up his hands and move to Switzerland.

He thought of emigrating after Qavam's government fell in January 1922 but reconsidered when his old friend Moshir, who was once again prime minister, offered him the governorship of Azerbaijan. In accepting this post, Mossadegh hoped to distance himself from the hostility he faced in the capital. No doubt he also hoped to replicate the success he had enjoyed in Fars.

Azerbaijan was another huge border province, dominated by tribes and supervised by a powerful neighbour – in this case, Russia. Mossadegh knew it well. As a boy, he had lived in the provincial capital, Tabriz, with his mother and stepfather, and had learned some Azeri Turkish. But Mossadegh had triumphed in Fars because of his autonomy there. Azerbaijan would be different. In Reza Khan, the country now had a war minister who took a controlling interest in any region that suffered unrest, cultivating allies among the local leaders and building his network of spies. Azerbaijan was such a region.

Reza's forces had recently smashed a rebellion in Tabriz, leaving the bazaar a smouldering wreck. Further west he was battling

another revolt, this one led by the Kurdish blackguard Simko Shikak.
Reza had a reputation for pressing for the appointment of rivals
to sensitive positions, only to undermine them. Mossadegh was
famous for his probity and patriotism. He could only be regarded
as a rival.

It was perishing winter when Mossadegh arrived on horseback,
with a high fever, to take up his post. Tabriz was sullen and tense.
Death sentences and prison terms had been handed down to the
captured rebels, and innocent citizens also languished behind bars.
(Mossadegh, typically, had them released.) Pay was in arrears.
Persia's honeymoon with the Bolsheviks was starting to sour, and
the Soviets were proselytising energetically in a city which they
considered part of their natural zone of influence. The red flag
had been solemnly hoisted over the Soviet consulate. Mossadegh
immediately riled the consul by having a troublesome Soviet citizen
arrested.

The most important challenger to Mossadegh's authority was
the tribal leader Sardar Ashayer. The sardar extorted produce
without pity from the local people. The territory under his sway
was the region's bread-basket and he only need give the word for
the supply of wheat in Tabriz to stall. The sardar also happened
to be one of Reza Khan's favoured warlords and an ally in the fight
against Simko.

By a strange coincidence, Najm al-Saltaneh's niece had married
the sardar in order to safeguard her estates in the region. But
Mossadegh did not shrink from a confrontation. He ordered the
arrest of an indebted official who had taken sanctuary at the sardar's house. The sardar responded by obstructing the wheat supply.
Mossadegh telegraphed desperately for wheat but was stonewalled
by landowners who answered to the sardar. The city mayor –
another of the sardar's stooges – reduced the amount of flour being
given to the city bakers, thereby sparking riots at the ovens.

Here, brutally distilled, was Persian politics. From the prime
minister to the humblest village headman, political survival
depended on filling the bellies of the people, and bread shortages
could quickly turn into serious threats to public order. Mossadegh

discovered this almost to his cost when he was in a local mosque for a memorial service and found himself surrounded by angry citizens demanding bread. Mossadegh did not hesitate to raise the stakes, promising to resign if there was not enough flour for everyone by the following day. 'I saved my skin,' he recalled, 'but coming back from the mosque I was not at ease for a single moment, and asked myself how on earth I would manage to keep my promise.'[3]

The following morning, Mossadegh convened an emergency meeting of the great and the good to discuss the bread situation, and this gave his military commander a chance to lure the sardar into a side room and arrest him. The mayor was dealt with in similar fashion and the other notables were astonished at the ease of Mossadegh's victory. He had the sardar's ammunition stores stripped and his weapons brought to Tabriz. At a stroke, the bread crisis was solved.

Security improved after the sardar's arrest and some local land-owners thanked Mossadegh for ending years of 'torture' at his hands.[4] But there was disquiet in Tehran at the detention of a man who was loyal to the central government. Mossadegh brushed off an attempt by his own cousin, the sardar's wife, to bribe him into releasing her husband. But now Reza Khan waded in, ordering Mossadegh to dispatch the sardar to Tehran, where he was placed in gilded captivity.

By arresting the sardar, Mossadegh had shown unwelcome inde-pendence, and it was the death knell of his governorship. Critical articles started appearing in the press, and gradually he lost control over provincial security. Small humiliations mounted up and even-tually he was prevented even from sending ten men to deal with an outbreak of unrest. He received pathetic telegrams from officials in outlying districts, deploring their powerlessness. 'As God is my witness,' Mossadegh wrote, 'it's as if I have been plunged in fire.' It is likely that Reza Khan was the author of his discomforts.

The horrendous winter also took its toll. Mossadegh had arrived in Tabriz in a high fever. To this was added an outbreak of stress-related bleeding in his mouth. When he finally resigned in the spring of 1922, he used the excuse of his failing health. So threatened did he feel, he returned to Tehran with an escort of 120 men.

Back in the capital he was named foreign minister, but soon the Moshir government was on its last legs and the eyes of all were fixed on Reza Khan and his increasingly overt manoeuvring for power. Moshir fell on his sword in late 1923, and Reza became prime minister.

Back in August 1922 Sir Percy Loraine had reported that Reza had markedly improved internal security. Simko had fled into Iraqi Kurdistan and socialist insurgents in the Caspian forests were in retreat. Reza had sidelined many of his former rivals, including Qavam, who was allowed to go into exile after being accused of involvement in a plot to kill him. Reza, Loraine wrote, had achieved this and more in spite of the Shah, the majles and the mullahs. Now the Shah's deficiencies would encourage Reza to bid for absolute power.

Ahmad Shah was a sad vestige of a warlike race. He had famously declared that he would rather sell cabbages than rule over Iran.[5] He commanded a residual loyalty among some patriots, including Mossadegh, but this was less for his virtues than the relatively benign nature of his vices. He had refused publicly to defend the Anglo–Persian Agreement, and had made no attempt to replicate his father's tyranny. And yet this was no way for a monarch to behave: vigilant in defence only of his allowance, perpetuating his rule from the Riviera. When the Shah returned in December 1921 from his second trip to Europe, Reza greeted him with a triumphal cavalcade from Bushehr to Tehran, but the minister's shows of military pomp were designed less to reassure the monarch than to intimidate him. Relations between the two men deteriorated as several governments came and went and Reza showed his contempt by rarely turning up to cabinet meetings. At length, with Moshir's resignation, the Shah was left with no one else to choose; he bowed to the inevitable and asked Reza to form a government.

In neighbouring Turkey, the Ottoman Sultan with his much grander lineage had been deposed by a nationalist soldier. Ahmad was terrified that Reza meant to be a second Ataturk. Mossadegh went to see his royal cousin. Having endorsed Mossadegh's concerns about the worrying train of events, the Shah regretted that he could do nothing. 'When I heard this,' Mossadegh wrote, 'I expressed my sorrow and never again went to see the Shah.'[6]

In August 1923 Ahmad steamed westwards for the last time. At Nice he waddled, round and dapper and solemnly unnoticed by the locals, up and down the Promenade des Anglais, his mind full of plots and suspicions, causing procedural squalls if a fellow Iranian spotted him – for how to take one's leave of the Pivot of the Universe when he passes you in the street? And later, when the attractions of bougainvillea and sharing a hotel with American millionaires wore off, he lapsed into self-pity. 'What did I do wrong?' he pleaded with a Persian visitor. 'Do you want me to be a tyrant in order that the people love me?'[7]

Back in Tehran Reza engineered a 'spontaneous' movement in favour of a republic, but the bazaaris and mullahs abominated such godless arrangements and stirred the rabble. Reza turned bayonets and rifle butts on an anti-republican crowd, giving a voluble preacher a taste of his horsewhip. But he got the message, and the bill to institute a republic was shelved.

In the words of Seyyed Hassan Modarres,* the bravest of the mullahs and an electrifying critic of Reza, 'however good the guard-dog is, it stops being useful the moment it bites the hand of its master's child, and must be banished'.[8] And yet others, appreciating Reza's success as a pacifier, only wanted him muzzled. Reza went to the seminary at Qom and, having poured honey into the ears of the clerics, declared the republican movement dead. He visited Modarres in his threadbare digs in Tehran, where the divine held a dervish's court amid scattered theological treatises and a brazier of hot coals for his pipe. Reza proved to be an effective arm-twister. His supporters forgave him the impurity of his beliefs, his shambolic oratory and his poker-playing with Sir Percy Loraine at all hours. They called him father of the nation and a symbol of all that was virile in Iran.

* The title 'Seyyed' indicates descent from the line of the Prophet.

Reza did not like critical journalists. The director of one paper had his teeth knocked out. The editor of another was whipped. Many more were arrested and their publications suppressed. A young poet who had dared lampoon Reza's republican ambitions was found at home in a pool of blood.

Again, the mob rose up. This time an American diplomat, Robert Imbrie, was murdered after taking photographs at a public fountain that was reputed for its healing powers. Imbrie had fled into a tea-house whose owner doused him with boiling water. Led by a mullah, the crowd caught up with Imbrie at the infirmary where he was being treated, and a camel driver bashed in his head with a stone.[9] Imbrie had been involved in negotiations that were being conducted by two US oil companies for drilling rights, and conspiracy theorists blamed the British, with their own much larger oil interests, for his death. Reza executed the ringleaders and imposed martial law. Every crisis was an opportunity to push forward the juggernaut of intimidation.

Reza continued his provincial forays. His subjugation of the Arab Sheikh Khazal was a masterpiece of theatre and diplomacy, for the sheikh had been Britain's protégé and Sir Percy Loraine was gulled into giving him up to captivity. Each victory was an excuse for Reza's supporters to erect bunting and triumphal arches, to call him 'Conqueror'.

Reza now went on pilgrimage to the holy places of newly-created Iraq, where he assured the top clerics of his devotion to Islam. A triumphal ode appeared under his name, presenting Iran as a sunken nation that had not, all the same, 'forgotten that it too, in its own time, was the crucible of civilisation'.[10] Not that Reza knew much about civilisation. He slept on the floor (his bed was too soft) and was incapable of pronouncing quite elementary words.

Ahmad Shah flirted with the idea of coming home but put it off when bread shortages once again plunged the capital into chaos. Another movement was whipped up, this one viciously anti-Qajar, with a blizzard of telegrams blowing in from all over the country and a sit-in of hirelings demanding an end to the dynasty.

It remained for Reza to bow to the will of the people.

*     *     *

Mossadegh had watched Reza's rise with misgivings, but was cheered by the fall in lawlessness and banditry that he had brought about. Seventeen years after his first attempt to enter parliament ended in disqualification on procedural grounds, Mossadegh had been elected to the fifth majles. But the parliament building was no longer a congenial habitat for a constitutionalist of the old school, especially one whose mother was a Qajar princess. Using his regional allies, many of them army officers who had been rewarded with provincial governorships, Reza had manipulated the elections in the outlying seats, and while Tehran returned a fair number of traditional moderates and there was a socialist rump, the majority was in thrall to the prime minister.

Deliberations in the chamber acquired a shrill, egalitarian tone. Mossadegh was unsympathetic to the republican movement and his decision to stand for the deputy speakership was unwise; he mustered a single vote, presumably his own. Titles were abolished, and Mossadegh al-Saltaneh became Muhammad Mossadegh, the name he had adopted when going abroad as a student, and by which the world would come to know him. Reza chose the surname Pahlavi, the name of an ancient Iranian language, thereby associating himself with a glorious, pre-Islamic past.

Mossadegh resisted Reza's attempts to buy his support with the offer of a government post. He acted as Reza's liaison with a kitchen cabinet which tried to steer the prime minister away from abolishing the dynasty. There was little mirth in these meetings, and the prime minister did not conceal his ambition. 'The British brought me to power,' he said, 'but they didn't know who they were up against.'[11] Reza's belief that he owed his throne to the British would sharpen the sense he had of his own vulnerability. Whatever they had given, they could also take away.

Mossadegh and the others hoped that Reza could be appeased with authority short of absolute power. But the opposite happened. With each concession, his confidence grew. In October 1925 pro-government deputies prepared a resolution abolishing the Qajars and entrusting the nation's affairs to Reza Khan until a constituent assembly convened. A procession of deputies filed through the basement of one of his palaces, where they were threatened or cajoled into supporting the plan. The celebrated poet Muhammad Taqi Bahar was one of a few opposition deputies to answer Reza's summons, but he resisted the blandishments of 'that strange and cunning man whose face lacked light'. That evening, a group of Reza's supporters shot and started hacking off the head of an unfortunate man they had mistaken for Bahar. The press tactfully ignored this grisly murder.

Two days later the resolution came to vote. Support for Reza in the chamber was strong and any opposition deputy showing his face would be risking physical attack. That morning the outgoing speaker, Mostowfi al-Mamalek, phoned Mossadegh (who was his cousin) to consult him on whether he should attend the decisive session. Mossadegh compared a parliamentary deputy to a gunner who is paid on the understanding that he will fire his cannon if the country comes under threat. In the same way, Mossadegh continued, the deputy is expected to defend the constitution. His resolve stiffened, Mostowfi joined Mossadegh at the parliament building.

Inside the chamber the usual spectators were conspicuous by their absence. Their places had been taken by agents and uniformed police. Reza's goons herded the deputies in. One growled at a hesitant deputy, 'Do you have a family, children? Do you care for them?'[12] The man took the hint – and his seat.

Mossadegh was one of five deputies who turned up to speak against the motion. Appalled by what was about to happen, he was overcome by emotion and retreated to the lavatories, where he wept hard. By the time he had composed himself and returned to the chamber, Seyyed Yaghub, a cleric and former constitutionalist, was justifying his support on the grounds that Reza was still needed to prevent the provinces from relapsing into chaos. 'In order to attain a new felicity,' he declared, 'one is obliged to tear up the old tree.'

Now it was Mossadegh's turn. Pale and balding, but not yet gaunt, he rose to defy the new dictatorship. He had ignored his usually reliable instinct for self-preservation and was starting a new and more radical phase in his career.

The orators Modarres and Hassan Taqizadeh, the latter of whom had been a celebrated advocate of the constitution, had already spoken against the resolution, but neither approached Mossadegh in power and logic. Mossadegh's was a passionate production, painstakingly prepared. It was not a defence of the old order but a denunciation of the new one, and his evidence was moral as well as legal. He succeeded in presenting himself as an advocate of both Islam and democracy, twinning the old faith with the modern cult of the nation. Only someone with a mastery of constitutional precepts could have done so.

He started by holding up a copy of the Qoran and bearing witness to Islam, obliging his adversaries to rise out of respect for the holy book. He said that anyone forgetting Islam and the nation was 'base and dishonourable and should be killed'. With this trumpet blast Mossadegh hoped to silence anyone who might question his religious sincerity – as well as to cast doubt on Reza's own claims to piety.

Next, Mossadegh countered suspicions that he was defending the family firm. He had been 'utterly disappointed' with the Qajars, and would not defend people who 'use the country in good times and disappear in bad'. For all that, Mossadegh discerned some advantage in the present situation. The country had a ceremonial Shah whose sole responsibility was to anoint a prime minister according to parliament's wishes. Was that not constitutionalism?

Mossadegh praised Reza's achievements, but then his tone became passionate and reproachful. 'So, the prime minister becomes sultan . . . is there such a thing as a constitutional country where the king also runs the nation's affairs?' He turned on Seyyed Yaghub, who had spoken in favour of the motion:

If they cut off my head and cut me into pieces and if Seyyed Yaghub assails me with a thousand curses I will not accept this! After twenty years of bloodshed! Seyyed Yaghub! Were you a constitutionalist? A freedom-seeker? I myself saw you in this country ascend the pulpit and urge the people on to freedom. And now it is your opinion that this country should have one person who is Shah and prime minister and magistrate all at once? If so, this is reactionary! It is despotism! Why did you needlessly shed the blood of the martyrs on the road to freedom? Why did you send them off to die? From the beginning you should have come out and said we lied and never wanted constitutionalism. You should have said that this is an ignorant people who must be beaten into submission![13]

Later that evening, in the Golestan Palace, the Crown Prince heard the cannon that proclaimed the fall of a dynasty. He expected to be imprisoned, but then came Reza's message that he should gather his personal effects, put on a commoner's clothes, and set out for exile without delay. The Crown Prince complained that he was penniless, but the treasury was sealed. The royal carriage was no longer at his disposal. Reza sent him a piffling sum to see him across the Iraqi border.

In years to come Reza would remain touched by contempt for the Qajars. He embarked on the resurfacing so beloved of usurpers, changing street names and replacing Qajar buildings with severe neoclassical confections. The press depicted the Qajars as unpatriotic and treasonous. There had been just one man among them, Reza quipped: Muzaffar ud-Din Shah's favourite daughter – and she was reduced in her old age to roaming Tehran's tree-lined avenues looking for fuel. Rubbing in his new prerogative, Reza took a descendant of Fath-Ali Shah to be his fourth wife: almond-eyed Esmat, who was famous for her bruised, voluptuous lips. Reza was constantly nibbling them, so the gossip went. Thus a softer light fell on a hard man.

In truth the Qajars could never be wholly wiped out. Thanks to the prodigious loins of Fath-Ali and Nasser ud-Din, there were too many of them. Mostly they went obscurely about their lives and were left alone, while a small number achieved high office under the new regime. Most found that the name had lost its draw. Well-born Qajar women struggled to find husbands for their daughters, and were forced to trawl the middle classes.

Several members of Mossadegh's paternal family – a bureaucratic family, rather than a royal one – adapted nicely to the new dispensation. Mossadegh's nephew Ahmad Matine-Daftary, who was also his son-in-law, became prime minister under Reza Shah, although later on the Shah had him imprisoned. Several of his Mostowfi cousins reached senior positions in an expanding, modernising bureaucracy.

Tiny, formidable and old, Najm al-Saltaneh remained the Qajar matriarch *par excellence*. But even she got used to her altered circumstances, throwing her energies into a foundation hospital which she had built, the Najmiyeh Hospital, living in a small house in the same compound and paying the labourers herself at the end of the working day. She never lost her foul tongue – nor her love for her elder son. On one occasion she turned up at Mossadegh's front door at three in the morning and the household was roused to receive her. 'Sit with me,' she ordered the future prime minister, and he did.[14]

Mossadegh's speech against the abolition had made him famous, and after it he was visited by Farmanfarma. The prince kissed his nephew's hand – an unusual act of humility – and exclaimed, 'Truly, you have brought the Qajars back to life!'[15] But Farmanfarma had mistaken Mossadegh's hatred of dictatorship for clan loyalty, and in any case the thrill did not last. A few weeks later, when Reza inaugurated an assembly to change the constitution and establish the Pahlavi dynasty, he was amused to spot Farmanfarma sitting in a sulk on the steps of the parliament building, his chin in his hands.[16]

Farmanfarma observed the eclipse of his family with revulsion. He was not alone in regarding the Qajars and the monarchical principle as one and the same, and he and his sister thought of Reza as a grubby dictator got up in royal plumage. But Farmanfarma had not survived at the top of public life by disclosing his true feelings. He had flattered Reza since the latter began his rise, visiting him regularly and referring to himself as Reza's 'old slave'. He had even supported the idea of a republic, or at least pretended to. But Reza had no need for a hanger-on from the old regime.

After becoming Shah, Reza resisted Farmanfarma's advances, seizing the luxurious house of one of his sons in central Tehran.

(Reza would eventually take over several of Farmanfarma's properties, and build his winter palace, the Marble Palace, on one of them.) White-haired and riddled with gout, the old prince took his decline philosophically, abstaining from politics but siring heirs with undimmed vigour. He ended up with thirty-six children from eight wives (not counting many more from concubines along the way) and many of these births necessitated a change to his complicated will, infuriating the elder children as bits fell off their inheritance.

Mossadegh's relations with his uncle cooled in the latter's old age. The family lost focus with Najm al-Saltaneh's death in 1932, but by then Reza's terror had reached its zenith and many political personalities refrained from meeting for fear of being accused of plotting. Having fallen out with Curzon over his supposed indifference to their imprisonment after the 1921 putsch, Farmanfarma later tried desperately to paddle back into favour. For once the British were immune to the old prince's charm. Sir Percy Loraine had a new horse to ride.

Mossadegh can only have felt extreme distaste for all the backsliding. He was already a man of significant pride – not the pompous, *l'état c'est moi* pride of a Farmanfarma, but the pebbly pride of a loner who values above all his reputation and integrity. He differed in almost every way from some of his mother's relations, Prince Firooz in particular. The glittering Firooz had passed on his Rolls-Royce to Reza Shah, a British chauffeur at the wheel. And Firooz saw no shame in becoming a member of the Pahlavi inner circle.

Reza was impervious to the manoeuvring; the Qajars were doomed. An imperial decree would bar anyone with Qajar blood from ascending the Pahlavi throne, disqualifying Esmat's sons as well as that from another Qajar wife. In time, even Firooz would fall – as would all the hangers-on – as soon as he was no longer regarded as an asset to Reza's mission to modernise Iran. 'When you have a whore,' as the new Shah put it, 'you use her, pay her and kick her out, and there the matter ends.'

It is impossible to understand Reza Shah's reign without appreciating the shame he felt at Iran's backwardness. Turkey would be his sole foreign destination; he refused to go further west for fear of being demoralized by the gulf which separated Persia from Europe. Some of his foibles invite derision – his banning of photographs of camels; his championing of the WC – but he should be judged by his significant actions, and Iran changed more thoroughly in the sixteen years of his reign than in the half-century that preceded it.

Reza was a dynamic man and he inspired dynamism in those around him. He promoted men like the judicial reformer Akbar Davar, who worked a fifteen-hour day rather than gossip over the water-pipe, and his court minister, Abdolhossein Teimurtash, as intelligent as he was brutal. Reza implemented an impressive number of reforms that were designed to turn the cracked empire he had inherited into a purposeful nation state. But he ended up, like so many of his fellow dictators, alone in his citadel. And much of the good he did was nullified by the way he did it.

At the next parliamentary elections, in 1926, Reza allowed Mossadegh and some of his other critics to be returned from Tehran. But Mossadegh did not attend the final session of the constituent assembly which set up the new, Pahlavi dynasty, telling a government emissary that he was not feeling well. He also refused to swear fidelity to Reza when taking up his seat in the sixth majles. Although Reza was not yet an undisputed dictator, this required considerable courage.

Mossadegh's cousin Mostowfi had agreed to form a government, and the Shah had insisted on a cabinet place for the ageing architect of the Anglo–Persian Agreement, Vusuq ul-Dawleh, who was now back from exile. The confirmation debate offered Mossadegh a chance to nail Vusuq for what he regarded as his treachery. Mostowfi pleaded with him to let bygones be bygones, but Mossadegh was not the forgiving type.

Persian politicians are not known for their economy in public speaking. Formless productions of eye-watering length are the norm, and quotations from the poets contribute to the sense of drift and abstraction. Mossadegh was capable of immensely boring speeches on policy, read in long monotonous gulps. But, in other circumstances, roused and inspired, he could be a quite different speaker. On these occasions his inhibitions fell away and he became cunning and lachrymose, a masterly manipulator of emotions. For a man who hated violence, he could be violent.

Mossadegh must have known that the new cabinet would be approved, and Vusuq with it. But he wanted to be on the side of right, and he put seven years of bile into his denunciation of the former prime minister. In one passage he went too far, accusing Vusuq of planning Iran's partition, and there was uproar. Then, with a change of gear, the nationalist lawyer became a mullah delivering a call to arms. Islam, he said, 'commands that every Muslim should defend his country, and if he wins he will have endowed the country and the religion with a new spirit, while if he loses, he will have drunk the sherbet of martyrdom in the path of God.' No one, Mossadegh complained, had ever heard an expression of remorse cross Vusuq's lips, but what could be expected nowadays, when 'there is no chance of punishment, when service and betrayal are one and the same,' and 'we stifle the spirit of freedom-seekers and patriots'? There is bitter poetry in these lines, which no other parliamentarian would have dared speak.

Vusuq, in an otherwise ineffective response, perceptively pointed out the difference between a statesman who does not shirk his duty even when the nation is close to collapse and the statesman who prefers to stay on the sidelines rather than shoulder an impossible task. With Mossadegh there is sometimes a strong sense of the latter, of a man who snipes virtuously instead of sullying himself with office.

For Mossadegh, as for Iran, the end of the Qajars was a milestone. He had started the constitutional era as a diffident reformer. Now, in the late 1920s, he found himself in the vanguard of a hopeless resistance. Who, apart from a cussed contrarian, would willingly occupy such a precarious position? But Mossadegh had become the most exuberant opposition politician operating in the country's sole forum for dissent.

There were attempts to stop him speaking but he got around them by tabling motions on subjects unrelated to the main debate, and then, in a style that ranged from intimate (sometimes inaudible) to bombastic and conversational (anecdotes about his mother), he sprang his argument on the very topic he was not supposed to be discussing. He was no stranger to self-righteousness, for instance threatening to leave Iran for ever because four foreign inspectors were working within the tax department. One Shah-loyalist noted his 'negativity on all subjects and his failure to express a single positive sentiment'.[17]

Reza was not yet so dangerously isolated as to require yes-men for advisers, and in these early years showed signs of appreciating Mossadegh's honesty and experience. He was sometimes summoned for informal chats and Reza even dangled the premiership before him – a hazard he sidestepped with another convoluted anecdote. Reza seems to have been intrigued by this noble who hated the monarchy's pomp and luxury, and who advised him to let his palaces crumble and to sit in an unadorned room with a dripping roof, if only the people were properly fed. He also took note when Mossadegh upbraided him for the Potemkin-style displays, featuring triumphal arches and scrubbed-up schoolchildren in gleaming clothes that were not their own, which greeted him during his royal tours of the provinces. The absurdity of these displays had been lost on Reza.

For his part, Mossadegh was impressed by Reza's energy and ability to get things done. He applauded the Shah's efforts to build a modern army and re-establish central authority over far-flung parts of the country, even when this involved smashing the tribes. He supported Reza's attempts to liberate Iran from the influence of the powers, and described another of the Shah's triumphs, his abolition of the capitulations – the old system of handing over sections of the economy to foreign interests – as a 'source of Iranian pride'.

He also broadly approved of Ali Akbar Davar's drive to wrest control of the legal system from the clergy and give it to European-trained judges and lawyers. Mossadegh did not express himself on Reza's educational reforms, under which new primary and secondary schools were built, as well as foreign-run technical colleges, but the efforts he spent educating his own children admit no doubt that he supported an expanded, secular system for all, including women. If there was a criticism to be levelled at Reza's education policies, it was rather that they were superficial and underfunded.

In sum, there was much for Mossadegh to like, and yet he was the most trenchant critic of the new regime, for his differences with the Shah were profound and philosophical. Mossadegh was an anachronism in an age that aspired to human perfection. His politics lacked the clean Nietzschean lines of the transformative dictators, and were unshaded by the revulsion that some of Reza's followers felt for the rest of society. The court minister Abdolhossein Teimurtash, for instance, considered himself a superman and believed that his compatriots 'should be struck, should be ridden, should be held by the stirrup leather'.

Again and again in Persian history one meets this same hatred of the elite for the rabble. It was typical of Mossadegh to speak out against the Tehran mayor whose policy of destroying old houses in order to widen roads saw many homes ruined before their inhabitants could save their belongings. It was all part of an effort to make Tehran look more western, but Mossadegh noted that the destruction of private property was illegal in the West.

Behind his comments lurked a suspicion of material aspiration, drawing from an ascetic ideal located in Iran's poetic and spiritual past. There is poetry in his question, posed in an article around this time: 'What would happen if the roads were not paved and the buildings and guesthouses went un-built? Where would be the harm in that? I wanted to walk over the earth' – and here, inevitably, politics intervened – 'and not suffer my country to be taken over by others.'

In 1926 Modarres narrowly escaped death while walking to class before dawn, pulling his camel's wool *aba* over his head so his assassins would not have a clear view of him. He was wounded nonetheless, and taken to a police hospital where he was assigned a doctor who was notorious for administering lethal injections. A crowd barged into the hospital and, lifting up Modarres's sick-bed, carried him to a different hospital where the doctors would not try to kill him. Reza, enjoying the air up on the Caspian, sent his sympathies.

Mossadegh struck back with humour, which dictators hate. In a speech he observed that Tehran had become a less dangerous place under Reza, before adding mildly, 'It is possible that Mr Modarres's neighbourhood is unsafe.'[18] During a debate on financial savings he proposed cuts in two sectors it was impolitic even to acknowledge: the secret police and the censors. Once, when mealtime approached and Mossadegh was still speaking, a deputy interrupted him to ask for a recess. Mossadegh said, 'Your tummy is rumbling, but I will keep my belly-full of beliefs.'[19]

Mossadegh's issue with the dictatorship was not just its emphasis on coercion, but also its showiness and lack of discernment. Reza fitted into the mould of contemporaries such as Ataturk, Mussolini and Primo de Rivera – men on a personal mission to transform their countries. Mossadegh was also a rationalist. 'Knowledge', he said, unconsciously echoing one of Ataturk's most famous aphorisms, 'is the sole means of distinguishing good from bad.' But knowledge did not only mean science and progress. It also meant using the favours one is born with – the physical and moral environment, religion, race and tribe.

Reza Shah reformed furiously. He scrapped the Arabic and Turkish names for the months and introduced their old Persian equivalents. He replaced the Arabic lunar year, in use since the Arab invasions, with the Iranian solar year, which starts on March 21, the vernal equinox. He developed a cumbersome civil service and later on laid the foundation stone for the new University of Tehran, to which boys and girls were admitted on equal terms. There was a tentative industrialisation, with a small number of new factories being built. In 1935 Reza would substitute 'Iran' for 'Persia' as the official name of the country – the name used by the people, not a European derivation from antiquity.

Mossadegh recoiled from measures that were harmful to the nation's 'Iranian-ness' and 'Islamic-ness', because they were the building blocks of Persia's identity. The Shah's historical distortions left him cold. The government privileged Persia's distant, pre-Islamic heritage over the more recent past, when the country's native institutions and culture had been sapped, so the theory went, by Arab influence. (In fact the Arab invasions had invigorated Persian institutions and culture, leading to a renaissance of statecraft and the arts.) Mossadegh admired the ancients, sponsoring a translation of Fustel de Coulanges' *La Cité antique*, but he had no truck with Reza's antiquarian fantasies, which led to a rash of mock-Achaemenid public buildings and a new vogue for pre-Islamic names. 'We should live as Iranians,' Mossadegh said, 'retaining the good things we have while accepting the good things of others.'[20]

The new men worshipped Napoleon, but Mossadegh found inspiration in Montesquieu's *De l'esprit des lois* of 1748, in which the Frenchman assigned to each form of government an animating principle (republican virtue; monarchical honour; despotic fear), introduced for the first time the separation of powers (legislative, executive and judicial), and suggested an assembly of secondary causes, such as climate and religion, which make governments different from each other. From here it was a short step to Mossadegh's 'Iranian-ness' and 'Islamic-ness', and his belief that a constitutional monarchy was the most appropriate arrangement for Iran. But it was obvious to everyone that under Reza the separation of powers was a sham. The Shah considered no sphere of national life inviolate.

Mossadegh spent much energy puncturing Reza's grandest ambition, which was to throw a railway from the Caspian Sea to the Persian Gulf. For Reza, Persia's lack of a railway was a shameful omission and he took charge of the project, casting a hypercritical eye over miles of track, haranguing labourers for their idleness and laying the last rail himself, in 1938. With its formidable natural barriers, plunging elevations and complex systems of switchbacks and tunnels, the Trans-Iranian Railway was (and remains) a spectacular feat of engineering, and it was financed indigenously through patriotic taxes on tea and sugar.

It was one of those ideas that Mossadegh demolished from a position of pretended support. His prediction of miles of gleaming underemployed track running through sparsely populated country proved accurate, and his suggestion of more roads self-fulfilling. Years before the railway was finished, the long-distance lorry had become the country's symbol of internal trade. Reza's achievement was of greatest use to the Allied occupiers who unseated him in 1941, when it was used to transit materiel for the Soviet war effort.

In the words of an acute modern historian of Iran, Peter Avery, Reza's trouble was that he held up the triumphs of the past to a people who knew better. 'They . . . know from experience better than almost any other nation on earth how transient are material achievements and pomp and glory . . . the New Order pointed to the ruins of Persepolis as reminders of what Iran had once been and must strive to be again. The Iranian people also see in those ruins a monument to the vanity of human success.'[21]

During the elections to the seventh majles in 1928, a drawn-out process again marred by vote-rigging, Mossadegh went to the Shah and demanded that the polling happen without hindrance. The Shah summoned Teimurtash, who assured him that the elections were being conducted freely, only for Teimurtash to tell Mossadegh out of Reza's earshot, 'I could hardly say anything else in the presence of the Shah! Why not draw up a common list of six government and six popular candidates and settle the matter in this fashion?'[22] Mossadegh refused to compromise.

In the event, the polls were horribly corrupt. Of the old guard, Mossadegh's friend Moshir and Moshir's younger brother, another veteran constitutionalist, Motamen al-Mamalek, were elected, but refused to take up their seats. Mossadegh and the dissident divine Modarres, who did stand, were not returned. Modarres failed to get a single vote. 'I assume that the 14,000 people who voted for me in previous elections changed their minds,' he said, 'but what happened to the vote I gave myself?'

Mossadegh and the others now resolved to leave public life. Of those obstinate souls who had refused to bless Reza's advance to absolutism, Mostowfi died a few years later, while Moshir and Motamen retreated completely from the public eye. The poet Bahar, who had barely escaped assassination on the eve of the Qajar abolition, was persecuted, jailed and exiled, and Modarres sent to prison in the deserts of eastern Iran. Only Hassan Taqizadeh, the veteran constitutionalist who had spoken against the Qajar abolition, joined Reza's gang, before he too fell under suspicion and was banished to an embassy abroad.

When Mossadegh left the majles his fame had never been higher, and his prospects never bleaker. He had done as much as anyone to show that Reza was the angel of death for constitutionalism. But the Shah's position seemed unassailable. Mossadegh was in the wilderness. He was forty-five years old.

# 6

## *Isolation*

Returning to Tehran after the fall of Seyyed Zia, Mossadegh and his family had gone to live at Najm al-Saltaneh's home in Yusufabad Street in the northern part of the city. Later they moved to a prominently placed house in a garden compound on the corner of Heshmat ul-Dowleh Street and Palace Street – so called because it led to the entrance of the Shah's Marble Palace. With the intensification of Reza's dictatorship, however, Mossadegh's instinct was to withdraw from the public eye. He let the Heshmat ul-Dowleh house to the Japanese Embassy, while the northern part of the same compound was developed by his son Ahmad, now an engineer, and he and Zahra moved to a complex of rooms in a garden owned by a niece.

As Mossadegh's grandson Majid would recall, the house was built modestly

and irregularly, and was surrounded by trees and a high wall. At the entrance to the garden there was a carriage gateway and, on either side of that, rooms for the gatekeeper and the gardener; a hedge of trees . . . hid the view of the main house. At the far end, after crossing an alley of trees, one came to a single, straight, raised storey, incorporating rooms of different sizes. French windows opened onto the terrace, and in front of the building to one side there was a high-roofed building, also opening onto the same terrace, with some colonnades. This big room was called the *hauz-khaneh*, or bath house, and it had a marble basin in the middle which was fed by a spring.

The water . . . was channelled across the room, and spilled
onto the terrace. Around the basin there was a tiled masonry
platform with scattered carpets and cushions, for resting on
during hot days.[1]

Mossadegh's room was on the first floor of another, L-shaped
building, whose lower section contained reception rooms. Much
of the house was out of bounds to visitors, in keeping with Iranian
tradition.

Mossadegh had spent much of his life participating in the social
round that was, and remains, inseparable from politics. Iranians are
delightful friends: warm, waspish and emotional. No conversation
is complete without consumption: tea in the winter, cordials and
fruit in the summer, followed by an invitation to stay for a meal.
The Tehrani in need of lunch needs only knock at a friend's door at
noon. The days are fluid and spontaneity is the watchword. 'Let us
go to so-and-so's house,' someone suggests, and with that the evening
is accounted for. People drop whatever they are doing to attend the
funeral of an acquaintance's mother. The structure of life is provided
by the calendar with its holidays and mourning days, and the seasons
with their different produce and entertainments. In Ramadan everything gets turned on its head. Life acquires a nocturnal character,
with discussion fuelled by stews, rice dishes, fruit and an array of
fried sweets, lasting until the dawn prayer and the onset of sleep.

Mossadegh was far from being a glutton, but he participated in
all of this. Standards of entertaining were maintained even when
the country was on the precipice. In the First World War, a crony
received at Mossadegh's house wrote that the two of them demolished a tray of rice and potato accompanied by a superlative lady's
finger stew and two portions of kebab, followed by melon.
Mossadegh spoke more than he ate. 'Then we occupied ourselves
with tea and conversation until an hour before dusk.'[2]

With Reza's dictatorship, the days of relaxing on bolsters and
plotting the country's future ended. The shutters came down on
chaotic Iran, and another Iran emerged, furtive and frowning from
the epic complexes of its ruler.

For Mossadegh it was significant that this change took place when he should have been reaching the summit of politics. Rather than fill the top offices, he spent the next thirteen years largely confined. There were times of depression, even of despair, but by and large Mossadegh stoically accepted his lot. Alongside the garrulous politico there had always been a reclusive Mossadegh: convalescing, his head buried in a textbook. This would now become the prominent feature of his personality, and in later life the popular image of him would be of an ascetic – frugal and cerebral.

Even this life was not without consolations. He had been an absent father for his elder children. Now he had another chance. In 1923 Zahra gave birth to her last child, a girl called Khadijeh, and in 1925 a first grandson, Majid, was born. Majid's mother, Zia Ashraf, was an inattentive parent, and he and Khadijeh were raised as siblings in the house of Mossadegh and Zahra, whom they called *Maman* and *Papa*, in the French manner.[3]

Mossadegh lovingly watched his charges grow. He supervised the children's homework after they started school, taught them backgammon and chess, and slipped them chocolate and sweets. They adored him in return and treated him with unabashed affection. Ideas about parenthood had changed since Mossadegh was a boy, when his father had been a spectral presence and Farmanfarma's children trembled to be near him. With Khadijeh in particular, a pretty, mischievous, sociable child, a keen pianist and tennis player, who was headstrong enough to run away from school and lose herself in the bazaar, Mossadegh had a remarkable bond, the kind that sometimes arises in Iran's extended families, confounding observers with its strange, cross-generational chemistry.

Mossadegh was affectionate but he expected to be obeyed unquestioningly, and in full. Having given the children instructions to do something, he would ask, 'What did I just tell you to do?' and they would repeat exactly what he had said.[4] Once, when Majid was impertinent, Mossadegh chased him around the garden brandishing some branches until Zahra intervened, took the boy to her breast, and forced her husband to kiss him and retire.[5] As a rule, Zahra tended to reinforce Mossadegh's authority. Her stock way of defusing a dispute was to side with her husband, saying, 'Whatever *Agha* [Sir] says is for the best.'

For the children, unaware of events outside the walls, it was a blissful existence, with a big garden to play in and family visitors coming through the gate – particularly on Fridays, when Zahra might give lunch to twenty people. The Persian New Year was marked with new clothes and Mossadegh's gift of money for each child. The twig effigy of the caliph Omar, anathema to traditional Shias, was ritually burned on the anniversary of his death.[6]

There was a large and changing staff, for Zahra kept alive the Qajar practice of taking in orphan girls as domestic servants, giving them a rudimentary education and marrying them off. Zia's house-keeper, a broad-shouldered Azeri Turk called Telli, had started her career as one of these interns, but never left. Telli moved in and out of the private apartments with impunity.

Mossadegh hated nepotism, laziness and profligacy. He expected the highest standards from the young people, so that they might, as he put it, be 'of use' to the country. Not for him the ducal spending of a Farmanfarma; he demanded thrift and tore a strip off the young 'Papoola' (his nickname for Ghollamhossein) when the latter spent his way into debt in Europe. Mossadegh deplored show-offs and spivs, and later on advised Majid to leave his car at home when attending courses in a poor part of Tehran, 'otherwise it will arouse jealousy on the part of the other students'.

Nowhere are Mossadegh's relations with his young dependents more charmingly preserved than in letters he addressed some years later to Ghollamhossein's son Mahmud. It was the autumn of 1949 and Mahmud was at boarding school in Britain. The experience was evidently not to the young man's liking and in a letter to his grandfather he complained about the weather and his new surroundings, as well as the school's prohibition of wirelesses. In his reponse, Mossadegh gave no hint of the political turmoil then prevailing in Tehran, but devoted frank and unguarded attention to Mahmud's concerns.

'I am your sacrifice,' he began, using the traditional intimate salutation,

I received your letter of October 1 and it caused me much happiness. I am grateful that you are well – thanks be to God – but can say nothing about your dissatisfaction with the weather and your situation, because you have not yet got used to them. Of course the sun does not shine in Britain, but on the other hand you will learn things which will be useful to this country, and things will not seem so bad once you have got used to the situation and I am sure that with every passing day you will get used to the way things happen there. On the question of the radio, you should observe the school rules whatever they are, and no student should receive something that another is denied . . . otherwise, son, it's possible that a lord would have lots of things that you would covet. In this instance I have nothing further to write, for you are very intelligent and logical, and will accept anything I say.

You asked after me, and the answer is that my ill-health knows no bounds. If Papoola sends you the newspapers you will be aware of what is going on here . . . definitely continue to write your news and these letters will aid you in not forgetting your Persian. I miss you enormously, but an education is more useful to you than anything else.

I am your sacrifice, my dearest Mahmud.

—— Papa[7]

As the daughter of Tehran's Friday prayer leader, Zahra naturally concerned herself with the religious side of the children's education. She said her prayers regularly, fasted during Ramadan, and invited her female relations to join her for *rowzekhani*, when a mullah would come to the house to recount the sufferings of the Shia imams, reducing his listeners to blubbering wrecks in return for a fat fee. Mossadegh, who teased his wife for her religiosity, abhorred these performances and tried to be out of the house when they took place. Despite the importance he attached to Islam as part of his cultural background, and his abstinence from pork and alcohol, he neither prayed regularly nor observed the Ramadan

fast. Indeed, years later, during the fasting month, he would derive
mischievous pleasure from sipping a glass of water during a parliamentary speech and then defending himself according to Islamic
tenets: 'I am ill . . . for the past twenty or thirty years I have been
under doctor's orders not to fast. If someone is ill and fasts, that
is against [religious] law because he is doing himself harm.'

Life was a mixture of Iranian tradition and European-inspired
innovation. Progressives like Mossadegh had rejected the practice,
common in their fathers' day, of taking several wives, and yet he
felt that other traditions were well worth keeping. He married
three of his children to their first cousins, a mechanism for
bolstering family unity and preventing the dissipation of wealth,
and the unsuspecting Ghollamhossein, home on university vacation
from Europe, was bounced into marrying a girl he had not seen
before.[8] For all that, Mossadegh was not a snob and he welcomed
his niece's marriage to a doctor from a middle-class background,
Yusuf Mir. Family lore has it that Zahra pretended to be ill and
asked for Mir; his ministrations were secretly observed by the other
women in the family, and they formed a positive opinion of him.

Mossadegh's financial situation was never less than comfortable,
but by the time of his retreat from public life much of his land had
been sold to finance his own education and that of his children.
He hung on to one estate, however, at Ahmadabad, in the agricul-
tural region of Savejbolagh, some sixty miles west of Tehran. It
was here that he found true seclusion.

A big holding even by Iranian standards, Ahmadabad was made
up of several villages that Mossadegh had bought from a Qajar
cousin. It was watered by way of underground water channels and
a tributary of the local river. Set in a garden at the centre of the
estate was a two-storey brick house surrounded by trees, punched
with big windows and with a slanting metal roof. It was comfortable, but far from luxurious.

Most of Mossadegh's land was tenanted and administered
through an estate office. Mossadegh himself grew watermelons,
but they were small, on account of the irregular water supply, and
rarely acceptable to the Tehran wholesalers. The area was malarial

and visiting children and grandchildren were put to work inserting quinine into capsules for distribution to the tenants. Quinine was expensive, so Mossadegh applied himself to finding a substitute, discovering after much trial and error that the boiled sap of juniper roots kept the infection at bay. One of Khadijeh and Majid's jobs when they came to Ahmadabad was to cut the dried sap into pellets, which Mossadegh and Ghollamhossein, who operated a free surgery every Friday, gave out to tenants.

With his natural authority and easy, humorous manner, Mossadegh was popular among his tenants. Rent was paid in kind and the law as it then stood allowed Mossadegh to keep three parts of the harvest, to the tenants' one part. Mossadegh favoured a more equitable, fifty-fifty division. And when, many years later, the government transferred thousands of hectares of land from landowners to their tenants, inspectors found the accounts at Ahmadabad to be exemplary.[9]

To begin with, at the start of what his family would call his 'first isolation', Mossadegh divided his time between Ahmadabad and Tehran. As the tempo of his work dropped, he made himself available to the government for informal consultation, and interested himself in the publication of *La Cité Antique* – whose translation he financed from his own pocket. In 1929, his mother opened the Najmiyeh Hospital, with half the beds reserved for the needy, and he became its trustee, devoting much time to the accounts. Mossadegh's involvement with the hospital grew after Najm al-Saltaneh's death, when caring for the endowment became a way of honouring her memory.

Increasingly, he attended to essential business by handwritten note or by using emissaries, rather than in person. 'I have a tendency to isolation,' he told a friend, 'and never leave the house to go anywhere.'[10] He occasionally slipped behind the wheel of his Buick to attend a memorial service, but usually communicated with old friends and relations via couriers. The Tehran postal service was now the preserve of Reza's spies, who pored over letters for subversive intent. Increasingly, the gateman was told to inform callers that '*Agha* is not at home,' or '*Agha* is at Ahmadabad.'[11]

He listened to the radio and read the newspapers, including those sent by friends from Shiraz, where he had spent some of his happiest days. When going out, he went bare-headed in defiance of convention – until Reza Shah, that inveterate meddler, obliged Iranian men to wear the peaked 'Pahlavi cap'. Sensitive to the cold, in winter Mossadegh wore loose trousers and a tunic made of soft, velvety wool called *barak*. He was no longer fussy about tailoring, and had these suits made up by the sheet-maker at the Najmiyeh Hospital.

As Reza's dictatorship got harder, so the list of casualties grew. Prince Firooz, whose brilliant brain had propelled him as far as the finance ministry, was convicted on trumped-up corruption charges and confined at home. Other personalities were jailed or killed. Tribal leaders, including the British patsy Sheikh Khazal, were strangled at their dinner tables or had fatal shaving accidents, while police chiefs competed to unearth dastardly plots, real and imagined. In 1938 the exiled Modarres was interrupted while saying his prayers, forced to drink poison and then beaten and strangled to death.

In this way Reza's promising new order degenerated, and the monarch showed the traits of dictators everywhere. Thousands were wrongly imprisoned and hundreds killed at his behest. Vast properties and other assets were confiscated. At the end of his reign it was discovered that Reza had acquired the most productive 10 per cent of the country's farmland. A climate of fear settled over the administrative class, with the emergence of a praetorian coterie controlling access to the Shah, who in turn learned to trust no one, particularly those who appeared to be closest to him. Poor Davar, who had been at the forefront of Reza's legal reforms, was driven to distraction by the monarch's irreconcilable demands for a modern judiciary, savage retribution, and land. In 1937, he sat down at his desk and swallowed a fatal dose of opium. Even the indispensable Teimurtash, who did more than anyone to turn Reza into the prowling, leonine tyrant he became, was the victim of his own success. He died in a jail he himself had built.

The Shah retained some popularity among the elite and the small (but growing) middle class, but the mass of ordinary people had the uneasy feeling that he had turned against their religion. Reza had long nurtured a hatred of the clerics. Many of his reforms were aimed at relieving them of their historic functions, such as registering births and presiding at marriages, and devolving these to secular professionals. In this, Reza was strikingly successful. By the end of his reign the destitute mullah was a stock figure in Persian towns and villages.

In step with his fellow reformers, Turkey's Ataturk and King Amanullah of Afghanistan, Reza ventured into social engineering. In 1928 he obliged his male subjects to wear European-style clothes and the Pahlavi cap in place of the brimless hat which many Muslims prefer because it allows their foreheads to touch the ground during prayer. He later decreed European-style headgear for men, which caused more confusion. In 1936 the chador was outlawed after the Queen and her elder daughters appeared in public unveiled and in European dress.

Reza did not hesitate to use force when the people resisted his edicts, turning machine guns on protesters in Mashhad and rampaging through the shrine at Qom with a whip after the Queen was slighted there. He was as distrustful of heterodox as he was of mainstream religion. 'I shall not permit any prophets to appear during my reign,' he declared.

The results of Reza's experiments in social engineering were tragicomic. Many Persian women did not set foot out of doors after the ban on the hejab. Others found ingenious ways around the regulations, bribing local policemen to look the other way during their weekly trip to the bathhouse, or, as in the case of Zahra, shopping through the open window of a car. Bidden to bring their unveiled wives to mixed tea parties, some bureaucrats contracted temporary marriages with prostitutes, who played the part of an emancipated spouse.

Mossadegh was by no means opposed to the idea of women leaving off the veil. His two daughters wore smart headscarves when going out, but more as a fashion statement than a pious gesture. What offended him was the arbitrary and extreme nature of the Shah's edict, and that it should be brutally applied – such as when veiled women were assaulted in the street and their chadors ripped from their heads.

Mossadegh had shown that he would not associate with Reza Shah, but it was not his character to court death or hardship. 'A broth is on the boil,' he told Moshir, 'and I will not be the legumes.' On the contrary, he went to great lengths to convince the authorities that he was harmless, and to deny Reza a pretext to arrest him. Fearful that his library contained volumes that might be considered seditious, he donated most of them to Tehran University. He avoided expressing political opinions in front of the servants in case they had been recruited as informants by Reza's secret police. This had become a common practice, and one of Mossadegh's cousins got around it by employing a deaf mute.

By the turn of the 1930s, Mossadegh was spending more time at Ahmadabad. Ghollamhossein would drive Zahra, Khajideh and Majid there at weekends, and Mossadegh would come out of the house when he heard the car and invite his guests to sit on the terrace and refresh themselves after their journey. The children had donkeys and carts to play with, or they would go into Mossadegh's room and trampoline on the springy metal bed he had brought home from Russia years before. After decades of frenetic activity and stress, the gentle rhythms of the countryside were a source of solace. 'I am content with this quiet village,' he wrote. 'I am in touch with no one on account of the distance that separates me from the city and from society.'[12]

It served Mossadegh's purpose for it to be known that he was at Ahmadabad and out of circulation. At the beginning of 1930, he wrote to an old friend, 'Most of the time I am at [Ahmadabad], engaged in farm work, or reading,' adding that he came to Tehran only 'when I have something specific to do'. He was without family during the week, waited on by the villagers, attending to the estate and monitoring the Najmiyeh Hospital from afar. At night he would play Turkish ditties on his tar, a string instrument he had been taught as a young man at Tabriz. In this case, isolation was a blessing, for he had a tin ear.

In early 1940 Mossadegh and Zahra took possession of a new
town house, built by Ahmad, at the northern end of the Palace
Street property. Built in a modernist idiom over two floors and a
basement, it also incorporated Iranian elements such as a private
internal courtyard where Zahra could garden, and a division
between the private apartments and the reception rooms at the
front of the house. This was now the family base in Tehran. Ahmad
and his wife (they were childless) lived next door. Zia Ashraf,
Ghollamhossein and Mansoureh, together with their respective
families, were also close by.

Mossadegh occupied himself with domestic details, but could
not remain indifferent to what was happening in the country at
large. One event would cause him as much agony as the signing
of the Anglo–Persian Agreement, and have an even greater effect
on his life. In 1933, Reza Shah renegotiated the D'Arcy concession
governing relations between the Persians and Britain's oil interest
in the country – the Anglo-Persian Oil Company.

In line with the D'Arcy concession, Persia had received an annual
royalty of 16 per cent of company profits, but enjoyed almost no
influence over the company's activities and no access to its accounts.
The arrangement had allowed the company, boosted by its status
as fuel supplier to the Royal Navy, and paying no Persian income
tax, to expand into Iraq and Kuwait and become one of the world's
great producers. For years, although oil revenues financed Reza's
new army, the Persians had fumed that the country was being
fleeced. Nationalist anger ran high against a company which channelled most of its profits back to Britain and which employed few
Persians in either skilled-worker or management positions.

In 1932 the Shah had been furious to learn of a dramatic fall in
royalties on account of the world economic crisis. He famously tossed
his copy of his dossier concerning oil negotiations into the stove,
declaring it void and in need of radical revision. His decision was
greeted with illuminations and festivals around the country, and a
flood of telegrams congratulating the monarch on his patriotic action.

Soon it became clear that Reza had overplayed his hand. Iran
could not steer the industry without the company's help, and the

country's foreign-exchange needs had spiralled thanks to his reforms. After negotiations and arbitration by the League of Nations, Reza was forced to accept a revised royalty, based on tonnage at an official gold exchange rate, that many considered little improvement on the original concession. The company was formally exempted from Persian customs duties and income tax. (It was, on the other hand, a big contributor to the British exchequer.) Finally, and most importantly, the term of the concession was extended from 1961 to 1993, which meant that for a further thirty-two years Iran would be denied the vast majority of the profits accruing from its main asset.

The government's propaganda machine declared victory, but Mossadegh keenly felt the humiliation. 'I longed', he wrote, 'to warn people about the harmful effects of [the concession's] renewal, but the circumstances didn't permit this, and it was impossible for anyone to utter a word in defence of the nation's interests.'

Why did Reza Shah agree to such a revision, which would surely invite patriotic odium in years to come? According to Hassan Taqizadeh, who as finance minister had put his signature to the new agreement, the Shah had started out adamantly opposed to an extension of the concession, but his attention had been caught by the company's undertaking to reduce the concession area – something of a red herring, as the company had never shown an interest in the territories which were now to be excluded. To others, the revised concession was proof that Reza, despite his nationalist rhetoric, was no less of a British lackey than the signatories of the Anglo–Persian Agreement had been.

News of the revised concession came the year after Najm al-Saltaneh's death, and it may be assumed that these events contributed to the physical and mental deterioration that Mossadegh now underwent. In the summer of 1933 Mossadegh wrote that he had suffered heart problems and was following a diet. His thoughts were morbid. 'At the end of the day, life in this world is nothing but unhappiness and I am sure this is the case for us all until we die. Let us hope things are better on the other side.'[13]

It was the beginning of a long period of ill-health, which

coincided with the apogee of Reza's tyranny, when Mossadegh expected arrest at any moment. At the beginning of 1936 he complained of malaria, fever and enteritis, and he let blood – a treatment that had all but died out in the West. 'If I let blood,' he wrote, 'I get short of breath and tight in the chest, and if not I am weak and powerless.'[14] He was also suffering from chronic insomnia. 'I have never enjoyed this life, and have always asked God to grant me death.'[15]

Later that year Mossadegh suddenly started to bring up large amounts of blood, and Ghollamhossein insisted that they go to Europe for treatment. Permission was granted and Mossadegh was hospitalised in Berlin, though no one could provide a medical reason for his condition. After the symptoms had subsided, Mossadegh went to see a neurologist, who asked him, among other things, what level of education he had attained and what he did for a living. Mossadegh replied that he was a doctor of law and political science, but that he farmed. The doctor replied, 'That in itself is a kind of illness – to have a doctorate, and be a farmer.'[16]

We have no record of Mossadegh's impressions of Hitler's Germany – whose rise had filled many Iranians with hope that the old Anglo–Russian hegemony was coming to an end – and certainly no indication that he echoed the casually pro-Nazi sentiments of many of his compatriots. He hurried back from Germany, apparently because he feared that Reza Shah would associate him with a dissident movement of expatriates which had gathered there.

# 7

# *The Tragedy of Khadijeh*

It was a hot summer's day in 1940. Mossadegh had come to Tehran
to procure quinine. He, Zahra, Khadijeh and Majid were at a rented
summerhouse in Shemiran, in the foothills of the Alborz mountains.
Shemiran was nothing like the high-rise jungle it is today. It had
not truly become part of Tehran. It was rural and sparsely populated and only Reza Shah's Rolls-Royce disturbed the peace.
Mossadegh's family stayed in simply furnished rooms in a big
garden, which also had a tent for meals and entertaining standing
over a pool in the middle.[1]

It was dusk when the local police chief and two constables arrived
at the gate. The valet said, '*Agha* isn't at home,' but the policemen
knew otherwise, and were eventually admitted and told to wait for
Mossadegh in the tent. When he entered, Mossadegh said, 'I've
been expecting you for the past ten years.' The policemen asked
him to accompany them in his own car and to bring what notes
and documents he had about the place. They would go to the town
house in Palace Street, pick up more documents, and then go to
the police station. They would look at what Mossadegh was writing,
ask him a few questions, and let him go. Mossadegh did not believe
the policemen's reassuring words, though he repeated them to his
wife as he left.

Several factors may have contributed to Mossadegh's arrest, all
involving the kind of real or alleged foreign links that obsessed
Reza Shah. Mossadegh had perhaps erred in employing a
Frenchwoman to tutor Majid and Khadijeh. He may have aroused
suspicions with his Berlin trip. Finally, and most tantalisingly, there

is evidence for a renewal of contacts between Mossadegh and his old crush Renée Vieillard. She wrote to him at least once in 1940, and her letter was returned, inscribed with the words, 'It is impossible to communicate with M. Mossadegh.' From that she 'understood that it was imprudent to write to that distant land, from which no echo reached us save a rare press dispatch. All that I know is that Mossadegh is alive.'

Khadijeh and Majid had been out bicycling when the police arrived for Mossadegh, and they were in the street, aghast observers, as their 'Papa' was driven away. In the days that followed, Zahra was sustained by her religious faith, and spent many hours in prayer. For the children, however, there was the stark fact of Mossadegh's absence. A man who had built a wall around himself to preserve his dignity and integrity – a man who knew his own frailties – now found himself at the mercy of an indiscriminate terror.

Mossadegh was taken to Palace Street, where the police sealed a cabinet containing his documents and some books pending examination. They then took him to the police station, where he was formally arrested, and from there to Tehran's forbidding central prison, where his personal possessions were confiscated and he was thrown into solitary confinement. His interrogation started the next day, and he may have considered this to be a good sign, for Reza's jails were full of long-term prisoners who had not been questioned, let alone charged.

Meanwhile the police returned to Palace Street and went through Mossadegh's papers and books. They found just one incriminating document – the constitution of a defunct political party. The investigator in question slipped the document to Ghollamhossein, who was accompanying him, and told him to stuff it out of sight, an act of selfless bravery which may have saved Mossadegh from the capital charge of treason.

Back at the central prison Mossadegh asked on what grounds he was being detained. One of the policemen told him, 'You've done nothing wrong, but you should stay in jail for the time being.' A few days later, having been told he was free to go, he was given the ominous news that he was to be transferred to the desert citadel of Birjand, near the Afghan border. It was obvious that, having failed to find a legal pretext to destroy him, the authorities had decided to distance him from his family and the public. Later on they could announce his death from natural causes. Mossadegh turned to a picture of Reza on the wall and quoted from Saadi, '"Oh, cunning tormentor of the helpless, how long will this charade go on?"'

After Mossadegh's arrest his family had received instructions to provide food and spare clothes for the prisoner, and they had moved from Shemiran back to Palace Street to be closer to him. Hearing that Mossadegh had been earmarked for a transfer, they got permission to send a family cook, Javad, to care for him. A friend in the police told Ahmad the precise time when Mossadegh was due to begin his arduous transfer. (Again, he would have to go in his own car, and meet his own expenses while in jail.) 'Be there', Ahmad's friend told him, 'if you want to see your father for the last time.'

On the appointed afternoon a party set out from Palace Street: Ahmad, Zia Ashraf and the two teenagers, Khadijeh and Majid. Opposite the central police station, the road was lined with a hedge. The family crouched behind it and looked through the gaps, towards the police station.

At around 6 p.m. an elderly man, trussed like a chicken, was hustled into the street. Even though he was weak, he struggled. He would not go. The policemen kicked him and the old man shouted, 'Whatever the government wants to do to me, it should do it right here!' He hurled himself onto the ground and the policemen dragged him towards the car. Mossadegh gripped onto the wheels of the car, but they prised his hands off the tyres and shoved him in with a cop on either side. Crouching behind the hedge across the road, Mossadegh's family watched, stupefied and appalled.

He tried to commit suicide as he was driven east, swallowing a lethal quantity of the opium-based tranquillisers his wife made up for his occasional use, but bringing them up again because of the bumpy road. The trip was also interrupted at Mashhad, where Mossadegh received medical attention, and yet again as they approached Birjand, so that the officer escorting him could shoot deer. (The dead game was beheaded and loaded up in the car.)

Arriving at the citadel, Mossadegh lent his car to the same police officer, who had been on leave and was returning to his post further south. It was typical of Mossadegh, at a time of agony and tension, to discern the human being even in someone wearing the uniform of a despised government.

Mossadegh was very feeble for most of his imprisonment, especially when the authorities put him in a tiny, suffocatingly hot cell. He was denied communication with his family, and the national police chief gave orders that the slightest negligence on the part of the Birjand police should be 'severely punished'. The prisoner was given a single book, on natural remedies, which was then taken away from him. His frailty compounded by the heat and a short, physically devastating hunger strike, he survived on the devotion of Javad and a remarkable volunteer from Tehran, a female nurse who was allowed to care for him provided she also live as a prisoner.

He spent a lot of time lying on his bed in his pyjamas. He was in a state of extreme tension, what a local official called 'chronic hysteria', and was convinced that the authorities intended to put him in front of a firing squad.[2] In fact, this was not the case. The prison governor was so nervous that his distinguished prisoner might try to slit his wrists, he personally supervised him whenever he shaved, and the police chief talked him into abandoning his hunger strike with the aid of a glass of milk, some biscuits and a Qoran.

Tension and emotion weakened Mossadegh further, and he would lie down and close his eyes before Javad revived him by breaking open capsules of camphor and holding them under his nostrils. He was assaulted by fleas, which Javad was also able to deal with. It is a striking image, that of the elder son of a Qajar princess, a minister several times over, and a future world statesman, standing trembling and emaciated in a tub of water in the corner of his cell, being subjected to a full-body shave.

Mossadegh's behaviour when his morale was at its lowest is highly revealing. The other political prisoners did not have cooks and carers. They received nothing to eat but bread and a little *kaleh joosh*, a poor person's dish made of fried onions, crushed walnuts and whey. Mossadegh made sure that Javad bought more bread than was needed, and ordered him to make extra food, all for distribution among the others. Mossadegh himself insisted on sharing his own food with the guard on duty, and gave out medicines from his own supplies.

Then, suddenly, came a remarkable stroke of luck. Ghollamhossein had been introduced to the Shah's eldest son, Crown Prince Muhammad-Reza, when the latter was studying at a Swiss boarding school in the early 1920s, and they had maintained friendly contact ever since.[3] Muhammad-Reza had also made friends with an ambitious Swiss of modest background, Ernest Perron, who had moved to Tehran and become his close confidant. It so happened that in December 1940, Perron was successfully treated for an intestinal problem at the Najmiyeh Hospital, which Ghollamhossein was now running. Ghollamhossein waived Perron's fee, and the Swiss's gratitude proved decisive.

As Perron recovered he was visited several times by the Crown Prince, and on one of these occasions Perron requested his help to get Mossadegh freed. Muhammad-Reza was a diffident, vulnerable young man, but he was not without compassion, and he duly signed the order – approved by his father, the ultimate cause of Mossadegh's incarceration – for the prisoner to be transferred from Birjand to Ahmadabad, where he would be under house arrest.

It was a cold winter's day more than five months after his arrest when the prison authorities informed Mossadegh that one of his servants had come to see him. Mossadegh assumed that this was to do with arrangements for his will, and that he would soon be executed. Instead, he was told that he was free. Before leaving Birjand, he presented a farewell gift of money to every one of the jail's 120 prisoners and several of the guards. He gave his left-over food supplies to the local police chief. A week later he was back at Ahmadabad.

Had he survived a few more months in jail, Mossadegh would have been freed under the general amnesty that was declared shortly after Reza Shah was unseated by the Allies in 1941. But he was so feeble when he was released, it is possible that the amnesty would have come too late.

The Crown Prince would appreciate the irony of his intercession in favour of the man who would mount the biggest challenge to his rule. 'At my urging,' he wrote, 'my father released many people from prison. Possibly I should regret it, but one of them was Mossadegh, the man who later bankrupted the country and almost ended the dynasty established by my father.'[4]

Mossadegh would not get over his incarceration. He came out with a new condition, rheumatism, and would never again walk any distance without a cane.[5] And there was a more private anguish, impossible to assuage. Mossadegh's arrest had left a second casualty – collateral damage from the scattergun paranoia of Reza Shah.

The victim on this occasion was Khadijeh, Mossadegh's beloved youngest daughter. She had been among the little group crouching behind the bushes when Mossadegh was dragged out of the central police station and shoved into his car for the trip east. Everyone watching, naturally, was touched by this scene, but for her the effects were of a different magnitude. After witnessing Mossadegh's forced removal, she and the others had gone back to the house in Palace Street, where she howled and screamed: 'Papa! Papa!' It was particularly terrifying for Majid, shocked to see his playmate in such distress. It was decided that Khadijeh should go up to her uncle's house in Shemiran, to be with her cousin, a girl of roughly her age, to whom she was close. But that did not work. A couple of days later, at first light, the gateman was startled to see a slight figure wearing only a nightdress streak across the garden towards the gate leading onto the street. It took the combined efforts of the gateman and several others to prevent her from getting out and to dress her properly. Then she went into a coma.

She awoke four days later, but she was lost. Much of the time she was quiet and subdued. She seemed to be deep in sorrowful thought. But whenever she got agitated, and especially when she wept and screamed for her father, it was difficult to calm her down. Sometimes it seemed as though Majid was the only person who could communicate with her. He would sit with her, speaking gently and holding her hand, and the fit would subside.

Tehran's doctors were perplexed. They dunked her in cold water. They tried a course of insulin injections, which induced a deathly calm; that meant traumatic scenes as members of the family and household chased Khadijeh around the garden before pinning her down and forcing her to submit to the needle. For a while the doctors told the family that she should be away from familiar faces, so she lived for a while with a nurse in a small house at the end of the garden, and ate meals on her own.

At other times she had visitors. Family members would come to see her and, if she was calm and in good humour, they would take her out for a drive or a stroll. Sometimes this worked well and she would return in good spirits. But Khadijeh's fits could not be predicted. On one occasion, Zahra declared her daughter cured, only for the girl to have a dramatic relapse.

It is not hard to imagine the effects of Khadijeh's collapse on the family. Her mother Zahra had a strong, conventional faith, the kind that demands no explanations, and this helped her overcome adversity. She was resigned to 'whatever God wills'. But Mossadegh himself was not pious. He could not take refuge in prayer. Also, he was without sensual props. He asserted time and again that the tragedy was his fault, and he wept for it in his room with the door shut.

Mossadegh ordered holes to be drilled in the walls of Khadijeh's room so that she might be observed unobtrusively – presumably to make sure she did not harm herself. Hopes rose and fell of a cure. In 1946 Mossadegh took her as far as Beirut, from where he hoped to cross to Jerusalem (then part of the British mandate of Palestine), which boasted a famous specialist, but Khadijeh had a turn in the hotel and the local doctor who was summoned advised him to turn back to Tehran. There was nothing, he said, that any specialist in Jerusalem could do.

Mossadegh would devote the rest of his career to fighting the legacy of Reza Shah and the ambitions of Muhammad-Reza Shah. For many, the traumas of an imprisonment and the agony of a daughter would have injected personal venom into political matters. But for Mossadegh, the division between the personal and the public spheres came naturally. He undoubtedly loathed both Pahlavis, but not for what they had done to him, but to Iran.

For all that, it would be remarkable if the events of 1940 had not had a profound effect on so compassionate a politician as Mossadegh. When he achieved ultimate power, he was absorbed in one issue alone, oil, but oil for him meant dignity, and he had an instinctive feel for the dignity of the ordinary Iranian. It is richly appropriate that one of his early acts as prime minister was to visit a notorious jail and recommend an immediate improvement in conditions, and that, on the day of his overthrow, he was close to setting up a refuge for mentally ill vagabonds, whose horrifying colony, in a suburb of Tehran, had moved and appalled him.

By that time, Khadijeh had passed into other hands. In 1947 she was taken to a clinic in Switzerland, where the doctors were kind and the pills were good, and where she was able to live in a pleasant environment, visited by her beloved Majid, who had moved to nearby Geneva. Eventually a lobotomy, which had been recommended to Mossadegh and Ghollamhossein by American doctors, was performed, and subsequently bitterly regretted, for it snuffed out the last light in Khadijeh's eyes.

She died in 2003, perhaps the last victim of Shah Reza Pahlavi.

# 8

# *The Prize*

Reza Shah did not achieve his main foreign-policy objective, which was to distance Iran from Britain and Russia and find new allies elsewhere. He improved relations with neighbours such as Turkey and Afghanistan, and, by marrying Crown Prince Muhammad-Reza to the sister of King Farouk of Egypt, consolidated his place in the declining circle of Middle Eastern monarchies.* He was puzzled and disappointed by the United States, whose interwar isolation and economic difficulties precluded ambitious overseas engagements, and turned to Hitler's Germany as an emerging power that had not trodden on Iranian feelings in the past. The Reich was delighted to win friends and contracts under the noses of the British and Russians. By the eve of the Second World War, Iran had a big community of German advisers, lecturers and spies, and Germany accounted for nearly half the country's overseas trade.

In the First World War, German propagandists had benefited from rumours that the Kaiser was a secret Muslim toiling for Islamic regeneration. In the Second, Aryan brotherhood between the Germans and their Iranian 'cousins' was the favoured theme. After the war began in September 1939, rapid Nazi gains convinced Reza that Germany was invincible, and he did not take very seriously

---

* The nuptial ceremonies, which were held in both countries, served to reinforce the reciprocal dislike that has existed for centuries between Persians and Arabs. A special train carrying the Egyptian visitors to Tehran ran out of food, water and electricity. The bride's mother moaned incessantly about the primitive facilities, and Reza Shah caused consternation when he announced that the bride's private fortune now belonged to Iran.[1]

Britain's demands that he expel thousands of Germans on the grounds that they constituted a third column of agents and saboteurs. He certainly saw no advantage in antagonising the side everyone expected to win.

Germany's invasion of Russia in June 1941 and the Nazis' lightning advance towards the Caucasus increased Iran's strategic importance. In the event of a German victory over the Soviets, Churchill anticipated a German assault on Britain's oil interests in Iran and Iraq, while, if the Russians held out, they would need reinforcing through Iran from the Persian Gulf. The British and their new Soviet allies pressured Reza to expel the Germans, but the Shah's concessions were too little, too late. Reza's prime minister was awoken at 4 a.m. on August 25 by the Soviet and British ministers, informing him that the country was being occupied.

Iran was in no state to deal with an invasion. Cabinet members had been concerned only to avoid the Shah's wrath and the majles had been busy with a bill to allow Reza to acquire yet more land. The Shah was perplexed by the Allies' actions and spent a lot of time pacing with an expression of thunder under the tall oriental plane trees outside his summer palace at Saadabad, running his hand along the manicured hedges and fuming at the collapse of his vaunted army. He summoned his top generals and tore off their epaulettes. The Shah's fury was also drawn by radio broadcasts from London depicting him as a tyrant and a land-grabber.

The anti-Reza broadcasts were directed by Sir Reader Bullard, the British minister in Tehran whose antipathy towards Iranians would draw comment from Winston Churchill. The Shah believed that the Allies had invaded Iran in order to force his abdication, and Bullard, for one, was determined that Britain's reputation should not suffer further from its association with a monarch whose unpopularity it 'would be difficult to exaggerate'. The Allies were soon discussing possible replacements and the Shah's nerve broke when he got news that the Soviets had advanced to within a few miles of the capital. Convinced that only by quitting could he save his dynasty, Reza abdicated in favour of the Crown Prince, whose hand he placed in that of the elderly prime minister before setting out on the long journey into exile – first, to the British colony of Mauritius, and eventually to South Africa. The following day, the prince was crowned Shah Muhammad-Reza, even if the British and Russians were still undecided about him.

Muhammad-Reza must have felt intensely lonely as his father and the rest of his family sailed off in a British warship, but he was more complicated than the shy, rather diffident youth that Bullard cared to see. The new Shah was, as the historian Homa Katouzian has written with admirable economy,

> a young, timid as well as intimidated man, suffering from a basic sense of insecurity which was further exacerbated by his own superficiality as well as lack of knowledge and experience. He disliked older men of knowledge and wisdom because he felt dwarfed by them. He enjoyed the company of women and sycophants but did not trust them. He was acutely worried about a foreign (mainly British) plot to dislodge him, and he therefore took extreme care not to displease them . . . he wished to increase his personal hold over the country, but lacked courage and decisiveness, and hoped that others would do it for him.[2]

The new Shah was also haunted by the memory of his father, who had terrified and inspired him, and whose fate he strove to avoid.

Mossadegh, one of those 'older men of knowledge and wisdom', visited the young monarch in October 1941, barely a month after he came to the throne. Mossadegh had asked Ghollamhossein to take him so he that he could thank the Shah for securing his liberation from jail. Muhammad-Reza was the sixth Iranian monarch Mossadegh had met, and the fifty-nine-year-old was over-generous with his advice on how the stripling of twenty-two should behave, illustrating his argument with barbed analogies. He compared Reza Shah to the Qajar tyrant Muhammad-Ali, who had bombarded the majles before fleeing into exile, and urged the young monarch to emulate Ahmad Shah, who had refused to endorse the Anglo–Persian Agreement. When the new Shah noted that Ahmad had been deposed, hardly commending him as a role model, Mossadegh replied that he had been deposed by the British, not the people.[3] In the case of Reza Shah, he went on, 'when the British wanted to depose Reza Shah all the Iranians raised their voices in agreement with them.'

It is hard to think of an analysis less likely to ingratiate Mossadegh with Muhammad-Reza. The new Shah soon let it be known that he would rather abdicate than be another Ahmad. For all that, Muhammad-Reza knew that he must show himself to be different from his father if he was to survive, and this is what he did in the early months of his reign, granting an amnesty to political prisoners and razing the jail in Tehran where so many of his father's opponents, real and imagined, had been imprisoned or murdered. The uproar against Reza had started before his ship was over the horizon, with deputies who had been famous for their obsequiousness now fulminating against the fallen dictator. Reopened newspapers and liberated politicians competed to abase the man they had once lauded to the skies.

For the Allies these were unimportant details. There was a war to win, and in Iran their concerns were to maintain the flow of oil and to supply the Red Army using Reza's railway and roads. They took over the country's security in the absence of a functioning army, deporting German suspects, interning prominent Germanophiles and keeping a close eye on the tribes. In Tehran the British and Russian ministers manipulated internal politics to a degree unknown since Ahmad Shah, choosing governments and subsidising friendly newspapers, but the results were disappointing. The deputies over-exploited their new freedom and operated a quorum veto to bring down a succession of weak governments. The corruption and hoarding were outrageous.

For the British, in particular, it was not a happy occupation, and Bullard's attempts to rehabilitate his country's image met with predictable failure. He told his superiors, 'The Persian now has a double pleasure in stealing, raising prices to famine level, and so on; he always blames the British. He never mentions the Russians, as the Russians might be a little rough.'[4]

According to a treaty signed in 1942 by Russia, Britain and Iran, Allied forces were to withdraw within six months of the end of hostilities, leaving the Iranians to decide their destiny. But the treaty was mocked by the facts. Iran had huge oil reserves that the belligerents would covet once the reconstruction of their own countries was underway. In the absence of a strong central authority, the country's minorities were beginning to stir, particularly the Azeris and Kurds, and there was a new, well-disciplined communist movement that seemed capable of threatening the young Shah. Many of the country's established politicians remained in thrall to one or other of the powers. A few went down on their backs for both. In short, Iran was rich, potentially unstable and susceptible to interference – qualities that guaranteed the close attention of the powers as they gathered their forces for the new Cold War.

With the end of dictatorship, politics came stomping through the capital. The number of newspapers soared, many of them sponsored by the British or Soviet legations, and no street frontage was complete without the fluttering banner of some new political organisation. The best organised of these groups was the country's communist party, the Tudeh ('the Masses'), which had formed as a loose front around Marxists who had been imprisoned under Reza Shah and would gradually come under Moscow's control. Having returned from exile, conservative old-timers also found a market for their ideas. Prominent among them were Mossadegh's two old sparring partners: Seyyed Zia, the coup-master of 1921, whose impressively funded party attracted anti-communist elements and British support, and the shrewd, inscrutable Qavam.

For several months after the invasion and the formal lifting of his house arrest, Mossadegh had shown little sign of wanting to resume a high-octane political career, and it was not until the autumn of 1942 that he returned to Tehran. He was sixty but looked ten years older. His standing with the public was higher than ever. There was general admiration for his painful purgatory and his refusal to deal with Reza Shah, and he was recognised as the pre-eminent representative of the patriotic and democratic ideals that had animated the Constitutional Revolution. It was an extraordinary revival in fortunes for the captive of Birjand.

Young activists beat a path to his door. An account by one, Nasser Najmi, describes the visit that he and other members of the newly formed Patriots Party paid to Mossadegh in the spring of 1943. Arriving at Palace Street, the group was greeted by Mossadegh's valet before being conducted through the courtyard and up a flight of steps to a first-floor room lined with chairs. Mossadegh entered wearing a homespun suit and smiling beatifically, and Najmi felt that this was 'the very man' he was looking for, with his 'elevated personality, political strength and unique qualities,' bidding them to sit and make themselves comfortable, resting his 'right hand on his chest in a gesture of extreme courtesy'.

Mossadegh arranged his feet underneath a low table which was covered with pills and medicines, and invited his guests to help themselves from a box of nougat. His voice was still feeble from incarceration, but the young activists were captivated as he expressed the hope that a new generation would rescue the country from occupation and uncertainty.

Reza's departure had left an empty space that the new parties and newspapers, the returnees and the young Shah were trying to fill. Iranian democrats had the chance to prosper as never before, while the Tudeh set down roots in factories and the majles organised itself into self-serving caucuses that were compromised by their loyalty to one or other of the powers. The Shah chafed at his own lack of real power. He had no intention of remaining a rubber stamp.

In 1943, as elections to the fourteenth majles approached, Mossadegh's admirers made it hard for him not to stand. Playing to pious, nationalist sentiment, one of them wrote puff pieces for the papers, stressing Mossadegh's historic opposition to the British and Reza Shah. In the event, Mossadegh was triumphantly returned, winning more votes than any other candidate in Tehran. He began his opening address in the chamber he had not expected to revisit with the rousing words, 'I haven't seen the Iranian people for twenty years. I do reverence to the Iranian people.'

There was an opportunity to set out his stall when the deputies connived in acquitting two court favourites on charges of vote-rigging and corruption. Mossadegh suspected the Shah of arranging a whitewash and suggested that the majles ask him to conduct a separate enquiry on their behalf, with access to the relevant files.[5] The speaker refused to hold a vote on the subject and there was a slanging match, with Mossadegh threatening never to set foot in parliament and his opponents yelling, 'So much the better! Off with you!' Mossadegh retorted, 'This is not a parliament – it's a den of thieves!'[6]

Mossadegh stalked out but his prestige was now so high that when he turned away in disgust, his supporters would call him back. Two mornings later, a crowd of students and bazaaris gathered outside 109 Palace Street, shouting slogans against the acquitted men and demanding that Mossadegh accompany them to parliament. Mossadegh set out with them on foot, but soon tired and had to be driven the rest of the way, while the marchers shouted, 'Long Live Mossadegh!' The crowd ignored soldiers' orders to disperse, lifting him aloft as they approached the parliament building, which was protected by soldiers with fixed bayonets.

Inside parliament news spread that Mossadegh and his supporters were at the gates. Gunfire was heard and several deputies rushed out to see what was going on. The troops had been ordered to fire over the heads of the demonstrators, who were trying to force their way into the parliament enclosure, but a handful aimed at the crowd. Mossadegh was unscathed but several demonstrators were injured and one student later died. Mossadegh fainted and another deputy was struck with a rifle. Both men were taken to the parliament sanatorium and dozens of Mossadegh's supporters succeeded in storming into the chamber. They only left when he asked them to. The bazaaris shuttered their shops in protest.

The episode had demonstrated Mossadegh's ability to manipulate a crowd, which would become one of his sharpest weapons. His protest against parliament had been rowdy and had ended in tragedy, but he had exhausted all other means of contesting the despotic actions of parliament and the Court. Mossadegh later apologised for the undiplomatic words he had used in parliament, but his conduct was strongly criticised by opponents on the Left and the Right. The deputies had, in fact, changed their minds and given him the mandate he sought, but the enquiry he eventually carried out did not get far.

Mossadegh's health and nerves had been undermined by the dictatorship. Why did he not take an elder-statesman role, rather than throw himself back into the fray? Part of the answer has to do with the Persian love of age and experience – the baby-faced Shah knew all about this – and the expressions of support that Mossadegh had received from young men who had known only the sterile politics of Reza Shah. This was a mighty force to resist, and while he remained an outwardly diffident participant, forever threatening to retire or go away, a sense of destiny prevented him from doing so.

His instinct in the past had been to stand on his own, declining formal alliances and playing the role of the contrarian outsider, but now he had a large number of supporters, some of whom would become favourites. Mossadegh would form no political dynasty, not only because of his aversion to nepotism, but because his children were occupied with other things. Ahmad, now a senior civil servant at the ministry of roads, was by temperament an intellectual and an artist. Ghollamhossein was a devoted personal physician but a political ingénu. In another age, Mossadegh's middle daughter Mansoureh might have carried the torch, for she was a committed activist and her husband, Mossadegh's nephew Ahmad Matine-Daftary, was a former prime minister, but politics was not yet considered an acceptable feminine vocation. It would be twenty years before women won the vote and were able to stand for parliament. As for Zahra, she preferred perennials to politics.

The composition of Iran's political elite was changing. Mossadegh found his closest supporters among a generation of able younger men, many of them from middle-class backgrounds, who had received their education under Reza Shah and were now prominent in the bureaucracy, academia and the press. They were inspired by Mossadegh's colossal personality and were prone to hero worship.

Prominent among these was a tall, balding bruiser from the trading town of Yazd: Hossein Makki.

Makki was the son of a merchant who travelled to Russia once a year to sell hats, and had none of the advantages of wealth and breeding that Mossadegh had taken for granted. He was an impenitent self-promoter and, though he had studied engineering, he made his name after Reza's fall as a bureaucrat, journalist and historian. Ahmad Mossadegh was a friend; he introduced Makki to his father after the old man took a liking to a book that Makki had written about Iran under the dictatorship. Makki was too young to remember many of the events he described, but he was inspired by the figure of Mossadegh – so different, he found, from the usual 'marionettes' performing their allotted roles on the political stage.[7]

Mossadegh quickly took Makki into his confidence and Makki in turn was charmed by the older man, with his modesty and frugality (drinking just a little tea when he returned Makki's call, slipping an orange into his pocket for later). And so began an intense political friendship, with Mossadegh writing Makki letters of easy, almost paternal familiarity, and Makki campaigning for Mossadegh at the 1943 elections and then helping out as dogsbody and adviser.

Makki introduced Mossadegh to another future ally, the provincial deputy's son Muzaffar Baghai, and he tried to bring Mossadegh and Qavam together. But the two Qajar survivors were far apart and Mossadegh recoiled when Qavam applied all his guile to rig the 1945 parliamentary elections. Makki was himself elected, but his alliance with Qavam did not last.

The majority of Mossadegh's family regarded Makki as a bumptious parvenu and an opportunist. But Mossadegh would have use for Makki, and others like him, because these men of the new Iran responded with an unquenchable enthusiasm to his call to arms.


To peruse the literature emanating from the propaganda bureau of the Anglo-Iranian Oil Company is to meditate upon the qualities of corporate ambition and social duty and their sublime enactment beneath the Union Jack. Photographs of hearty Iranian employees at play on the basketball court, neat lines of workers' cottages and a display of native flowers at the Abadan Gymkhana attest to a happy and well-cared-for community, while behind the scenes throbs one of the world's most remarkable industrial complexes, centred on the great refinery at Abadan and spreading like a smile of civilisation across one of the world's least hospitable regions. The future of the British Empire may be uncertain. Not that of Anglo-Iranian.[8]

Iranian oil had helped drive the Allies to victory, and crude production continued to rise during post-war reconstruction, from 19,190,000 tons in 1945 to 31,621,000 tons in 1950. The high demand for oil during the post-war reconstruction of Europe enabled the company to achieve a rapid expansion in pre-tax profits, which rose from about £29m in 1946 to some £41m in 1949, before more than doubling to around £86m in 1950. Anglo-Iranian was a private company, but its Iranian operation was Britain's largest single overseas investment and it was an important source of revenue for the shattered British economy, with taxes to the home exchequer greatly exceeding royalties to the Iranian government. Finally, there was the symbolism of it all, for the British Empire had been forced to retrench on all fronts, India was independent, and Anglo-Iranian, with its growing involvement in Iraqi and Kuwaiti oil, was a rare example of rising British prestige. Clement Attlee's new Labour government was socialist at home, nationalising industry and planning a welfare state. Abroad, particularly in Iran, red-faced men went around in tailcoats as if nothing had changed.

The British Embassy's daily bulletin gave much space to Anglo-Iranian puff, but it had little effect on Iranian public opinion because it was not believed. The company was not indifferent to the needs of a burgeoning workforce, and its efforts to recruit Iranians at management level were hampered by the disdain of Tehranis for the baking flats of Khuzestan, but the biggest obstacle to Anglo-Iranian's success in its endeavours, and as a consequence the biggest factor in its unpopularity, was Anglo-Iranian itself.

Under the concession agreement, the company was bound to provide housing, healthcare and other amenities for its Iranian workers, but in 1949 some five-sixths of them (more than 40,000 men) had no official housing of any sort, and many lived in hovels. The company's much-vaunted training programme was inadequate; even without attrition, the company was training only about half the number of Iranians needed to fulfil its obligations with respect to Iranian participation in the higher grades.

Anglo-Iranian regarded the provision of amenities for dependents of Iranian workers as the responsibility of the government, effectively asking the Iranians to invest philanthropically for a population whose problems had been created by the company and whose labours benefited Britain more than Iran. The Iranians declined to do so. In 1950, the town of Abadan had only enough electricity to supply a single London street. Of 20,000 school-age children, there were places for just 2,500. The company argued that conditions for Iranian workers in the rest of the country were no better, or even worse, but there was no British elite lording it over the rest of the country as there was in the concession zone. This being England, society was organised into classes: a top class of Europeans and some British-educated Iranians, a second class of white-collar Iranians and imported Indians, and, at the bottom (and much the largest), a third, blue-collar class.

Racial segregation was practised not only at work, but also in housing allocation and the use of buses, cinemas and clubs. Just one club was mixed, with a majority of Iranian members, but this did not mean that the Iranians controlled the club. It was controlled by the company management – by the whites. From British India, the company borrowed a cantonment culture and colonial nomenclature. The Britons were 'sahibs' and their wives 'memsahibs'. Back in England they were nice middle-class people. Out here, under the blazing sun, they were kings.

Their attitude is encapsulated by correspondence from 1950, when a British employee wondered if it was beyond the company to clean up the filthy bazaar that lay next to the great refinery. The answer was that 'we should not interfere too much and, anyway, if we gave a little they would ask for more so it was best not to give at all.' So the company gave as little as it could get away with, and was loathed everywhere, while the Tudeh Party experienced a surge in popularity in the concession zone.

For Iran's nationalists it was a truism that the company's employees were spies. Starting in 1931, the company had enjoyed close relations with the industrial intelligence unit in Britain's Secret Intelligence Service (SIS), also known as MI6, contributing to a stream of reports, mostly on Soviet Russia and Germany. Flouting an agreement that agents should only be recruited through Britannia House, the company's headquarters in London, the SIS's Baghdad station established a network of company assets in World War Two. Anglo-Iranian was nervous because, if the Iranians came to know about the network, the effects on the company's prospects could be disastrous. After the war, the SIS agreed to disband the network but Anglo-Iranian executives assured the SIS that they would volunteer any information 'of real inside importance' – and it can only be assumed that they did.[9]

In the summer of 1946 the industry was paralysed by a general strike that was caused by, among other things, the company's refusal to pay wages on the Friday holiday as required by law, and this in turn sparked ethnic violence involving the province's indigenous Arab population – old British clients from the days of Sir Percy Cox and before. The company capitulated on the Friday wage but did not learn its lesson. Rather than address the wider Iranian concerns, it simply redoubled its propaganda efforts. It was another example of 'the stupid attitude of the Europeans out here – to antagonise rather than cooperate with the Iranians. Even among quite intelligent people here, this racial antipathy is to be found – and unless it goes, this company will.' These words were not written by a Tudeh agitator but an Englishman called L. P. Elwell-Sutton, a scholar and sometime employee of Anglo-Iranian and the British Embassy in Tehran, whose later book, *Persian Oil*, devastatingly laid bare the company's ethos.

Elwell-Sutton was an exception and his former colleagues in the company and the embassy would never forgive him his siding with the natives. It did not seem to matter that he was right.

*   *   *

The Allied occupation had been significant in another way, for the United States had modified its long-held policy of benevolent inaction in Iran, landing a military force to operate a section of the great railway and sending technical missions of assistance. Then, in August 1944, the British-backed prime minister, Muhammad Saed, reluctantly acknowledged that the government was considering applications by the Anglo-Dutch corporation Royal Dutch Shell and two American companies, Socony-Vacuum and Sinclair, for oil concessions. It was obvious that Saed's government was preparing to entrust more of Iran's mineral wealth to the capitalist West. Rumours also swirled that Socony-Vacuum stood to get a concession in the northern provinces, which the Russians regarded as their sphere of influence. In this way, the Cold War started in Iran long before it did in Europe, and the early advantage lay with the Soviets.

Many Iranians had been thrilled by the Soviet defence against Hitler, and the Tudeh basked in Stalin's glory. Six Tudeh MPs had been elected at the 1943 parliamentary elections, advocating socialist reforms under the monarchy, and the party also supported a burgeoning trade-union movement. In the north of the country, the Soviets drilled for mineral resources without authorisation, while in Tehran Bullard complained that the 'behaviour of the Soviet Ambassador in general resembles that of a Commissar in a Baltic State rather than of a diplomat in a foreign independent country.' Bullard's own pro-consular style more than qualified him to make this sort of assessment.

The Soviets reacted swiftly to news of the impending concessions. An abrasive assistant foreign minister, Sergei Kavtaradze, was dispatched on a tour of the northern provinces under Russian occupation. Ending up in Tehran, Kavtaradze sat down with Saed and demanded an oil concession to cover the same provinces, but the prime minister rebuffed him by saying that all concessions were off the table until the war's end. Kavtaradze's rejoinder came on October 24, 1944, in an infamous press conference at the Soviet Embassy. He repeated his demand for a concession, denounced the 'unfriendly' actions of Saed's government, and obliquely invited Iranians to bring it down.

By any measure, Kavtaradze's behaviour as Iran's guest was extraordinarily coarse, and it had an immediate effect, pushing many neutrals to harden their opinion of the Soviet Union and causing consternation among the Tudeh. Up until now the party had been able to dodge the vexed question of where its loyalties would lie if Iranian and Soviet interests collided. Now Iran's pro-Tudeh press bent over backwards to explain the difference between a good concession (Russian) and a bad one (British or American), shrieking all the while for the downfall of the 'crypto-fascist' Saed. With the wartime allies at loggerheads, and no mutually acceptable government likely to emerge, the Tudeh and its Russian backers arranged a shocking escalation.

A few days after Kavtaradze's press conference tens of thousands of Tudeh supporters marched from the party building to parliament, calling for Saed's resignation and the granting of the concession. The effect of this well-disciplined crowd chanting slogans and waving banners on the rather chaotic and basic town of Tehran might have had a decisive effect in favour of the Soviets – were it not for Kavtaradze, scheming ineptly behind the walls of his embassy. Photographers and reporters were on hand when lorry-loads of armed Red Army troops arrived to 'protect' the marchers as they approached parliament. The images they captured, of bayonet diplomacy by a 'friendly' neighbour, a stone's throw from Iran's sovereign legislature, could hardly have been more damaging.

From being the wronged party, overlooked in favour of western interests, the Soviets now looked like bullies. Tudeh members turned in their cards in droves, but still Kavtaradze refused to go home, and the country seemed ominously poised between the communists on the one hand and Seyyed Zia's right-wing goons on the other. Then one man came through the middle to confound them all: Muhammad Mossadegh.

His momentous speech to parliament following the Tudeh rally, and the bursts of un-parliamentary applause which interrupted it, showed his ability to articulate the popular mood. Mossadegh was too iconoclastic and too attached to the principle of private property to be a communist, but he had been regarded by the Tudeh as not unfriendly to them. He was certainly aware that, by speaking passionately against the northern concession, he would become their enemy, but that probably did not worry him, for he did not shrink from subjecting political alliances to the needle light of principle.

He started his speech by settling scores across a dozen years, showing the pivotal importance of the D'Arcy Concession as Reza Shah had renegotiated it in 1933, and which Mossadegh unpicked, clause by ignominious clause. Mossadegh favoured what he called 'negative equilibrium' in foreign affairs, which meant rebuffing all foreign claimants to concessions and privileges, but D'Arcy redux was thirty-two years longer in duration than the original, and this pointed in quite another direction. Kavtaradze was known to have claimed a far bigger area than that covered under D'Arcy, and it later emerged that he planned for much of northern Iran to be a Soviet 'security zone'. The awful truth was that Reza's disadvantageous 1933 concession was a benchmark, and the Soviets were determined to better it.

Amid bursts of applause, Mossadegh made it clear that he regarded Kavtaradze's behaviour as a breach of the assurances of non-intervention that Iran had received from the Bolsheviks after the 1917 revolution. 'If the Saed government went,' he asked, 'and its successor also did not want to agree [to the concession], what would [the Soviets] do? Would the Soviet government cut relations each time the Iranian government turned down one of their requests?' Mossadegh proposed that the Russians have first refusal on any northern oil and that they join an international consortium to extract it, but he also issued a threat: 'The people of Iran do not take kindly to countries that betray them; where possible, they nail these traitors to the wall.'[10]

This cannot have pleased Kavtaradze. Nor can Mossadegh's sarcastic quip, which got play around Tehran: 'Mr Kavtarazde arrived too late, and now he is going home too soon.' The vice-commissar did not in fact return to Moscow until Mossadegh had steered legislation through the majles prohibiting any government from negotiating a concession with a foreign interest without first getting permission from the deputies. Kavtaradze lashed out against the law and flew away.

The Tudeh and their newspapers poured vitriol on Mossadegh – especially when he refused to endorse a bill to annul the revised D'Arcy Concession. Mossadegh was playing a tactical game, for he expected the bill to be rejected by the current parliament, allowing the British to say (as Mossadegh told the bill's sponsor), 'You claim that this concession was renewed during a period of [Reza Shah's] dictatorship, and that it is illegal – well, now you have a free parliament, which has declined to reject it.'[11] Mossadegh's words suggest that he was already searching for ways to annul the D'Arcy Concession.

Mossadegh was not alone in contemplating action against southern oil, but he knew he must offer an alternative to Anglo-Iranian. He regarded oil both as a weapon and as a goal in Iran's struggle for true independence. Iran's poverty demanded that it develop its resources for the benefit of the people, but the country had neither the financial means nor the technological expertise to do so. Mossadegh proposed an indigenous oil industry financed by advances against future sales and employing foreign technicians alongside Iranian managers. 'Let us negotiate with every state that wishes to buy oil,' he declared, 'and get to work without delay to liberate the country.'[12]

Mossadegh's message was attractive but simplistic in the extreme, for the international oil industry was changing in ways that would make his scenario impossible. Internationalism permeated western political and economic thinking in the aftermath of the war, with the Bretton Woods agreement on capital flows and globalism slipping its halter. The dominant 'Seven Sisters' of the international oil industry – Anglo-Iranian, Royal Dutch Shell and the American 'five', Standard Oil of New Jersey, Standard Oil of California, Socony-Vacuum, Texas, and Gulf Oil – were becoming an all-powerful cartel across the Middle East. Supported by their governments, which regarded stability in the energy sector as a condition of containing communism, the majors reached co-ordinating and integrating agreements or bought each other's oil – as in the case of Standard of New Jersey and Socony-Vacuum, which undertook to buy a huge proportion of Anglo-Iranian's output. New and developing sources were being tapped in Kuwait, Iraq, Bahrain, Qatar and especially Saudi Arabia, and all were following a concessionary model.

There would be little toleration for independent spirits under the new dispensation, and no enthusiasm for an independent Iranian oil industry caring little for cartel rules. Mossadegh was vulnerable on this score, and an Iranian communist leader told a bitter truth when he taunted him, 'Are you really so naive as to suppose that they will let you extract oil using domestic capital? . . . You expect them just to give you the wherewithal to set up shop – bang in front of the oil company?'[13]

Ahmad Qavam, still known by his theoretically defunct title, Qavam al-Saltaneh, had profited from Reza's departure and become a giant once more. He lacked Mossadegh's popular touch but arguably surpassed him as a tactician. He was cold, rich and well tailored, and his life after the Qajar abolition was a long raspberry blown in the direction of the Pahlavi family. His eyes were sensitive to the light and hidden by dark glasses, contributing to his inscrutability. Mossadegh was his opposite – helpless, heroic, asking to be read. Qavam doled out land to his supporters; Mossadegh, squares of nougat.

Qavam had met the Shah when the latter was a tousled four-year-old, patting him on the head and slipping him some gold coins. Twenty years later, ushered into the sovereign's presence, he murmured, 'Good Lord! You *have* grown!' It was the contempt of the Qajar nobility for the Cossack line, and Qavam was widely rumoured to favour a republic with him as president. For his part, the Shah sardonically referred to Qavam as *'le père du peuple'*, a moniker that Qavam encouraged and which the Shah, whose main attribute was his yawning sense of inadequacy, no doubt coveted.

Qavam knew where his and the country's interests overlapped, and here he conducted his politics. He concealed his aims and beliefs with displays of tactical artistry, and this equipped him to deal with a foreign crisis which arose in 1945 – and which parliament made him prime minister in order to resolve. In November of that year, in a sign of the USSR's continuing ambitions, Soviet-backed separatists declared an autonomous regime in the north-western province of Azerbaijan, and, the following month, a smaller one in Kurdistan, the Red Army in each case preventing Iranian forces from intervening.

It was an early experiment in satellite creation, with the Soviets showing no sign of preparing to withdraw from Iran – as they were treaty-bound to do, now that the war had ended. But the experiment was tactical. For now, the Soviets were less interested in accumulating dependencies than forcing the Iranians to give them their northern oil concession.

Qavam had been educated in tsarist Russia and had tea estates in the Soviet-occupied zone. He knew his adversary. He opened negotiations with the Soviets after his appointment in January 1946, and soon won their confidence. In April, well after the last American and British troops had exited Iran, and as Harry Truman's new American administration applied pressure on the Soviets, Qavam approved a deal under which Iran and Russia would set up a combined oil venture across the northern provinces in return for Soviet recognition that the Azerbaijan crisis was an internal Iranian matter, and a promise to withdraw their forces without delay.

Qavam was popular in Moscow, and he was truckling to the Soviets in other ways, bringing communists into his cabinet and giving the Tudeh latitude to hold strikes. The British distrusted him but wanted the Russians' demands met as far as possible. This was, of course, because they feared that Persian intransigence on the question of northern oil would have a symmetrical impact on their own activities in the south.[14]

Any parliament with Mossadegh in it would surely have impeached Qavam for making policy on the basis of an unauthor-ised foreign concession, but the majles was in recess and Qavam ruled as a virtual dictator, with a new political party, the Democratic Party of Iran, to follow and adore him. The law was also on Qavam's side, for it allowed fresh elections only after the last of the foreign troops had left the country. The Red Army duly hurried home after reclaiming arms they had doled out to their Azeri clients, whom they now urged to reach terms with the government.

Qavam then surprised everyone by dramatically changing direction. His overtures to the Soviets, it turned out, had been a ruse to get the Red Army out of the country. An anti-communist tribal uprising gave him an excuse to turn against his Tudeh friends; he drove them out of government, suppressed their newspapers and unleashed his party workers on Tudeh offices. He also started showing marked pro-American tendencies, buying US surplus war materiel and asking a US firm to draft a development plan. Qavam's triumph came with the reconquest by government forces of Azerbaijan, which also killed the Kurdish 'republic' of Mahabad. The Soviets were furious but continued to hope for confirmation of their oil concession by the next majles, which Qavam had predicted would be pro-Soviet.

Again, the Soviets were disappointed. Qavam rigged the 1947 elections, stealing a slim majority, but now his luck ran out. His party fell apart, mainly because it was a kleptocracy united by avarice. The deputies rejected Qavam's Soviet oil concession almost to a man and, striving to be even-handed, imposed a legal obligation on the government to renegotiate Anglo-Iranian's southern oil concession and 'regain the nation's rights'. At the time, Sir John Le Rougetel, who had succeeded Bullard as British ambassador – the British legation had been upgraded to embassy status – warned Anglo-Iranian that this law 'may give the Persians the right to nationalise the petroleum industry'.[15] The significance of this prophecy eluded most people at the time.

The premiership finally slipped from Qavam's grasp in December 1947, to the Shah's satisfaction, for the dilatory youth of Bullard's description was no longer satisfied with tennis and ribbon-cutting. On the contrary, the Shah nowadays gave the impression that his royal birth confirmed an innate aptitude for affairs of state. Nothing pleased him so much as the trip he made in 1947 to the newly 'liberated' parts of Azerbaijan, where the warmth of the reception convinced him that he, not Qavam, had saved the country. In 1947 he was divorced from his lovely Egyptian wife, who had failed to sire him an heir and who in any case pined for the Nile. In 1951 he would take a second, Iranian wife, the even lovelier Sorayya Esfandiari – who failed him in the same way.

The Shah came late to intrigue, guided by his fathomlessly manipulative twin sister, Ashraf, who of all the Pahlavi children most resembled Reza Shah in pluck and want of scruple. Separated from her brother when he was sent away to boarding school, she had accompanied her father into exile after his abdication, amusing herself in Mauritius, the exiles' first port of call, by buying all the shoes she could find in the local bazaar. (Reza had been more concerned for his supply of opium, which he pretended was for his cook.) Beautiful, high-spirited and fiercely independent, Ashraf was devoted to her brother, if exasperated by his repeated failures of nerve. She had a lively rivalry with her elder sister, Shams, and cultivated parliamentary deputies in an attempt to build support for the throne.

The Shah now wanted to increase his powers and harness the country to the West. He feared the British, who had brought him to power and who might (or so he believed) dispense with him, and he admired the United States. Friendship with the West, he believed, would allow Iran to disengage itself further from the Soviet Union.

Obstacles needed to be cleared, and these included Iran's obligation, imposed by its own parliament, to renegotiate the Anglo-Iranian concession by reaching a supplemental agreement providing more funds for development. Negotiations between the company and the government turned on Iran's demand for higher revenues from its oil – but they turned slowly, for the Iranian side was under heavy fire from nationalists and the Tudeh.

The Shah was impatient both for power and progress on the supplemental agreement, and his chance came after February 4, 1949, the day he narrowly escaped assassination at the hands of a young man with a Tudeh affiliation, Nasser Fakhrarayi. The Shah was extraordinarily lucky. Of the five bullets to leave the assailant's revolver, two grazed the royal person and three passed through the peak of his hat. The Shah reacted by lunging at his assailant, twisting his body as he did so to present a narrower target, and was lucky that the sixth cartridge failed to explode, for it would probably have been fatal. The revolver jammed and Fakhrarayi was killed.*

The Shah's narrow escape fed his sense of mission – now anointed with a miracle. Housed in a cabinet, his bullet-ridden uniform was a conversation piece at the Officers' Club, while the royalist press and toadying mullahs harped on about divine intervention. The Shah banned the Tudeh and steamrollered a raft of constitutional amendments through a hastily convened constituent assembly, which gave him the right to dissolve the majles and a new senate. He congratulated the assembly on furthering the cause of constitutionalism. In fact, he had accomplished a judicial *coup d'état*.

Mossadegh was in the doldrums once more. He had tried to prevent Qavam's election rigging of 1947, writing open letters, addressing public meetings and taking sanctuary in the Shah's palace in the hope of forcing him to intervene on the side of democracy. To no avail: the monarch was not yet ready to take on Qavam, and Mossadegh was lambasted at every turn for his 'negativity'. He withdrew from the race and slunk back to Ahmadabad, where he suffered another sharp deterioration in health.

Now parliament came within an ace of asking him to become prime minister after Qavam's fall, even though he was in Ahmadabad and not seeking nomination, but he had been hurt by Qavam's criticism of the 'negativists' and wallowed in self-pity. He told people that he had retired from politics and mutely referred unwelcome visitors to a doctor's order, displayed on the wall, instructing him to refrain from speaking. He later complained that parliament did

---

* The Shah's suite showed less spirit than the monarch himself. The Shah's half-brother Ghollamreza, Le Rougetel reported, 'threw himself flat on the ground, while the others retreated by imperceptible degrees to a distance of about 20 yards.'[16] The Shah's bodyguard only found their courage after the assailant threw away his revolver and raised his hands above his head. They opened fire on him and he died of his injuries.

not consult him and that he might as well be dead for all the attention he received. It was an epic sulk.

Watching Qavam and the Shah slug it out, Mossadegh wanted neither man to win, but rested his hopes in young admirers like Nasser Najmi, to whom he wrote in the winter of 1948, 'The pain is great and there is no doctor; let us hope that one of you guides our benighted ship to shore.'[17]

# 9

# Victory or Death

The Soviets and the British both regarded Iranian nationalism as political froth, generated by unscrupulous politicians and easily dealt with. They operated on the assumption that Iran contained jingoists in abundance, but not a single patriot. And yet national feeling had existed since the turn of the twentieth century, first among the elite, then on a much wider scale. Now, nationalism had grown to such a degree that it was poised to take over politics and set the country's course, for after oil nationalisation Iran's history would be about secular nationalism fighting religious nationalism, with the Left in attendance and the Shah fearing all.

Mossadegh was the first and only Iranian statesman to command all nationalist strains because his probity could not be doubted and because he elevated national independence over everything else, turning it into an existential question that needed an answer before the other questions could even be asked.

Ordinary Iranians were disregarded by almost everyone who mattered in public life. In general, the men who decided Iran's destiny made policy on the premise that deals would be done, that no one would get everything but everyone something, and that the people would swallow the lie that their interests had been served. But this was no longer the case. Iran's parliament was grubby, but to a degree it reflected public opinion. New pressure was being applied, from the press, from the merchants in the bazaar – and increasingly from a few outspoken clerics, for the ayatollahs were now clawing back prestige after the ravages of Reza Shah. Meanwhile, foreign visitors still wrote about sleepy,

medieval Iran – unchanging Iran. It was what they expected to
see, so they saw it.

The British view was that the recent unrest in the oilfields was
a political glitch. They focussed on communist troublemakers and
ignored the wider threat posed by a people fully awakened. The
British believed that the company had done the Iranians a huge
favour by finding and extracting oil. Now the natives were stamping
their feet but this owed nothing to a maturing sense of nationhood
and everything to the infelicities of the oriental mind. When it
suited them, company directors hid behind the letter of the concession agreement. Few saw that it was the spirit of this document,
a disadvantageous concession negotiated by a defunct dictator,
which damned it in the eyes of so many. And almost everyone,
from the communists to the religious Right, could unite to decry
an arrangement whereby, in 1947, the Iranian government received
royalties of £7m and the British government £15m in income tax.

The company was prepared to negotiate a supplemental agreement that would give the Shah more money to modernise his
country, but would not recognise Iran's operational ownership of
its own resources. Anglo-Iranian was firm: there would be no caving
in to the government's demands, a 50:50 profit-sharing arrangement
of the kind that other companies had negotiated elsewhere in the
world, and a statutory revision of the agreement every fifteen years.

Pressured by the Shah, who wanted a quick result, Iran's chief
negotiator settled for an increased royalty and a new minimum
annual payment, but by the time the supplemental agreement came
before the majles, public opinion was roused. One deputy had
called for the industry to be nationalised, and the veteran constitutionalist Hassan Taqizadeh, recently returned from exile, sensa-
tionally disowned the 1933 concession which bore his signature. The
opposition bayed that the concession was illegal. However beneficial the small print, a supplemental agreement would imply the
opposite.

The debate started on July 23, 1949, a few days before the majles
went into recess prior to elections. The British and the Shah were
in a hurry and no one expected the next majles to be any less

nationalist, so tremendous pressure was applied in favour of rati-
fication, with deputies being bought and pro-Court journalists
painting the opposition as British lackeys trying to save the company
from paying an increased royalty. In an atmosphere of intimidation
and dread, there was no telling which way the majority would
jump, and Hossein Makki and the other nationalists in parliament
were resolved to filibuster until the end of the session, and in this
way stop the supplemental agreement from coming to a vote.

Makki needed an elder statesman's clarion call. One evening he
went to Palace Street and implored Mossadegh to write the deputies a resolve-stiffening open letter, but Mossadegh was in one of
his self-pitying moods and waved him away. Makki spent a fruitless
hour trying to break Mossadegh down before leaving him with the
words, 'Woe betide the nation that spends fifty years nurturing a
politician for its time of need, only for such a man at such a time
to duck his responsibilities.'[1] It was a well-aimed jibe, given
Mossadegh's image as a shirker, and after Makki had left the old
man sat for hours on his own, deep in thought, before eventually
taking out pen and paper.

Fearing assassination, Makki was not staying at home, so early
the next morning Mossadegh telephoned another nationalist deputy,
Abdolhossein Haerizadeh, and asked him to take his letter to the
majles. Makki read out Mossadegh's missive as soon as he was
handed it, and while it was not a masterpiece and started with a
reproach to the deputies for not consulting him earlier – 'Is he an
oil expert?' one retorted – it had a galvanising effect.

Certainly Makki himself was inspired enough to perform heroics,
particularly on the final day of parliamentary business, when, half-
stupefied from lack of sleep, a high fever and the stimulant meth-
edrine, he filibustered for well over ten hours, ending all hopes of
a vote before parliament was dissolved. Makki's colleagues urged
him to carry on talking even if it meant keeling over and dying
– and they were not joking. For the new nationalists, it was nothing
less than victory or death.

It was past midnight before Makki, confident that the vote
could not be taken before the end of the session, finally stopped

speaking. In the rapture of the moment, Makki's fever miraculously subsided.

The disciplinarian Reza Shah had fathered Iran, and his son tried to adopt his mantle, but Muhammad-Reza's irresolution was often exposed and he turned in misery to the surrogate parent he so resented: the British Empire. He may have been the unquestioned head of the armed forces, and able to pervert elections and dismiss governments at will, but the King of Kings often found himself scurrying to a foreign functionary – Bullard, Le Rougetel and, from the spring of 1950, Le Rougetel's successor, Sir Francis Shepherd – for guidance and reassurance. The Shah needed to be told that the British approved of what he was doing, and this did not make him seem very father-like. The Mossadegh family referred to him contemptuously as 'that boy' – except for Mossadegh himself. Even in private he called the Shah 'His Majesty'.

From the time the British made clear that they would brook no tinkering with the supplementary agreement, and its fate hung in the balance, Iran came anarchically alive with the realisation that more than oil was at stake. Britain's prestige was again being tested, this time in a spread-eagled Middle Eastern monarchy. The banned Tudeh were making a come-back, working the underground presses and building support in the provinces. A people susceptible to messianic signs contributed to an atmosphere of drama and skulduggery. It was a high-water mark for conspiracies and their theorists. Even the journal of a sophisticated French-educated Iranian such as Ali Shayegan, the dean of law at Tehran University, alludes to the practice of besmirching one's opponents – as well as one's friends. The most common accusations concerned membership of a semi-clandestine fraternity – the Freemasons, say, or the Bahais – in the pay of the British (who else?) and dedicated to debauching Iran. The novelist Iraj Pezeshkzad has rightly described the anti-British paranoia that gripped the country as an illness, and it is an irony of the British Empire that, at the very moment when its power had waned decisively, Iranians considered it invincible. Expatriate students, glimpsing the White Cliffs of Dover for the first time, reported experiencing unsettling palpitations and presentiments. There was something about the damp little island that was both repellent and entrancing. It was touched by evil, and yet, in the majestic logic and stability of its institutions, it showed the way.

Mossadegh himself regarded Britain's constitutional monarchy as the best model for Iran's government. And yet his hatred for the British as a malignant force in his country's affairs, and his intuition for what he regarded as the Anglo-Iranian Oil Company's essential evil, was profound. Not for him the glib modern distinction between a people and their government. In a democracy as smooth as Britain's, one was bound to reflect the other.

In no country that was colonised by the British may these attitudes be observed to the same degree. But Iran was never formally colonised, and there was to be no formal independence. Here, in the poisoned ambiguity of a relationship that was never defined, and in which the British were automatically assumed to be hiding something, mistrust became a pathology.

There was no such pathology with regard to the United States – not yet. But, as the Shah and the British pondered solutions to the oil impasse, and the opposition considered ways of prolonging it, the Americans' hands-off approach to Iran was giving way to a closer engagement. It was what the Shah desired, for he considered the US to be Britain's natural counterweight, and now, revelling in post-war wealth and productivity, a source of aid and arms. The Truman administration had undertaken to protect the northern Mediterranean, investing massively to stabilise Turkey and Greece and keep them out of the Soviet orbit; what, Muhammad-Reza asked, about Iran?

Although the Americans sympathised broadly with the Shah's plans to carry on his father's programme of modernisation, and while they acknowledged the Soviet menace from the north, they could not make up their mind about the sovereign himself. The first question was whether he had the mettle to see through his vaunted seven-year plan of investment and reform. The second was whether the US should help him become a dictator.

These questions were bound up with money and prestige. The recent example of China's Chiang Kai-shek, who had absorbed millions of dollars of US help only for the communists to drive him into the sea, was a persuasive argument against anti-Red largesse. And so, to the Shah's frustration, the argument over aid and arms ground on in Tehran and Washington, and his representations acquired a sour, resentful undercurrent.

On one matter, however, the Shah, the Americans and the British were at one, and that was the need for the supplemental agreement to be ratified and Iran to begin receiving increased revenues which would permit investment and reform. For that, a new parliament was required.

Mossadegh would never be a very determined retiree, though he was affected by lordly indecision and his famous charm soured if he was not paid enough attention. He remembered how the previous elections had been rigged, and as the polling for the sixteenth majles approached in the autumn of 1949 he worried that this would be repeated. His young acolytes flattered him, calling him 'Iran's great national leader', and he was susceptible to the argument that there was no one but him to save the day. As he wrote later, 'After much consideration, I concluded that if I sat silently, I would be doing wrong.'[2]

He now shared the stage with another formidable personality, Ayatollah Abolqassem Kashani, who had been exiled in 1949 at the Shah's behest but continued to influence events back home. Kashani was the latest in Iran's line of charismatic political clerics. A few years younger than Mossadegh, educated at the seminary at Najaf, in Ottoman Mesopotamia, he had taken part in a religious rebellion against the British in the First World War which cost the life of his father (also a prominent cleric) and fuelled his own abiding Anglophobia. The British gave Kashani further grievance when they jailed him during the Second World War for being a German fifth columnist, and he had known rough treatment and exile after that.

Now he was a thorn in the establishment's side, denouncing the oil company and its Iranian stooges and godfathering a group of armed fanatics called the Warriors of Islam. Kashani aspired to lead a worldwide Islamic revival, but in theological terms he was decidedly junior to Shiism's top ayatollah, Seyyed Hossein Burujerdi. Burujerdi believed that the clergy would lose public respect if it involved itself in politics, but as the Shah grasped for power and Anglo-Iranian showed its talons, the perils of abstinence became apparent.

Kashani appealed both to Muslim fanatics and the western-educated secularists who had gathered around Mossadegh. Before his exile, the ayatollah's house near parliament had been the haunt of journalists and politicians of all stripes, as well as the usual straggle of beggars and supplicant widows. His political engagement raised his prestige among Tehran's pious bazaaris, who were ready to slam down their shutters and march at his word. Using contributions from the guilds, he filled the bellies of his supporters hundreds at a time. Even now, from Beirut, he remained a vital presence in Iranian politics. His devoted network of supporters saw to that.

For anyone of Mossadegh's generation, the idea of cooperation between lay and ecclesiastical leaders was normal, even if Mossadegh on occasion showed disdain for the stock figure of the coarse, hypocritical priest. The rapport between the two men was warm, but they had little ideological common ground. They had a shared hatred for monarchical dictatorship and the Anglo-Iranian Oil Company, but Kashani abominated other things that Mossadegh did not: the sale of alcohol and women without the hejab. Kashani's backers, the Warriors of Islam, believed that parliament should repeal all un-Islamic laws and consider its work done. This view of politics was at odds with Mossadegh's, which centred on a strong representative parliament to check the Shah and the army.

Mossadegh had always taken his own decisions, and he had spent his career fastidiously side-stepping the violence that was an integral part of Iran's social and political life. Now, in his late sixties, he became a politician of the masses, chumming up to Kashani and others, such as the rabble-rouser Muzaffar Baghai, who did not baulk at brutality and intimidation. These men drew support from the Tehran bazaar, a vast community of traders, porters and guild leaders, with a demi-monde of mobsters and hoodlums – the 'thick-necks', as they were called – with names like Icy Ramazan and Skull-Cooker Mehdi, whose understanding of morality admitted pilgrimages to Mecca as well as roistering on an epic scale, and who were usually prepared to switch allegiances so long as the price was right.

Elections to the sixteenth majles were held first in the provinces, and they were conducted so dishonestly that even the British were shocked.[3] The machinery of fraud was operated by two members of Princess Ashraf's clique: the Shah's court minister, the suave but insubstantial Abdolhossein Hazhir, and the ambitious chief of the general staff, General Hajji Ali Razmara. For their part, the supporters of Mossadegh and Ayatollah Kashani were determined to stop royal placemen from winning the twelve most important seats of all, in Tehran. Their candidates would be mainly national-ists – but supported by religious militants, Kashani's seminarian supporters and conservative bazaaris.

An upper house, a senate, was also being convened, and Mossadegh was a member of the college from which Tehran's fifteen 'elected' senators – another fifteen were appointed by the Shah – would be chosen by secret ballot. But Mossadegh had no faith in the vote, and before it began he announced theatrically that the government had already decided who would be 'elected'. Drawing a sealed envelope from his pocket, he declared that it contained the names of the winners. The ballot was duly held, and when Mossadegh's envelope was opened and his list of names read out, they corresponded, with one omission. (He had tactfully left off the name of his own nephew and son-in-law, Ahmad Matine-Daftary, who continued to have good relations with the Court.) Mossadegh's own name was not among the winners.[4]

On the morning of October 13, after hundreds of telegrams alleging fraud had arrived from the provinces, Mossadegh prepared to walk to the Marble Palace to demand that the tainted majles elections be annulled. Tormented by premonitions of bloodshed, he had barely slept the previous night, but his resolve stiffened when the chief of police threatened violence if he went ahead. 'We will endure whatever befalls us,' Mossadegh replied.

Several thousand people thronged the area around 109 Palace Street when Mossadegh came out to march the few hundred yards to the palace gates. Kashani's supporters yelled religious slogans but Mossadegh ordered them to stop. 'Silence is our slogan!' he announced through a megaphone. In this way he was able to camouflage the differences between his supporters. As the assembly moved off, Mossadegh would recall, 'Other than the sound of footsteps, there was no sound at all.' An agent provocateur shouted, 'Mossadegh for President!' but was immediately silenced.

Hossein Makki would later claim that Mossadegh and he linked arms on the way to the palace – Mossadegh's cane was in his other hand – but another account suggests that Mossadegh was arm-in-arm with Hossein Emami, a member of the Warriors of Islam who had achieved notoriety by assassinating an outspoken secularist, and who had been freed through the court minister Hazhir's intercession. Given Mossadegh's pluralist views, Makki's account is the more plausible, but Emami seems to have been close by when Mossadegh arrived at the palace gates and Hazhir received his letter to the Shah and a demand to take sanctuary inside.

Mossadegh had warmed up by now, and he poked Hazhir in the chest, shouting, 'Abdolhossein Hazhir! Do you have a conscience? If so, tell me the elections are free!' Then he said, 'Go and tell the Shah that this is the house of the people, and the people want to come in.'[5] Then there was an argument between Hazhir and Hossein Emami, with Emami threatening, 'If I don't kill you I'm a bastard!' Mossadegh told him to shut up.

The Shah and Hazhir now showed tactical acumen. They let just twenty of the marchers into the palace, including Mossadegh, who made the mistake of sending the crowd home. With Mossadegh thus disarmed, Hazhir was free to toy with the royal guests, regaling them with superb food and solicitous conversation. Realising their mistake, Mossadegh and his colleagues abruptly went on hunger strike, accepting only water when Hazhir invited them to eat, but Mossadegh weakened physically after just a few hours and Zahra showed her disapproval of this dangerous tactic by sending in a kilo of homemade biscuits. For three nights, the fasters held out – until Zahra's biscuits became impossible to resist. In the meantime, the Shah denied all knowledge of electoral fraud. Thus Mossadegh's first mass action ended in fiasco.

Eventually Mossadegh and his supporters left the palace and went back to Palace Street, where they cemented their alliance by setting up a new umbrella group, led by Mossadegh, called the National Front. The mood was far from exultant; the Tehran elections were at hand, and Hazhir was doing his best to rig them.

The count for votes cast in Tehran was being held at the Sepahsalar mosque, next to parliament, and over the next few days this substantial Qajar pile was the backdrop for a game of cat-and-mouse over sealed ballot boxes, with government agents trying to tamper with them and Mossadegh's supporters standing guard. Royalist thick-necks piled in but were repulsed by rival groups loyal to the Warriors of Islam, while pro-Kashani seminarians raised a ruckus from the rooftop of an adjacent theological college. Mossadegh's secretary arrived with nuggets of intelligence, and Zahra sent food. 'You must defend the people's votes until your dying breath,' ran Mossadegh's instructions, and with two-thirds of the votes counted, he, Kashani and five more National Front leaders were on course to capture seven of Tehran's twelve seats.[6]

Faced with a major reverse, the government dropped all pretence at propriety. Mossadegh and Kashani's election watchdogs were overwhelmed and locked in a room in the mosque. Mossadegh rushed by car to the palace to remonstrate with Hazhir – to no avail. Then the authorities moved the count to another building and denied access to the opposition. As the count continued the fortunes of the government's candidates miraculously revived, and soon enough the sole National Front representative on course to win a seat was Mossadegh himself, in twelfth place, with every chance that he too would be eliminated before the end of the count.

And so, with this blatant electoral theft, a parliament seemed poised to form that would end Mossadegh's national movement before it had even begun. Mossadegh had exhausted his options because they were exclusively peaceful and constitutional. The Warriors of Islam, on the other hand, did not consider themselves bound by constitutionalism and the law.

It was the middle of the month of Moharram, when Shias commemorate the martyrdom of Imam Hossein, when Hazhir sauntered into the Sepahsalar mosque, by now returned to its intended function, to receive phalanxes of black-clothed men as they trooped in beating their chests and venting a mourning chant. The intensity of these occasions, with the participants staggering under the weight of iron standards and the air thick with lamentation, lends itself to intrigue – and so it was that evening, for in a corner of the mosque lurked the assassin Hossein Emami.

Emami had vowed publicly to kill Hazhir three weeks before, then witnessed the fraud at the Sepahsalar mosque. Now he advanced and shot Hazhir, the bullet traversing the base of the left lung an inch below the heart.[7] Emami's weapon jammed and he tried to hit Hazhir in the face with it before he was seized. The following day the court minister died in hospital. The Warriors of Islam demanded that the elections be held again – only this time, freely.

Hazhir's death robbed the Shah of one of the few subordinates he trusted completely. He reacted with typical inconsistency, ordering the detention of opposition figures of all stripes, including Mossadegh (who was placed under house arrest at Ahmadabad), but also agreeing to rerun the Tehran poll. The Shah and his advisers were undoubtedly influenced by a fear of yet more assassinations – including, perhaps, the monarch's own – and there was, indeed, an immediate abatement of tension in the capital. The royal volte-face had confirmed the efficacy of violence as a political tool. The national movement was saved.

Robbed of his protective court minister, the Shah now felt intensely vulnerable to his chief of staff, Haj Ali Razmara. The Shah distrusted Razmara, but could not easily dispense with him, as he was popular in the army and had admirers among the British and Americans. Here, Mossadegh and his supporters might come in useful. A point in their favour was that they had a visceral dislike of Razmara, suspecting him of dictatorial tendencies, and would attack him without relent if given a platform to do so. The Shah decided to give them that platform, and it was one of the most crucial miscalculations of his reign.

Barely a month after they were arrested, the Front's leaders were free. Kashani's religious supporters held a big campaign meeting. Returning to Tehran, Mossadegh declared that Iran would never accept a parliament that had been set up through the intrigues of foreigners.

The Shah had blinked and in the rerun poll Mossadegh was returned as Tehran's top deputy. Kashani (in absentia) and six other National Front leaders were also elected – all but one from the capital. The legislature was 100-strong but its Tehran members enjoyed an influence out of proportion with their number. Mossadegh and his allies would exploit this to nationalise the oil industry and capture the attention of the world.

In June 1950 the Shah let Kashani come back after eighteen months of exile. Mossadegh was there to embrace him on the tarmac – the mullah and the doctor of law, pledging mutual devotion. The people had flocked to the airport by bicycle, car and donkey, and makeshift triumphal arches swayed precariously over the route into town. Kashani was driven home through the packed streets with unruly supporters on the bonnet of the open-top Buick, while the alleyways ran with the blood of ewes that had been sacrificed in his honour. The long narrow road where Kashani lived had been covered in carpets, and the seminarians shouted, 'God! Independence! Freedom!'

Kashani's conception of a political principle was more elastic than Mossadegh's. He had maintained good relations with the unabashed Anglophile Seyyed Zia. He received the families of jailed communists and zealots like the leader of the Warriors of Islam, who was theoretically being sought in connection with Hazhir's death but felt safe enough to give humdinger speeches in the ayatollah's house. Kashani aspired not to office but to a cleric's spell-binding authority. He would not descend to the ranks of ordinary deputies and appear in the parliament, nor would he formally join the National Front. He would watch severely over these bodies – another of Iran's fathers.

The coalition formed by Mossadegh and Kashani would have as fundamental an effect on Iran as the Constitutional Revolution itself, inspiring urban and provincial Iranians alike. Kashani was respectful to Mossadegh, his senior in age and his equal (at least) in political courage. The ayatollah carefully crafted his statements to parliament so that Mossadegh would not be embarrassed when he declaimed them. On June 18, 1950, for instance, Mossadegh read out Kashani's declaration that the Iranians would dispose of their oil as they saw fit, and his call that the country would not submit to another dictatorship. Kashani described himself as the 'voice of the people'. As time would show, the cleric's words belonged more properly to the layman who uttered them.

The Shah was squeamish about imposing a dictatorship, but he was prepared to close down parliament if he felt the alternative was chaos or the erosion of his own power. By his lights he had done the National Front a favour by admitting them into parliament, but no sooner was Mossadegh back in the chamber than he launched an impertinent attack on the monarch and Princess Ashraf. The court was unhappy and Sir Francis Shepherd, in one of his marathon lunches at the palace, reported the Shah as saying that the National Front was even more dangerous than the Tudeh, and as referring to Mossadegh as 'our Demosthenes'.[8]

The Shah had appointed the timorous, venal Ali Mansour to be prime minister, but Mansour angered him by courting the National Front and dallying over the supplemental agreement. Rather than try to force the agreement through parliament, as the Shah and the British had hoped he would, Mansour deputed a parliamentary committee – Mossadegh, inevitably, was its chairman – to examine it and make recommendations. By this time the Shah's tic, his desire for a 'strong' government, was re-emerging. The obvious choice to set up such a government was Razmara.

Haj Ali Razmara was one of those talented and problematic

generals that Iran's army produced from time to time, winning the
monarch's attention by competently running a cherished institution,
and his suspicion for the same reason. Educated at St Cyr, the
French military academy that had produced General de Gaulle,
Razmara was married to the sister of Iran's leading avant-garde
novelist. He was stocky, laconic and ruthless enough to attract
comparisons with Reza Shah, but the junior officers respected him
for working hard and living modestly. Razmara had proved himself
on the battlefield, commanding the forces that had liberated
Azerbaijan in 1947, and he and the Shah were now in close cooperation on defence plans against a possible Soviet invasion. For all
that, the Shah still did not fully trust his chief of staff. Razmara's
enemies whispered that he had been behind the royal assassination
attempt of the previous year, while his friendship with Princess
Ashraf probably went beyond the platonic. Above all, there was
Razmara's ambition. He promised foreign diplomats that he would
end the oil impasse and provide the firm, efficient leadership they
despaired of finding in the Shah.

Ordinarily, the British and the Americans would have baulked at
promoting this budding generalissimo, but these were not ordinary
times. The optimism engendered by the fall of Reza Shah had given
way to despair, and both western powers considered Iran to be in
danger of collapse. Nancy Lambton, Britain's most influential Iran
scholar at the time, had written in an influential paper of a general
hatred for the 'ruling class'. She evoked the febrile atmosphere in
the capital, where conversation might veer from a fancy dress ball
attended by outlandishly dressed members of the royal family to
the suicide of a soldier sent on guard duty while suffering from
pneumonia.

Western worries were compounded by the tense international
situation. In June 1950, communist North Korea had crossed the
38th parallel, drawing in the United States and its allies and raising
fears of a wider conflagration. In Tehran the US ambassador, John
C. Wiley, raised the spectre of 'the complete disintegration of the
country and its absorption immediately or eventually into the Soviet
bloc'.[9]

Mossadegh and his allies in turn focussed obsessively on the grand themes of national independence and democratic reform, and one is struck by their apparent indifference to the poverty and wretchedness suffered by the vast majority of their countrymen. It might have been expected for the capital's top deputy to rail at these maladies and suggest solutions, but Mossadegh's speeches, statements and letters from this time are dominated by his opposition to the government, and particularly to the supplemental agreement. This agreement would inject vital funds into the economy, helping civil servants, whose pay was now in arrears, and allowing the government to start implementing the Shah's development plan. But Mossadegh had not returned to parliament to fill bellies.

Here, months before he came to power, is the conundrum of Mossadegh and his movement. For the National Front, the question of spending oil revenues and lubricating a reforming state could not be addressed while the state was in servitude. No cosmetic alleviation should conceal the flaw running through the country. That had been the way of traitorous leaders of the past and as a consequence the flaw ran as deeply and painfully as ever. Repeatedly, National Front leaders told their supporters that if Iran did not control its own oil, it would be better if it stayed underground or was consumed by fire. Mossadegh declared that he was more interested in what he called the 'moral aspect' of oil nationalisation than its 'economic aspect'.

In these remarks the western powers identified hysteria, irrationality and caprice – anything but an authentic movement of national independence. And yet Iran now had, for the first time, exactly that. Around the world, decolonisation was bringing independent nations to life and the Iranians looked on enviously. Caught up in what they believed to be a life or death struggle, it is perhaps understandable that Iran's nationalists turned their backs on the relative security offered by the supplemental agreement. In the search for a nation there was no room for petty bookkeeping.

To start with, the British government and their supporters in the press damned Mossadegh with faint interest. The Tudeh Party seemed more threatening. Later, as he grew in stature, they rarely neglected to underestimate him, and discussion of Mossadegh acquired a tone of highly varnished condescension – used so often by the British against any adversary they did not understand. The correspondent of *The Times* sketched Mossadegh with the strokes of a caricaturist: 'He weeps with sincere emotion at the spectacle of his own patriotism, which is as genuine as it is hysterical, and if ardent love could make Persia strong and prosperous without the help of knowledge, sagacity or diligence, Dr Mossadegh would be an ideal prime minister.'[10] And barely had Sir Francis Shepherd arrived to take up his post in Tehran than he treated his superiors to a disquisition on the 'oriental mind'.[11]

The Americans drew on different traditions. There was a strongly anti-colonial conscience among many foreign-service officers, but the State Department's Bureau of Near Eastern, African and Far Eastern Affairs was young and in awe of Britain's experience. George McGhee, the assistant secretary of state with responsibility for the region, and a self-confessed Anglophile, described the Iranian nationalists as a 'so-called "opposition"', while in Tehran, Wiley and other US diplomats shared the British view that the Iranians were incapable of governing themselves – even if they were more sympathetic to the idea that the Iranians should be helped out of their pathetic disability.

There was a third foreign body with a controlling stake in Iranian affairs – the Anglo-Iranian Oil Company. Here, progress had been made at a glacial pace. The board had barely advanced past a state of Victorian paternalism and was condemned by one of its own directors as 'helpless, niggling, without an idea between them, confused, hide-bound, small-minded, blind', and generally ineffective.[12] The company's scabrous chairman, Sir William Fraser, had learned his industrial relations in the Edwardian era. But no longer could Britain boss around the rest of the world, and Iran was not the monolithic dictatorship that the company had dealt with in 1933. Finally, other rival companies, notably the American giant Aramco, were signing concessionary deals whose generosity to the producer nation would make the supplemental agreement look like parsimony itself.

Separately and together, these three groups of foreigners tried to shape Iran's future at a critical time, and eventually they prevailed upon the Shah to hand the premiership to Razmara. They had high hopes of the plausible, hard-working general.

Mossadegh was at least a generation older than most of his colleagues in the National Front. They venerated him and many of them would have laid down their lives for him. So it is not outlandish to suggest that he could have disciplined and moderated them as they bayed like animals in the parliament chamber, slamming down their wooden desk tops until they splintered on their hinges, and as the sulphurous atmosphere of threat and counter-threat consumed Razmara's premiership. But Mossadegh did not urge civilised behaviour on his comrades. He allowed their passions to fertilise his own. Things became so heated that the parliamentary speaker interrupted one barrage of nationalist invective with the words, 'Isn't this meant to be a constitutional country?'[13]

It was, and Mossadegh was meant to be its champion. He personified constitutionalism. His understanding of democracy was based on a profound knowledge of its guiding principles and an intuitive appreciation of how, and with what limitations, it might be applied in Iran. But Mossadegh and his colleagues would disrupt the full eight months of Razmara's premiership, blocking his every legislative move – while at the same time keeping his government alive for fear that the alternative would be parliament's dissolution and an out-and-out despotism. It was a travesty of the parliamentary democracy that Mossadegh had suffered to achieve.

The nationalist argument is that the alternative would have been uglier. The Shah had brought Razmara to power without a parliamentary vote and Mossadegh was not alone in detecting what he called the 'bitter taste of a military dictatorship' inspired by foreigners. Martial law; unlawful arrests; sham elections; censorship: Mossadegh knew these all too well, and was determined they should not recur. But Razmara was no longer in uniform and the reforms he brought before parliament – including decentralisation and land redistribution – deserved a respectful hearing. He was denied even that, and summarily damned as a second Reza Shah. Since he was a secretive man, and on the defensive for much of his premiership, his real intentions are hard to judge.

Mossadegh joined the uproar when the general first arrived in brown pinstripes to present his cabinet to parliament. Someone quipped, 'Stand to attention!' and there was pandemonium as desk tops were slammed until they splintered on their hinges and the nationalists hollered their opposition – Mossadegh and the younger hotheads, Baghai and Makki, loudest of all. From the public gallery someone shouted, 'Death to Dictatorship!' and Razmara's supporters gamely retorted, 'Long Live Dictatorship!' Mossadegh interrupted the prime minister's speech, shouting, 'America and Britain brought you to power!' and fired a salvo at the departing cabinet: 'Get lost! Shut the door and don't come back!'

Suddenly Mossadegh collapsed and the shout was heard: 'Ye Gods! Mossadegh has died!' Theatrical he was, but not morbidly so, and he came round with a dose of oxygen. Outside the parliament, Kashani's supporters hurled stones and tried to overturn the prime minister's car as he was driven away.

The nationalists picked up the bill for the smashed desk tops but a tone of vilification had been set. In parliament Mossadegh uttered the most threatening public words of his career: 'As God is my witness – even if they kill me, tear me to shreds – I won't submit to this sort of person . . . I will strike and I will be killed! If you are a soldier, I am more of a soldier. I'll kill you right here! I'll shed blood!'[14] Later on, Kashani said the prime minister's pen should be snapped, a metaphor for execution. Photographs of the slain court minister Hazhir circulated in parliament, black-bordered.

Razmara was not scared. He remained a soldier, in spite of the suit. 'After my death,' he predicted, 'the people of Iran will put up my statue!' He tried without success to divide the opposition, offering bribes and promising the Islamists he would shred their judicial files and bring in pious government. He cosied up to the Soviets, signing a trade pact and looking the other way when the Tudeh leaders launched a jailbreak. He met everyone – the Shah;

the ambassadors; the oil company. With Ernest Northcroft, Anglo-Iranian's portly, bespectacled Tehran representative, he had a fixed weekly rendezvous. He was on shifting sands because the only solid support he enjoyed – from foreigners – was a liability in the eyes of his countrymen. The Shah responded in his usual way, by undermining the man he had brought to office.

There were now several opposition newspapers, and they attacked Razmara relentlessly. Headlines and editorials were rousing, and journalistic standards low. *Shahed*, perhaps the country's best-selling morning paper, did not limit itself to attacking the prime minister's patriotism and integrity, but accused him of forcing female guests at the Shah's wedding to Sorayya Esfandiari into un-Islamic *décolletée* dresses. The paper then explained in un-Islamic detail what *décolletée* meant: 'A dress that leaves the upper part of the body completely naked and leaves quite uncovered the arms and elbows and shoulders and armpits and the whole back and upper portion of the chest and half the ladies' beautiful breasts . . .'[15]

*Shahed*'s owner, the nationalist deputy Muzaffar Baghai, was a bull-necked battler with intellectual pretensions and a taste for arrack. He could not be arrested – as many of the other editors were – because he enjoyed parliamentary immunity. Whenever his paper was closed down, he reopened it under a different name. The police tried stopping distribution but the nationalist deputies doled out copies on the street corners. On one occasion a thick-neck called Mad Mustafa and his goons were sent to destroy the *Shahed* presses, but the nationalists withstood the assault together with reinforcements from the Warriors of Islam. In the ensuing siege, Mossadegh spoke to Baghai by telephone and urged the defenders to flee, as he had been tipped off that the authorities intended to kill them. The confrontation came to a peaceful end after Mossadegh led a sit-in by nationalist deputies in the parliament building which drew attention to Baghai's plight. The spectacle of worldly Francophones fighting alongside Muslim fanatics showed how elastic alliances had become.

Mossadegh spent much of the second half of 1950 ensconced in a committee room in the majles, deciding the fate of the supplemental agreement. Anglo-Iranian and its supporters were in no hurry for the commission to reach its conclusion, believing that, as Iran's economic situation got worse and the need for oil revenues more acute, it would become easier to depict the nationalists as pig-headed adventurists indifferent to the nation's plight. Instead, the commission's long duration worked in the nationalists' favour, allowing them to bring the more conservative members round to their view. Mossadegh was instrumental in this process, explaining his views patiently and precisely to men who, while not devoid of national feeling, were instinctively more conservative than he.

The company was perhaps his biggest ally, for Anglo-Iranian's Tehran representatives continued to deserve the worst accusations of meddling and intrigue. The company bombarded editors with crib sheets lauding the agreement, while Northcroft urged Razmara to ban unfriendly newspapers, sack the government's representative on the oil commission (too impartial), and be more forthcoming in directing its members to a satisfactory conclusion.[16] Still, the company's position did not improve. The supplemental agreement was now so loathed, and the culture of odium so entrenched, that no one was prepared to defend it.

In Washington there was a new realisation that Anglo-Iranian was its own worst enemy, and the State Department privately deplored the British government's determination to 'permit the AIOC to operate as it has in the past, bribing deputies and Government officials'.[17] The Americans had moved ahead of the British on policy, too, for they understood that the agreement needed sweetening if it was to stand a chance of getting past the majles. The Foreign Office eventually came round, but the company dug in its heels. When, in July 1950, Shepherd proposed that Anglo-Iranian make an advance to help Razmara meet a prospective budget deficit of £28m, Northcroft replied by proposing £6m over six months, which Razmara dismissed as 'useless'. Sir William Fraser insisted there was only one solution to the impasse, and that was to ratify the agreement.

Northcroft had spent much energy deflecting Iran's demands for a 50:50 profit-sharing arrangement along the lines that Venezuela had recently negotiated with Shell. Then, in August 1950, the Iraq Petroleum Company (which was owned by Anglo-Iranian) agreed to pay Iraq a higher royalty than Iran stood to gain under the supplemental agreement. The Foreign Office recognised that the company would have to improve their offer in line with the Iraqi terms, but then the emerging oil kingdom of Saudi Arabia trumped everyone, for the profit-sharing agreement it signed with Aramco in December 1950 was the most advantageous any Middle Eastern oil-producer had negotiated to date. Under this arrangement, the Saudis would receive an average royalty of thirty shillings a ton, nearly double the amount Iran stood to earn under the supplemental agreement. By now, Sir William Fraser had grumpily endorsed advances of almost £30m and no longer excluded discussion of the 50:50 principle. But his concessions came too late.

By October 1950, when the nationalists launched impeachment proceedings against Razmara, few public figures in Iran referred to the AIOC without attaching an acid epithet – 'usurping' was one, 'marauding' another – while the Warriors of Islam warned that, if the supplemental agreement went through, the filth would spread and 'women's chadors will be ripped from their heads'. During the impeachment proceedings, Makki tore into the company for besetting 'Iran and its people with . . . vast and astonishing misfortunes'. Razmara's finance minister was hounded from office and went in fear for his life. None of this was conducive to an informed debate on the future of Iran's oil, and Shepherd would denounce 'the demagogy of [the] minority' and the 'threats of [the] gutter press'.[18] For once, the ambassador was right.

The impeachment was a piece of theatre, designed to make the government yet more despised. Then, on November 25, 1950, after the oil commission rejected the supplemental agreement, Mossadegh pulled a rabbit out of his hat. On that day, the nationalist members of the commission moved a historic resolution: 'In the name of the prosperity of the Iranian nation and with a view to helping secure world peace, we, the undersigned, propose that the oil industry of Iran be declared as nationalised throughout all regions of the country without exception; that is to say, all operations for exploration, extraction and exploitation shall be in the hands of the government.'

Events now moved with great speed and violence. On 27 November, Ayatollah Kashani issued a fatwa calling for oil nationalisation and his and Mossadegh's supporters embarked on a terrific propaganda onslaught, with rallies and screaming editorials and a flood of supportive telegrams coming in from the provinces. Rumours flew that Razmara was planning to seize power in a coup, and it was widely known that he had struck a secret deal with the AIOC for a profit-sharing agreement and a big advance to meet government expenses. Razmara had not divulged the details of this deal, for while it may have been feasible six months earlier, the prime minister doubted his ability to sell it in the current frenzy. The Shah was now against his general, sounding out potential replacements and soliciting Mossadegh's assurance (which he gave) that the National Front did not intend to install a republic. Mossadegh told the court minister, Hossein Ala, that he did not want the premiership. That would take him out of parliament, where he was now absorbed in getting nationalisation into law.

On 4 March, 1951 Razmara came to the majles and told the oil commission that nationalisation would be impracticable and that Iran was incapable of running its oil industry. Three days later, he was dead.

Mossadegh was busy with other members of the oil commission when a fellow-deputy came in and whispered that Razmara had been shot. Mossadegh said loudly, 'Well, he shouldn't have made that speech!' and got back to work.

The assassination had been carried out by a member of the Warriors of Islam, but there is strong evidence that Mossadegh had prior knowledge. Around the turn of 1951, Mojtaba Navab-Safavi, the leader of the Warriors of Islam, had discussed killing Razmara with several National Front leaders, and either Makki or Haerizadeh (the eye-witness accounts differ) claimed to be attending the meeting as Mossadegh's representative. Makki, for one, gave his approval of the proposed assassination, and Navab-Safavi asked him to convey what had been discussed to 'absent friends' – by which he meant Mossadegh.[19] Two days after that, Kashani also endorsed the plan.

Mossadegh never admitted to knowing in advance about the attempt on Razmara's life, but it is unlikely that he was kept unaware of so momentous a meeting involving his closest allies. He was not simply a benign presence in the National Front, but its unchallenged strategist, as evidenced by his brilliant plan to achieve oil nationalisation. If he did not run the Front as a strict hierarchy, or a personal fief, this is because he was not at home in such hierarchies and the Front contained strong characters who were prepared to answer him back. For all that, National Front meetings were generally held in his house, and his colleagues invariably sought his approval for major decisions.

Mossadegh was not a violent person, never raising a hand against a member of his family or a servant – neither uncommon at the time – and not shooting animals for sport. He kept a small ivory of Gandhi in his room at Ahmadabad. But Muslim nationalists in the Middle East usually admired Gandhi's struggle against the British and his religious tolerance more than his ideology of non-violence. Stemming from Hinduism, this ideology was alien and even puzzling in Iran, where vegetarianism was unknown and mainstream Shia Islam was full of gory stories of martyrdom. On a rhetorical level, Mossadegh's attitude to political violence was ambiguous. During an earlier conversation with Mossadegh, Iraj Eskandari, a Tudeh leader he had known for years, had described Iran's northern provinces as the Soviets' 'security cordon'. Mossadegh withdrew a pencil sharpener from his pocket, unscrewed the blade, and held it towards Eskandari, saying, 'You're like a son to me, but if I hear that phrase "security cordon" one more time from you, I will use this to cut out your tongue!'[20]

It is probable that Mossadegh did not attend the meeting with Navab-Safavi either because he was indisposed or because his colleagues had anticipated the subject of discussion and wanted to distance him from a nasty business. Characteristically, Mossadegh did not exult in the prime minister's assassination in the way Kashani and some of his nationalist allies did, but nor did he say anything to suggest that he found it tragic or repugnant. In the same way he had expressed no regrets at the earlier murder of the Shah's court minister, Hazhir.

With Hazhir's killing, the Warriors of Islam had saved the National Front in its infancy. Now, by slaying Razmara, they removed the last obstacle to oil nationalisation and a government dominated by the National Front. Mossadegh was in debt twice over to the militants, and Navab-Safavi knew it, impressing on the nationalists that he expected them to implement Islamic law if they came to power. But this is not what happened, and after Razmara's death Mossadegh cold-shouldered his former allies without compunction, doing nothing to dissuade the authorities from breaking up the organisation and jailing its leaders. Mossadegh was himself threatened by the Warriors, but never considered acceding to their demands. He was not thinking of implementing Islamic law. His attention was fixed obsessively on oil.

Much later, living out his final years soberly at Ahmadabad, he would describe his fellow members of the sixteenth majles with understanding, distinguishing those who were fighting for Iran's independence at any price from others whose desire for independence was tempered by doubts over how to achieve it.[21] In the heat of battle, though, he subscribed to the same Manichaean world-view as his followers. He was at his most excitable, fainting, bursting into tears and wallowing in old-mannish bathos – such as when he presented his German camera to a colleague, writing, 'I will have no use for it in these final days of my life.' He would live for another seventeen years.

His ailments were debilitating, but not life-threatening. He was in and out of bed with a temperature, receiving guests at Palace Street in the pyjamas that would become the recurring motif of all future caricatures. He was lethargic from uraemia, for which his doctor ordered complete rest: an impossibility, as the patient acknowledged. Everything seemed indexed to the oil issue and he put out petulant vows on the subject – not to get well; never again to set foot in parliament – which none of his colleagues took seriously. He was moved to lovely metaphors, comparing an increase in the banknote issue to pouring water into a glass of buttermilk – its colour staying the same even as its properties weaken – and claiming to have had a dream in which a 'celestial figure' urged him to 'break the chains that bind Iran's feet'.

His engagement with politics was deep and joyful. Later the cares of office, and of managing the crisis of his premiership, would wipe the broad uninhibited smile from his face; now was the time of his life.

Razmara's death was oddly disregarded in the lunge for nationalisation. On the afternoon of his assassination the oil committee returned to work and the following day, very exceptionally, no mourning holiday was observed. No mullah could be found to speak at his funeral. Something was happening that was more important. In the words of Muhammad-Ali Safari, a young reporter at *Bakhtar-e Emrooz*, a prominent nationalist newspaper, Iran during this period was marked by the 'most extraordinary scenes of pride and magnificence . . . the people of Iran compensated for years and perhaps centuries of humiliation and revilement.'

The prime minister's death had one crucial effect, and that was to persuade pro-British deputies that they could not resist the nationalist tide. On March 14, barely a week after the assassination, and with Hossein Ala now prime minister, the majles unanimously voted oil nationalisation into law. Affected by the prevailing atmosphere of intimidation, even those deputies who had been instructed by the Shah to stay away and prevent the quorum turned up and voted in favour. Tehran and other cities erupted in joy. In a poor country that is unable to flex its muscles abroad, the only way to show belief is to go out of doors, shout, and hope that the foreign press does its job. But shouting slogans against Anglo-Iranian had never been a simple act, for the belief in the British bogey had often dissuaded people from expressing themselves.

The majles oil committee got back to work after the Persian New Year holidays, for although the nationalisation law had been signed by the Shah, the manner of its implementation had yet to be determined. The company, the British government and the Shah united around the kind of arrangement that Razmara had proposed before his death, under which nationalisation was acknowledged in 'principle', while a new company was set up with Iranian representation on the board, and profits shared. To Shepherd, Hossein Ala dangled the possibility of an arrangement whereby the government deputed Anglo-Iranian to run the industry on its behalf.

These schemes, of course, would make a mockery of nationalisation and let the company keep its influence in Iran. Mossadegh and his allies moved fast. On April 25 the majles oil committee approved a bill providing for the dispossession of Anglo-Iranian and the establishment of a new Iranian company whose statutes would be ratified by the majles. Compensation would be paid to the 'former Anglo-Iranian Oil Company', as Mossadegh and his friends now called it, for the loss of its concession.

For the British there was one way to salvage the situation, and that was to bring back Mossadegh's old enemy, the Anglophile Seyyed Zia, as prime minister. Zia had told the British that he would accept a 50:50 deal with the company. Sir Francis Shepherd and his colleagues were not concerned by Seyyed Zia's tremendous unpopularity, or his reputation as a stooge. They were fixated by the idea of saving Anglo-Iranian.

When he presented the repossession bill to the majles, on Thursday, April 25, Mossadegh was aware that Zia was on the verge of the premiership, and he warned his fellow-deputies of the possibility that 'in the very near future an event takes place that completely undoes the work that you have accomplished'. Mossadegh demanded that the majles vote on the bill at the earliest opportunity: 'Don't let the people's sacrifices and the services you have rendered go to waste.' But the majles, while in awe of Mossadegh's authority and intimidated by the nationalist mob in the streets, contained many pro-British and royalist deputies.

The following day being a Friday, the day of rest, the repossession vote was set for Saturday April 27. Then came the unexpected news of Ala's resignation. He was annoyed at having been kept in the dark by Mossadegh, and felt unable to implement repossession. With Ala's departure, the majles's agenda changed. Before they voted on repossession, the deputies would have to nominate a prime minister, and there seemed no alternative to Seyyed Zia, who had gone to the royal palace and was waiting to kiss hands.

There was an alternative, of course: Mossadegh. But Mossadegh was famous for his aversion to office.

The mood in parliament on the morning of April 27 was electric. The public gallery was packed and worried-looking senators paced up and down the corridors. The square outside was filling with ordinary people, curious to see how the crisis would end. The majles speaker was in consultation with the Shah, so it fell to the deputy-speaker, Jamal Emami, to propose a candidate for prime minister. An experienced political operator, Emami did not want to be seen to be foisting Seyyed Zia on the country, so he proposed Mossadegh, confidently expecting him to refuse. Only then would Emami propose Seyyed Zia, thereby avoiding accusations of a stitch-up.

If Zia came to power, Mossadegh knew that nationalisation would be a dead letter and that he and his supporters would be jailed or exiled. On the other hand, if repossession could be ratified, the majles would have done its job and the onus would be on the government to implement it. He seized the opportunity that Emami had unknowingly presented.

'*Ghabbalto*,' he said in Arabic. 'I accept.' It is the word that bridegrooms use in their marriage vows. The deputies gave a roar and in the straw poll which followed Mossadegh received 79 votes out of 90 present. In fact, Mossadegh's support in the majles was nothing like as strong as the vote suggested. As Shepherd wrote, 'Members were extremely doubtful of the wisdom of the oil resolution, but having passed it they seem to have taken the easiest way out in confiding to Mossadegh the solution of the problem which he himself had created.'[22] Mossadegh declared that he would accept the post only if repossession were ratified that very day. Seeing that his stratagem had backfired, Emami scrambled to prevent repossession from coming to vote, but his procedural objections were overruled and the bill became law.

Muhammad-Ali Safari wrote in *Bakhtar-e Emrooz* that the celebrations by Mossadegh's supporters outside the parliament building lasted until 2 a.m. Safari himself got home at three in morning. 'Long live the memory of those glorious days.'

# 10

# Mossadeghism

It is not often that Iran finds itself at the centre of the world, and when it does, as preachy westerners like to point out, it is generally for the wrong reasons. Now, for the first time since the advent of modern communications, Iran was at the centre of world politics, though the title that *Time* magazine would bestow upon Mossadegh at the end of 1951, 'Man of the Year', was less an acknowledgement of his achievement than an expression of rage and befuddlement.

The *Time* cover, with a clenched fist piercing the Persian plateau and the oil derricks idle while Mossadegh looks on, evokes the moral contest that lifts world affairs from mere discussion of surpluses and bottom lines. What Mossadegh and his supporters considered a victory of right over wrong was for the British a theft and a violation. Besides, there was disquiet across the white world at this latest show of oriental bad form. It was bad form to flaunt the rules as they were laid down in London and Washington. To do so when communism threatened freedom everywhere was a further betrayal. To this outbreak of nihilism and ingratitude, the British attached a name, which soon gained currency across the Atlantic: Mossadeghism.

The danger was that Mossadeghism would spread and infect others. 'If Britain gives in to the Persians,' the *Daily Express* argued, 'then the time is near when we give in to the Egyptians and hand to them the Suez Canal – and Sudan. If we bow to Tehran, we bow to Baghdad later.'[1] Most Britons agreed with the Attlee government's argument that nationalisation was an illegal violation of an agreement that had been freely entered into by Reza Shah and the

AIOC. There was support for the government when it froze Iran's sterling accounts and stopped exporting sugar, iron and steel to the country. Solving the crisis was a different matter, however. The world had been preoccupied with war on the Korean peninsula when the nationalisation bill went through the majles. Having not given the question much thought, Britain's press barons and their editors had little to suggest.

Newspapers aligned to the Conservative Party knew they wanted action from the government, but did not know what form it should take. The *Daily Mail* of April 4, 1951 called on the government to 'do something about Persia before the rot spreads further'. The *Daily Express* urged resistance to the 'law of gangsters'. Reacting to Iran's claims that it was only doing what the Attlee government had done in Britain, the *Express* differentiated between British socialists, who were nationalising the country's property, and the Persians, who were 'trying to grab something which does not belong to Persia at all'. One Whitehall mandarin described as 'bunk' Iran's alleged moral entitlement to even 50 per cent of the profits of 'enterprises to which they have made no contribution whatever'.

Only the *New Statesman*, representing the views of the left wing of the Labour Party, sympathised with the Iranians. 'Persia', it wrote, 'has nothing for which to thank the Labour government. Moreover the proportion of profits retained in Persia is miserably low.'

The outrage and discussions returned to the man himself: this gnarled trunk of mischief with his veneer of old-world charm. Mossadegh understood nothing of the oil industry, nothing of modern power politics. Again and again, over the summer of 1951, the emissaries and delegations tried to tutor their bed-ridden rival and to make him see how, by picking a fight with the world's most powerful interests, he was condemning himself and his government. Again and again, he pretended not to hear, sent them away with a smile.

He was abandoning the trappings of the westernised oriental gentleman. The mild dandification of his youth had given way to flaming old age, its truculent honesty and absence of pretension.

He had no weakness for girls, boys, money, wine, the pipe or Karl Marx. Any of these vices would have made him more understandable, and, as a consequence, easier to deal with. But to his western interlocutors he was a riddle. They found him in his camel's wool *aba*, or cackling on his haunches in bed, or lying low with his hands fluttering up and down under his neck. It is possible to sympathise with Mossadegh's rather unimaginative visitors when faced with such a man.

Sir Francis Shepherd had come to Tehran after a torrid posting in Indonesia, where he had almost been killed during the war of independence against the Dutch. The foreign secretary, Ernest Bevin, had promised him 'a place where we never have any trouble with the natives' – and then sent him to Iran. Personally courageous – at the height of anti-British feeling he might be glimpsed in his Rolls-Royce with a huge Union Jack fluttering from the bonnet – Shepherd failed utterly in the first duty of a diplomat, which is to understand and interpret the actions of his hosts. His dispatches in the early days of the Mossadegh premiership were absurdly sanguine. Mossadegh's ascent was a 'blessing in disguise because he will prove a failure in a very short time'. Here, again, is the British diplomat who allows his hatred for the Persians, 'however understandable', to cloud his judgement. His descriptions of Mossadegh himself were romantic, mildly slanderous, and useless as an aid to policy-making. 'He did not make a pleasant impression on me when I saw him the other day,' the ambassador wrote on 6 May.

> He is rather tall but has short and bandy legs so that he shambles like a bear, a trait which is generally associated with considerable physical strength. He looks rather like a cab horse and is slightly deaf so that he listens with a strained but otherwise expressionless look on his face. He conducts the conversation at a distance of about six inches at which range he diffuses a slight reek of opium.* His remarks tend to prolixity

* This is the only reference I have seen to Mossadegh's alleged use of opium, and

and he gives the impression of being impervious to argument. He refused to be called 'Excellency' and does not use the ministerial motor car.[2]

Citing the threat posed to him by the Warriors of Islam, Mossadegh spent the first three weeks of his premiership sleeping in a cot in the parliament building. It is doubtful whether the militants would have dared assassinate a figure of his immense popularity, but the constant tension told on his health. He made periodic attempts to resign in disgust at the court's intrigues, but he expected, as usual, to be talked out of his decision.

There was a farcical scene one morning during his stay in the majles, with Mossadegh clutching a resignation letter and Hossein Makki forcibly preventing him from leaving the room to deliver it. The two men grappled and grunted near the door, and eventually Makki was able to turn the lock, but not before hurting his elbow. Sinking into a chair, the prime minister admitted defeat, and Makki angrily went home. The prime minister was not the apologising sort, but he wanted Makki's signal that there was no bad blood between them, so he telephoned the younger man and insisted he be his guest for lunch. Makki was sore and showed reluctance, so Mossadegh declared that he would not touch his food until he joined him. To this emotional blackmail Makki had no answer, and he hurried back to the majles.

Shepherd visited Mossadegh in his 'lair' in parliament, and relayed a detailed description – part spy novel, part bedroom farce. On crossing the spacious hall at the entrance to the majles, he wrote, 'I became aware of footsteps behind me and turning round found several unshaven types who were walking behind in a way that made me feel like Molotov scuttling into a conference in Paris.' At the top of a grand staircase,

there was [an] ante-room containing four more thugs. I was then taken into a sort of board room occupied by three more.

may be discounted as casual defamation.

Mossadegh's bedroom opened out of this. It was a small room with a French window looking out into a garden and contained two other doors, each of which was blocked by a wardrobe. The Prime Minister, who was wearing two suits of pyjamas, one khaki and the other green, was stretched upon a bed in one corner. He is certainly in an unhealthy state and is not able to walk much so that there is some excuse for his living near the scene of his labours, but the thugs and the blockade of wardrobes are certainly unnecessarily bizarre.'[3]

The caricaturists loved him. He was, wrote Anthony Eden, Britain's once and future Foreign Secretary, 'the first bit of meat to come the way of the cartoonists since the war'.[4] The work of a caricaturist is to take some facet of a person and turn it into a stupendous, carbuncular motif. Mossadegh was a dream, with his long, mournful nose and billiard-ball head, and his sudden changes of mood and demeanour.

There was now a voluminous literature devoted to the oriental troublemaker. *Time's* appreciation of its 'Man of the Year' was a pastiche of the *Thousand and One Nights*. 'Once upon a time,' it began, 'in a mountainous land between Baghdad and the Sea of Caviar, there lived a nobleman' – and the nobleman turned out, as in Burton's beloved version of the tales, to be cunning and to revel, sprite-like, in his own irresponsibility. 'His weapon', the magazine went on, 'was the threat of his own political suicide, as a wilful little boy might say, "If you don't give me what I want I'll hold my breath until I'm blue in the face. Then you'll be sorry."' The nobleman had the whole world 'hanging on his words and deeds, his jokes, his tears, his tantrums,' but behind his 'grotesque antics' lay 'great issues of peace or war, progress or decline'.[5]

In early June the prime minister dispatched his emissaries, including Hossein Makki and the provisional head of the newly formed Iranian National Oil Company, Mehdi Bazargan, to take over the southern oil facilities. The missions entered Abadan amid scenes of delirium, with tens of thousands of people on the route and kisses planted on the dust-caked official cars, while verses were declaimed comparing the British to the tyrants of Persian mythology. There was angst amid the jubilation, though, for the British had dispatched warships to the Persian Gulf and paratroopers were in a state of readiness on Cyprus. Later, the cruiser *Mauritius* would anchor opposite Abadan, where it sat within easy range of an Iranian navy ship. Makki, who boarded the Iranian vessel to jolly up the crew, reckoned the *Mauritius* could cripple it with one shell.

Anglo-Iranian's general manager was Eric Drake, and the tenacity and superciliousness he displayed during the crisis (and in an unapologetic interview he gave in later life, along with the refined Lady Drake), mark him as the quintessential company man.* Drake was in constant communication with Britannia House and Northcroft's replacement in Tehran, Norman Seddon, as well as Shepherd himself. His instructions were simple: to obstruct the Iranians at every turn.

The two sides duelled for most of June. To the emissaries, Drake expressed bland ignorance of the nationalisation law, and pointedly billetted them in the dingier kind of company housing – so stiflingly hot, the Iranians were forced to lug their cots onto the lawn to sleep. He ignored Bazargan's demands to provide information about the workings of the industry and to hand over three-quarters of the export proceeds the company had received since nationalisation. (The government proposed putting the remaining 25 per cent into a mutually acceptable bank, against future compensation claims.) But he was powerless to prevent the Iranians raising the national flag over the company headquarters, to the strains of a navy band and roars from a mighty crowd, and he suffered the indignity of watching Bazargan slip behind his desk during a meeting, and refuse to budge.[6]

Drake and the Iranians conducted point-scoring tours of the pitiful Iranian workers' dwellings and an airborne sweep over the great Abadan refinery, which the Englishman hoped would drill into his adversaries a sense of their inadequacy. This latter trip may

* The company recognised him as such, and he ended up chairman of British Petroleum, Anglo-Iranian's post-1954 incarnation.

have inspired Drake to concoct a 'dream' which he related to Makki and the others. In this dream, Drake was piloting a plane when Makki, one of the passengers, announced that he would now take over the controls even though he had not flown before. Drake refused to hand over, arguing that he was responsible for the plane and the lives of its passengers, so Makki asked whether he might press a black knob on the instrument panel to satisfy his desire for some measure of control. Again, Drake demurred, pointing out that pressing the knob would cut the engines dead, but suggested that once the plane was landed, Makki should arrange for a press photographer to take a picture of him, at the controls, from an angle that suggested the plane was flying at a great altitude. Bazargan and the others were much amused by Drake's 'dream' – which had no effect whatever.[7]

Drake and his subordinates then set about making Iran's new assets impossible to exploit. Mossadegh insisted that oil be sold in the government's name, so Drake ordered tanker masters to pump their oil ashore, effectively ending the export of Iranian oil. Then began the gradual evacuation of the British staff and their families, while the remaining workers wound down refining operations and deliveries of crude from the fields came to a halt. 'There was no question of violent resistance,' Drake would recall, 'but it's extraordinary how pieces of the plant would go wrong.'[8]

One stifling afternoon, Bazargan was awoken from his post-prandial nap by the first shipload of evacuees. 'I was flabbergasted,' he wrote; 'at a time when it seemed possible there would be an attack on Abadan, the British were embarking of their own accord in order to leave Abadan, with all its power and bounty and prestige!'[9]

For Iranian nationalists the drama of the repossession, which culminated in Drake fleeing to Iraq under fear of arrest for sabotage, and the occupation of the refinery by Iranian troops, amounted to the liberation of occupied territory. Events were followed avidly in Tehran – not least by Mossadegh. The prime minister was in constant contact with Bazargan, Makki and the others, issuing detailed instructions and urging them to avoid provocative actions.

Mossadegh tried to give the British technicians every excuse to stay. He diverted customs receipts to pay salaries and told Iranian workers to carry on obeying their British managers so long as the instructions they received were consistent with nationalisation.

According to Grady, the US ambassador, Mossadegh was backed by at least 95 per cent of Iranians. The Abadan evacuation marked a nadir in fortunes for the Attlee government, which had opposed this move by the company – but not strongly enough to stop it happening. Churchill, who was now the leader of the opposition Conservatives, was aghast. 'It is only when the British government is known to be weak and hesitant', he warned, 'that these outrages are inflicted upon us and upon our rights and interests.' It took a sophisticated Iranian nationalist to grasp that the British departure from Abadan did not amount to surrender. On the contrary, it was the harbinger of a long, embittered revenge.

Iran and Britain would spend much of the next two and half years engaged in oil negotiations, but never would there be mutual understanding. Both felt wronged and expected redress, but neither understood the grievance nursed by the other – or else they dismissed it as humbug. For Mossadegh, the nation's oil represented life, hope, freedom. For his opponents, it symbolised a stronger, more intrepid England, something to cling on to as the empire collapsed. Mossadegh did not see why the British could not accept their new, lower status. After all, they would be amply compensated for nationalisation and retain full access to Iran's oil. The British could not understand a statesman prepared to forego prosperity and justice in order to satisfy some spiteful reflex from the past. Both were surprised by the other's intransigence.

The Americans, who began the dispute as peace-brokers and ended it irreversibly implicated, saw things from their own perspective. The US was preoccupied with the communist threat. The day after North Korean forces invaded the south, Truman had expressed his fear that Iran would be communism's next target. 'If we stand by,' he told an aide, 'they'll move into Iran and they'll take over the whole Middle East. There's no telling what they'll do if we don't put up a fight now.'[10] For the president, nothing was as important as saving Iran for the free world – not Anglo-Iranian, and certainly not Muhammad Mossadegh.

Over the summer of 1951 the Iranians received three negotiating missions, one composed of senior company executives, a second led by an adviser to President Truman, the millionaire diplomat Averell Harriman, and a third by a bluff minister in the British cabinet, Richard Stokes, with whom Mossadegh would find himself in cheerful disagreement. All three, from varying angles, tried to reinterpret nationalisation to enable the British to carry on controlling the industry, and all were rebuffed.

Meanwhile, against the odds as Bazargan later boasted, a handful of heroic Iranian technicians succeeded in maintaining oil production to the extent that 'not for a single day did the country's automobiles, or its bakers' ovens, or its bathhouses' shut down for lack of fuel. The Iranians looked after the installations and oilfields well. Nationalisation united the country to an extraordinary degree, with women donating wedding rings and civil servants handing back some of their pay, while the prime minister himself declined to draw a salary and paid his own passage when representing Iran abroad.

Mossadegh had manoeuvred brilliantly, outwitting domestic and foreign rivals to get nationalisation onto the statute books, but the triumph of repossession turned out to be pyrrhic on almost every level. Soon enough, reality would bite – the reality that he had shut down an export business on which the country depended. How would the prime minister lower the expectations he had raised? How to lay the ground for the inevitable retreat?

The foreign delegations drummed into the Iranians their unpreparedness to step into Anglo-Iranian's shoes, and it was true; Mossadegh and his advisers had not anticipated Britain's determination to engineer a world embargo on Iranian oil. A few months before nationalisation, he had declared that even if Iranian production were to fall by two-thirds following nationalisation, the country would not suffer a loss in revenues because Anglo-Iranian would no longer get the lion's share. 'Oil nationalisation', he said, 'will bring no economic suffering in its train.'[11]

The Persian capital Tehran had been barely touched by modernisation at the time of Mossadegh's birth in 1882. Two traditional wind towers, for diverting the breeze into the house below, are visible in the middle ground. The Alborz Mountains, snow-capped for much of the year, provided the city's water.

Wearing the traditional *kolah* hat and a fashionable moustache, the young Mossadegh (*second left*) stands to the right of his maternal uncle, Prince Abdolhossein Mirza Farmanfarma (*centre*), in this family group. Farmanfarma took a paternal interest in Mossadegh, whose own father died in 1892, but relations cooled because of Farmanfarma's unabashed Anglophilia.

Mossadegh's first cousin, Farmanfarma's son Prince Firooz, was an architect of the ill-fated Anglo-Persian Agreement, under which Persia accepted de facto protectorate status in 1919, and which Mossadegh bitterly opposed. Here, Firooz (*far left*) accompanies Ahmad Shah (*centre*), the last of the Qajar line, on a state visit to Britain shortly after the agreement was signed. Lord Curzon, Britain's foreign secretary and the accord's most enthusiastic supporter, is on the far right, with Prince Albert, later George VI, third from right.

Mossadegh as governor of Fars after his return from Europe in 1920. A local newspaper described him as a symbol of 'unity, consensus and stability' in this strategic southern province, where, free from close government control, he displayed his talents as an administrator and conciliator.

Persia's strongman Reza Khan shows off a new toy during his rise to power in the early 1920s. He acquired the Rolls Royce from Mossadegh's cousin Prince Firooz.

A parade to mark Reza's coronation in 1926, when he replaced the Qajars with his new Pahlavi dynasty. Reza realised that Iran needed firepower if it was to become a modern state, but his vaunted army collapsed when Britain and Russia invaded in 1941.

The loving mother: shrewd, acidulous and besotted with her elder son, Najm al-Saltaneh, seen here in old age, was a member of the ruling Qajar dynasty and the single greatest influence on Mossadegh.

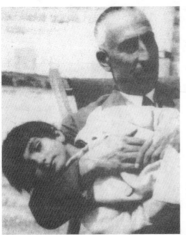

Mossadegh with his youngest daughter Khadijeh, whose mental breakdown after she witnessed his arrest in 1940 profoundly affected him.

A demonstration by the viscerally anti-American Tudeh Party shortly after oil nationalisation. Mossadegh repeatedly raised the Communist bogey in his dealings with US officials, but never believed that the party seriously threatened him.

Mossadegh was described by Anthony Eden as 'the first bit of meat to come the way of the cartoonists since the war'. With his mournful nose and billiard ball head, he soon became recognisable around the world.

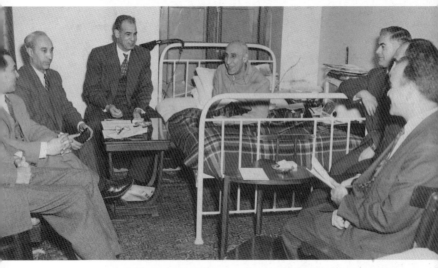

As prime minister, Mossadegh famously ran the country from his bed. Of his close associates, Hossein Makki (*centre, beside Mossadegh*) went from being a devoted admirer to a bitter foe.

Mossadegh and US President Harry Truman: the Iranian prime minister wowed America when he visited in 1951, but he soon lost the trust of a new superpower that was unwilling to relinquish its traditional friendship with Britain.

An anti-Mossadegh crowd, possibly dating from February, 1952, when mobs were mobilised to dissuade the Shah from leaving the country. Note the ugly assortment of weapons on display. Unsavoury characters such as these played a key role in the coup.

Charming and ambitious, Ayatollah Abolqassem Kashani helped bring Mossadegh to power, only to abandon him in favour of the Shah.

General Fazlollah Zahedi, who from 1952 was being groomed by the British as a successor to Mossadegh, and who took power after the coup.

Shah Muhammad-Reza Pahlavi and Queen Sorayya flew to Rome in despair after the apparent failure of the initial coup attempt on August 15, 1953. Little did they know that it would very shortly be successfully revived.

Shah-loyalists celebrate the success of the coup atop a tank in a Tehran street.

The coup-masters: (*from left*) US Secretary of State Foster Dulles, Winston Churchill basking in his last months of power, President Dwight D. Eisenhower and Anthony Eden, Britain's Foreign Secretary, on the White House lawn in 1954. Transatlantic ties seemed as warm as ever in the aftermath of Mossadegh's overthrow, but the Suez Crisis of 1956 would strain them almost to breaking point.

The legend in his aba, pacing out his house arrest at Ahmadabad. 'Good days and bad days go past,' he told the Shah. 'What stays is a good name or a bad name.'

It was moonshine. Within weeks of nationalisation, the US oil majors and Royal Dutch Shell had decided that it would not be in their interests for concession-busters to prosper. The six sisters rallied around their wronged sibling, refusing to extract or buy Iranian oil – even at a substantial discount – and pressuring tanker owners not to take Iranian crude to market. George McGhee, the US assistant secretary of state, was trying to establish 50:50 profit-sharing as the standard concessionary formula, and regarded nation-alisation as a dangerous precedent. Anglo-Iranian quickly overcame the supply shortfall by tapping other sources, while the emerging Middle Eastern exporters, Saudi Arabia and Kuwait, compensated so effectively for the absence of Iranian oil that production in the non-communist world actually rose over the year following nation-alisation.

In November 1951, *The Economist* wrote that 'the world's refinery arrangements have not waited on events in Abadan. With a small sacrifice in quality at other refineries, 55–60 per cent of Abadan's refining capacity has been replaced . . . while Dr Mossadegh talks, the world's oil industry gets on with its work and Persian oil is being left in a backwater.'[12] Mossadegh and his colleagues had anticipated none of this. They believed that the West needed Iranian oil more urgently than Iran needed revenues from that oil. The French-educated mandarin and majles deputy who would become Mossadegh's main oil adviser, Kazem Hassibi, had described the Iranian industry as 'a child which the Western world would fondly nurture in any circumstances'.[13] And the nationalists were convinced that the Attlee government would go to any lengths to avoid a repeat of the energy shortages that had crippled Britain during the severe winter of 1950–51.

In the event, Attlee took a hard diplomatic line, while Mossadegh, even after intensive tutoring on the realities of the market, continued to inhabit what Truman's envoy Averell Harriman called a 'dream world', expecting foreign staff 'to work on his terms, foreign oil companies to buy and distribute oil on his terms, and Iran to get all of the profits'.[14] Later in the dispute, Mossadegh would pour scorn on those Iranians who had supposed that oil could be 'extricated with the utmost ease from foreign dominance, and exploited, and that gold would flood from London to Tehran'. But no one had bought into this assumption more damagingly than he.

The British also deceived themselves, and their efforts at diplomacy were aimed at persuading Mossadegh to accept something less than nationalisation as it is understood around the world. A mission of senior company executives was an exercise in wishful thinking – 'so steeped in colonialist pride,' as one Iranian negotiator recalled, they were 'not prepared to say or hear anything about nationalisation'.[15] Averell Harriman alone seemed to appreciate that what the nationalists really feared was the physical presence of the company and its ability to influence internal Iranian affairs, but the plan he endorsed did nothing to assuage these fears. In fact, the scheme had been authored by Stokes of the British government, and would have handed the industry to a British-run operating agency, allowing, as Harriman admitted, for the 'complete return of British control'. Stokes told the British government that it was essential, 'from the point of view of the Company's future, public opinion at home and our balance of payments, to keep effective control of distribution of Persian oil in [the] world market'. Under his plan, he had computed, Iran stood to earn three times as much as it had received in 1950. But Mossadegh was not hanging on for a better deal. He would accept nothing but nationalisation.

Mossadegh's rejection of the Stokes plan, and his decision to evict the last of the company staff when it became clear that the British would not cooperate, ended a rancorous negotiating season. Stokes advised the Shah that the 'only solution' was a 'strong government under martial law and the bad boys in prison for two years or so'. The Iranians had seized highly incriminating documents which staff of Anglo-Iranian had been trying to hide, and which provided further proof of the company's malign interference in Iranian public life. It is not difficult to imagine the outraged reaction in Britain were it discovered that an Iranian company had influenced ministerial and other appointments and bribed newspaper editors to run articles in its favour. This is what Anglo-Iranian had done in Iran. The British press painted the company as the innocent victim of Iranian spite and Shepherd got the BBC's Persian service to deny the documents' veracity.

The Americans stumbled through the crisis. They were instrumental in persuading the British to accept 50:50 profit-sharing and the 'principle' of nationalisation, and to abandon some very advanced plans for a military intervention.* Harriman himself brought Mossadegh to the negotiating table, getting him to reconsider his refusal to deal directly with the British government because, as he saw it, Iran's opponent in the dispute was Anglo-Iranian. But both parties expected the Americans to do more.

The embargo which the British hoped would break Mossadegh's resolve was above all an American embargo. At the same time, the Truman administration was considering making a loan to Mossadegh's government. The British saw the loan as an incentive to Mossadegh to defy them; the Americans saw it as a way of protecting a broadly pro-western prime minister from his communist rivals. Mossadegh exacerbated these tensions with operatic flair. Upon being warned in a meeting with Harriman and Shepherd that Iran's oil industry might collapse, he retorted, 'Tant pis pour nous. If the industry collapses and no money comes and disorder and Communism follow, it will be your fault entirely.'[17] In fact, Mossadegh believed the Tudeh menace to be overblown, and he had been appalled when the security forces opened fire on pro-Tudeh rioters who had gathered in protest against Harriman's arrival on July 15, killing several.

In trying to drive a wedge between the two giants, Mossadegh was using the traditional expedient of the less strong, and which Iran, during the long years of Anglo-Russian rivalry, had refined into an art. In private, the British complained that America's indulgent

---

* These centred on an invasion of Abadan to restore British control of the refinery, to which end the Sixteenth Independent Parachute Brigade was brought to a state of readiness. The Americans were dead against military intervention, arguing that the Soviets would launch a symmetrical invasion of northern Iran, and Attlee, discomfited by the sabre-rattling of some members of his cabinet, vetoed the idea at the eleventh hour.[16]

attitude brought out the worst in Mossadegh, encouraging him to believe that, whatever happened, the US would step in and save him. Henry Grady advised his government to distance itself from British policy, which 'may well lead to disaster'. Grady had taken up his posting in the hope of establishing a flow of aid and credit to Iran, and thus binding it to the West. In September 1951, he told Mossadegh that for 'technical' reasons a promised loan would not materialise. The real problem, both men knew, was British pressure. The same pressure would lead to Grady's recall, in September, and his replacement by the solid Anglophile Loy Henderson.

For a while in 1951, strains appeared in the alliance between Britain and the US, but the opportunity detected by the nationalists in Iran turned out to be an illusion. Whatever their differing concerns, Britain and the US were not rivals, and their ties of history, strengthened by the common struggle against communism, were stronger than any challenge Mossadegh could mount.

In the eyes of an undiscerning public, the titans of nationalisation were a triumvirate uniting the three main elements in Iranian life: the government, represented by Mossadegh; the monarchy, by the Shah; and clerical authority, which Kashani claimed. The Shah wobbled from the start.

Muhammad-Reza Shah was not an unpatriotic man and he was attracted to oil nationalisation as an eventual goal, but he believed that Iran had no alternative but to do a deal with the company. Still, he could not openly resist the wave of nationalism that was sweeping the country. Certainly, he would not indulge Shepherd's extraordinarily reckless demand for Mossadegh's removal, which would surely imperil his throne. He would grit his teeth and wait.

It may be imagined how galling this was to the young king. Muhammad-Reza had eked out extra powers for himself, married a beautiful young woman who would, it was hoped, give him an heir, and mapped out a path to development that kept Iran aligned with the West. Now he found himself superseded by a geriatric prime minister whose popularity vastly exceeded his own and who insisted that he must reign, and not rule. The Shah felt alone and unloved but he had few confidants he could trust, and tended to unburden himself to foreigners. Henderson, the new American ambassador, must have been startled when the monarch revealed his distress during their first one-on-one meeting – repeating again and again, 'What can I do? I am helpless.'[18]

Mossadegh was implementing his long-cherished plan for the monarchy: to make it a political irrelevance. He harboured no republican designs, and had filled his cabinet with moderate, even conservative figures, but he did not allow the Shah to influence policy and restricted his ability to appoint officials. Mossadegh received Hossein Ala, who had gone back to being court minister, with his usual courtesy, and the cabinet went dutifully along to wish the Shah luck when he was admitted to hospital for an appendectomy, but the prime minister often pleaded indisposition when summoned to the palace and his responses to royal messages could be mischievous and flippant. On one occasion Ala told him of the Shah's worries of a British attack and Mossadegh responded by comparing Britain's bluster to his own in Neuchâtel all those years back, when the boys had stolen grapes from the neighbours and Mossadegh had sworn to kill them. Mossadegh particularly asked that this analogy be transmitted to the monarch.

Mossadegh returned the Shah's distrust for him. He was not alone in suspecting the Shah of having had a hand in Razmara's assassination, and when, early in his premiership, the Shah warned him that his life may be at risk, Mossadegh refused the offer of an armed guard if it was composed of the same men who had guarded Razmara. Mossadegh recounted this exchange with the Shah to parliament, adding gleefully that he had quoted to the Shah the following couplet, 'If my protector is that person I know him to be, he uses rock to protect glass.'

The Shah was the sum of his contradictions. He was an avowed moderniser, but he was also superstitious and in thrall, so the queen noted, to his Swiss svengali Ernest Perron, that 'diabolical . . . homosexual' who intrigued without relent and pried into the royal couple's private life.[19] The Shah longed to be loved, but he lacked Mossadegh's spontaneity and humour; he was stiff with his subjects and demanded formality from his courtiers. The patriot Shah became international when it was convenient. He saw nothing odd in summoning three American doctors and three nurses to perform his appendectomy, or in presenting his wife with a customised Rolls-Royce as his country embarked on a titanic struggle with the British.

Mossadegh's patriotism could be quixotic, but no one could plausibly suggest that his sense of national identification was less than complete, or that he was more at home with foreigners than with his own compatriots – accusations that were levelled at the Shah. Mossadegh acknowledged the beneficial effect of his long years in Europe, but they had served to strengthen his Iranian identity. Muhammad-Reza, on the other hand, had acquired European manners while in Switzerland, and his school days were among the happiest of his life.[20] His new wife, Sorayya, had a German mother and had been partly raised in Europe. She admired anything European and was shocked by Iran's squalor. Her alienation can only have sharpened his sense of not quite belonging to the land he ruled.

In many ways, the Shah was a tragic figure, sensitive and intelligent but taking no pleasure from the burdens of his station. Sorayya found him shy and endearing in private but wounded by the slightest rebuke. The monarch drove his Packard convertible at imprudent speed along the twisting passes of the Alborz mountains. When flying, he wished never to land. These were expressions of the Shah's fatalism and his desire for liberation. Mossadegh, too, was a fatalist and wanted freedom from the cares of office, but rather than camouflage these traits, as the Shah did, he magnified them, turned them into glinting angles of his personality. Indeed, as the attention of the world surrounded him, and he was the object of increasing scrutiny, Mossadegh became an accomplice in his own caricature.

Mossadegh's international persona was established with oil nationalisation and the attention of the world. Vernon Walters, Harriman's translator and a future deputy director of the CIA, described a charming, rather repetitive old wizard, very small and slight, feeble and deaf when it suited him.[21] Harriman's biographer drew attention to Mossadegh's astonishing physiognomic versatility; at will, it seemed, the prime minister could transform himself from a 'frail, decrepit shell of a man into a wily, vigorous adversary'. He was too much the *galant* when meeting Mrs Harriman: 'He took hold of her hand and didn't stop kissing until he was halfway to her elbow.'[22] A few months later, when Mossadegh went to the United States, he was met at Union Station in Washington by Dean Acheson, Truman's secretary of state. Acheson recalled watching 'a bent old man hobble down the platform supporting himself with a stick . . . spotting me at the gate, he dropped the stick, broke away from his party, and came skipping along ahead of the others to greet us.'[23]

It was generally agreed that Mossadegh had a profound hatred for the British and all their works. 'You don't know how crafty they are,' he told Harriman. 'You don't know how evil they are. You do not know how they sully everything they touch.'[24]

In these and other tellings, which generally have the savour of an after-dinner anecdote, Mossadegh is usually in bed, by turns winning and manipulative, and never afraid to upstage himself by dissolving into laughter. 'I have had a bad day,' he greeted Harriman one day in an ecstasy of hypochondria; 'this morning I fainted three times.' Acheson was charmed, Shepherd driven to white-knuckled distraction. Flying back home after being flummoxed by the old man, Averell Harriman confessed, 'I am simply not used to failure.'

Like the Shah, Mossadegh behaved differently with foreigners than he did with Iranians, though, in contrast to the Shah, he was less himself in their company. His act was calculated to unnerve; the more he mistrusted someone, the more playful, gnomic and inconsequential he became. Few foreigners knew where they stood with him. Vernon Walters wrote: 'One minute one had the impression that Mossadegh was really trying to find a solution [to] the oil problem, that an agreement was in sight. But the next conversation he would take up on a note that made clear that any agreement was remote. He seemed to enjoy this. It was like dangling fish on a line.' After two months in Tehran, Walters wrote, he and Harriman 'realised that Mossadegh simply did not want to arrive at any agreement because he did not feel he could sell it to his nationalists'.

Mossadegh at this stage was as much of a nationalist as anyone. The prime minister wanted a deal, but it seemed to him that the return of the British, in any guise, would nullify the main benefit of nationalisation, which was political independence. Those who took him seriously, like Harriman's oil expert Walter Levy, came away with a good idea of what Mossadegh might stomach. On the strength of several hours' discussion with the prime minister, Levy told the British that the company would have to give up its operating and distributing monopoly, and the British government would have to give up its shareholding. Mossadegh's insistence that no Briton should sit on the board would not preclude the presence of other, less noxious foreigners – continental Europeans, for instance.

*Tant pis* for him; the company was not interested. In the words of the dauntless Sir William Fraser, 'When they need money they will come crawling to us on their bellies.'[25]

## II

# *Winning America*

It was the last real chance for a civilised solution to the crisis and it came on the sidelines of another self-defeating British display.

The British had reacted to nationalisation by freezing Iranian assets in British banks and lodging an appeal with the International Court of Justice at The Hague. But Mossadegh had not recognised the court's competence, arguing that the dispute was between a sovereign state and a private company, and he had therefore ignored an interim ruling by the court that Iran should suspend repossession.

The British now took their complaint to the United Nations Security Council, against American advice and, ultimately, to the detriment of their own cause. Britain's delegate to the United Nations, Sir Gladwyn Jebb, had made his reputation in the council following the invasion of South Korea, when he had debated skilfully with his Soviet counterpart. On the matter of Iran, he drafted a resolution better suited to a truculent House of Commons than an international body which had begun to fill with newly independent nations. 'The plain fact', as Jebb saw it, 'is that by a series of insensate actions, the Iranian Government is causing a great enterprise, the proper functioning of which is of immense benefit not only to the United Kingdom and Iran but to the whole free world, to grind to a stop. Unless this is promptly checked, the whole of the free world will be much poorer and weaker, including the deluded Iranian people themselves.'[1]

To Security Council members such as India, which had recently won independence, and Turkey, with its memories of being invaded by Britain at the end of World War I, the Iranians appeared far from deluded. India's prime minister, Jawaharlal Nehru, had already declared in favour of the Iranian nationalists, while the two communist members of the council, the Soviet Union and Yugoslavia (China's seat was still in nationalist hands), objected to the question being considered at all. In the corridors, meanwhile, the talk was of recent events in Egypt, where Mossadegh's example had emboldened parliament to abrogate the country's treaties with Britain and patriotic militias were assembling to attack British troops guarding the Suez Canal – of which the British government was the biggest shareholder.

Mossadeghism was on the move, and so was the man himself, for Mossadegh had decided to reply to Jebb's resolution in person. For the performer, whose stage hitherto had been poor, shabby Iran, it was a chance to shine, and his 49-day absence from the country turned into a public-relations triumph. Not only did Mossadegh outsmart Jebb in the council chamber, but his charm and sincerity convinced many ordinary Americans that he was a decent man who wanted the best for his people. Finally, although it had not been his intention, Mossadegh's trip established him in the vanguard of the non-aligned movement a decade before it came formally into being.

Arriving in New York on October 8, Mossadegh and Ghollamhossein were driven in the Iranian ambassador's Cadillac to a state-of-the-art hospital in Manhattan. (The rest of his party went to a hotel.) There was nothing particularly wrong with Mossadegh, Ghollamhossein recalled later, but admission to the New York hospital would protect him from exhausting calls from well-wishers and journalists.

A more important reason for Mossadegh's choice of accommodation was probably his distrust of his own delegation. Mossadegh was accompanied by fifteen advisers, translators and assistants, including cabinet ministers and his eldest daughter, Zia Ashraf. This group was only hazily aware of his second motivation in coming to the US, which was to use the administration's good offices to try to reach a deal with the British. Mossadegh wanted his exploratory talks with the Americans to be held in absolute secrecy. He wanted the freedom to float ideas he might later disown – and which any ill-wisher in his group might manipulate against him. Later, if it came to finalising a deal with the British, he would seek advice from his specialists.

The hospital was a sumptuous institution. Mossadegh and Ghollamhossein had their own suite on the sixteenth floor, where the prime minister was spoilt by an army of doctors and nurses, and where he received, besides visiting diplomats from various countries, a team of American negotiators led by George McGhee. But this did not come cheap, as Ghollamhossein learned from the pages of a local newspaper, which informed its readers that the suite occupied by Iran's prime minister cost the princely sum of $450 a night.

Mossadegh was aghast when he found out. 'What have we gone and done?' he exclaimed, and Ghollamhossein hurried off to inform the hospital administrators of the prime minister's imminent departure to prepare for his Security Council appearance. The doctors protested. They had not completed their tests, for which they gallantly proposed to waive all fees. The Mossadeghs also insisted, and Ghollamhossein was dispatched to buy parting gifts for the doctors. And so, having borrowed $5,000 from an expatriate businessman, and arranged for more money to be wired from Tehran, father and son extricated themselves from the tender attentions of the New York Hospital, $14,000 and several Iranian carpets the poorer.[2]

They moved into an apartment at the Ritz Tower Hotel, where the other members of the group were staying. The American press had billed him as a great eccentric, and he did not disappoint. There was a remarkable scene in the Ritz Tower, where America's ambassador to the UN, Ernest Gross, called to see him, along with Vernon Walters, who had been re-engaged as translator. The Americans found Mossadegh in bed, and, as it turned out, in no mood to talk. In Walters' recollection, after Mossadegh had been introduced to Gross, the prime minister peered cautiously from behind his enormous nose and inquired, 'Ambassador, what are you Ambassador to?' 'Oh,' said Mr Gross, 'I am ambassador to the United Nations.' With that, Mossadegh let out a shriek as though he had been stabbed with a carving knife, tossed convulsively from one side of the bed to the other and sobbed wildly, huge crocodile tears pouring down his cheeks. Now this was a much more violent outburst of weeping than any I had seen previously; Ernest Gross was equally appalled by the outburst. I could not resist saying to him, 'Mr Ambassador, I don't think this is the day to continue the discussion.' He said, 'My God, neither do I.'[3]

Mossadegh made a better impression on ordinary Americans. Over the course of his stay in their country, many took a liking to the bed-ridden patriot, and Mossadegh reciprocated their sympathy and interest. He made much of the common ground between Iran's struggle and that of the colonists of 1776, and appealed for help in freeing Iran from 'the chains of British imperialism'. He was so appreciative of the laudatory articles that were written about him by the celebrated war reporter Marguerite Higgins, he sent Ghollamhossein to the journalist's apartment with a carpet in thanks. Mossadegh was deeply impressed when he heard that Higgins had refused the carpet lest her objectivity be compromised, and told Ghollamhossein, 'Here lies the secret of the success of this society.'

Mossadegh's first appearance before the Security Council took place on October 15. Crowds had gathered outside the UN building in Flushing Meadow, and Ghollamhossein worried for his father's powers of endurance. 'Papa,' he urged, 'today is an important day. Don't give up. Whenever you get tired, just tell me . . .' An ambulance was on hand in case he swooned. Mossadegh took his place in the chamber to great excitement, and 'perhaps no meeting of the Security Council', The Times of London sourly reported, 'has opened with less dignity – thanks to the air of drama given to the personality and foibles of Dr Mossadegh. Long after he took his seat he was surrounded by photographers and a band of admirers.'[4]

The newsreels tell a different story: of Mossadegh sitting dignified and erect while the flashbulbs pop.

He read in French, and his sober performance could not have been further from his histrionics in the Iranian majles. He situated the Iranian struggle in a wider quest for human liberty, for the Second World War had 'changed the map of the world. In the neighbourhood of my country, hundreds of millions of Asian people, after centuries of colonial exploitation, have now gained their independence and freedom. It is gratifying to see that the European powers have respected the legitimate aspirations of the peoples of India, Pakistan and Indonesia, and others who have struggled for the right to enter the family of nations on terms of freedom and complete equality . . . Iran demands that right.' He sat down after fifteen minutes and a cabinet colleague read on, for two compelling hours, detailing Britain's historic interference in Iran and calling for the rights of the weak to be protected.

Jebb's reply came the following day, and he began with a salesman's eulogy to the company, complete with glossy photographs which were passed around the delegates, showing beaming Iranian employees. But Jebb's tone was wrong again, and he rashly described Iran's actions as a danger to world peace. If that was the case, Mossadegh replied, Britain, which had nationalised many of its industries, should be arraigned 'for having sapped . . . the pillars of peace . . . whatever danger to peace there may be lies in the actions of the United Kingdom government.' It was Britain, after all, who had a flotilla of ships circling the Persian Gulf. 'Iran has stationed no gunboats in the Thames.'

The council was impressed, and the delegate of nationalist China reminded the British that 'the day has passed when the control of the Iranian oil industry can be shared with foreign companies'. Seeing their moral authority slip away, the British accepted an escape route offered by the French, in the form of a resolution adjourning the debate until the International Court of Justice had given its verdict. Jebb accepted with a bad grace. Across the world, the news bulletins were full of Mossadegh. Back in

Iran, the newspapers were cock-a-hoop and the Shah sent Mossadegh a congratulatory telegram.

It was at such moments that the United Nations achieved its full dignity, when a small, defenceless nation was able to address a big one on terms of equality, and when right, for once, triumphed over might. But still there was no deal.

Mossadegh had been talking to McGhee since his arrival in the US, and they were making what the American considered to be good progress. The parameters of an agreement were soon in place, with nationalisation preserved and the board of the National Iranian Oil Company (consisting of three Iranians and four neutrals) entering into a contract with a neutral company for access to technicians and know-how. The refinery at Abadan – which, McGhee was delighted to learn, had not been nationalised – would be sold to another neutral company and the National Iranian Oil Company would undertake to sell oil to Anglo-Iranian at wholesale prices for a fifteen-year period. By refusing to cooperate with nationalisation, Mossadegh said, the British had forfeited the right to keep technicians in Iran; he would not let them back, in whatever guise. But McGhee was optimistic. Under the proposed deal, financial gains for Iran and the company would resemble those of a 50:50 profit-sharing arrangement. The 50:50 formula would not be undercut.[5]

Now it was up to the British. They had already agreed to 50:50. Jebb had trumpeted, yet again, their consent to nationalisation. The Americans would take the proposals to Churchill's new Conservative government, which had been elected on October 25. In the meantime, Mossadegh would stay in the US with his team. If the British were willing to negotiate along the principles outlined by the Americans and approved by Mossadegh, talks between Iran and Britain could start immediately.

Mossadegh had come to Washington DC after his triumph in the Security Council, stopping for a symbolic photo op beside the Liberty Bell in Philadelphia, and was received cordially by Truman and Acheson. (He began his stay with another bonanza of hospital tests, which revealed that he was an old man with nothing much wrong with him.) It was McGhee, with his appreciation of Mossadegh's 'countless jokes and sallies', and his own ready humour, who was assigned to look after the prime minister and continue their discussions. With McGhee, Mossadegh seemed always at ease, making a fuss of the American's pyjama-clad son or visiting his farm and talking crops and irrigation to the estate manager. It is an unusual and touching image, the prime minister of a proud old country whiling away many dozens of hours with a little-known official from the new superpower, and forming relations of trust and affection.

Years later, McGhee speculated that Mossadegh's Anglophobia may have 'doomed from the start our efforts to facilitate a deal', but he was writing long after Mossadegh's removal from power by the Americans, and the idea that Mossadegh was responsible for his own ruin had become a convenient orthodoxy. In fact, all the evidence suggests that Mossadegh was serious in his pursuit of a deal, although he feared the moment when he might have to unveil it. In proposing a deal, even a demonstrably advantageous one, Mossadegh would be exposing himself to the fury and jealousy of the Tudeh, the landowners and the Court.

At the same time, to continue without a deal seemed equally perilous. The popular support which Mossadegh enjoyed in Iran, and the sullen acquiescence of the majles to his staying in office, could not be counted upon. As he told Truman, the situation at home was grave, with salaries in arrears and a mounting budget deficit. The burden on the government was enormous, for out of a population of around 15 million, some 2.25 million were civil servants. The country could not go on forever supporting 70,000 idle workers and their families in the oil fields.

Mossadegh was risking much by staying in the United States until Britain's new foreign secretary, Anthony Eden, composed his response, and he seems to have felt acutely imperilled by the news of political turmoil he was receiving from home. So there is a sense of liberation and abandonment in his meetings with the intelligent, un-implicated McGhee – and in the prime minister's detachment from his own party.

This detachment is one of the remarkable features of Mossadegh's American stay. The prime minister almost invariably negotiated with McGhee alone. Walters was usually the only other person in the room. (He and McGhee would sit on opposite sides of the foot of the prime minister's bed.) Between meetings, Mossadegh might consult a few colleagues on generalities – notably his oil adviser, Kazem Hassibi, who had been summoned from Tehran – 'indication', as Hassibi put it, 'that there might be a chance for a settlement'.[6] The details, however, he kept secret, and he insisted that McGhee treat their discussions with the utmost discretion.

Paranoia of this kind does not spring unbidden. For centuries, Iranian public life had been overshadowed by treason and betrayal. Mossadegh was striving to save his country; his foes waited for him to fail. He was on his guard against one suspected informer, Iran's ambassador to Washington, a Shah-loyalist called Nasrullah Entezam. The prime minister had astonished his hosts by slamming the door of the Oval Office in Entezam's face in order to exclude him from a meeting with President Truman.[7] Mossadegh also spent much energy trying to dissuade his party from accepting the hospitality of a rich Iranian businessman who was close to Entezam. To his chagrin, some of them succumbed; the businessman had an excellent cook.

All in all, the atmosphere in the prime-ministerial party cannot have been carefree. There had been much competition for a place on this most prestigious of junkets, and Hossein Makki had been offended by his exclusion in favour of Mossadegh's nephew and son-in-law, Ahmad Matine-Daftary. McGhee was surprised when Mossadegh told him that he would send any putative deal to the majles without endorsing it. Such was the prime minister's opinion of the majles, he feared that his endorsement might make its passage more difficult.

Mossadegh seems to have done little to lighten the mood in his party, whose members were not encouraged to express themselves independently. McGhee described the Iranians as 'insecure and afraid to speak frankly'. On one occasion, when the Americans solicited their opinion on something, there was a stilted silence before Mossadegh interjected, 'You see? They all agree with me!' It is likely that not all of them knew what they were agreeing with.

In the end, it was not Mossadegh, fretting in Washington, who scuppered a deal, but the British. Reporting after his first meeting with Anthony Eden, on November 4, Acheson wrote simply, 'Mr Eden's view was that the proposal was totally unacceptable.' The British could not agree to their elimination from Iranian oil production. They also argued that the proposed solution would have a destructive effect on all foreign concessions in the Middle East.

McGhee brought the news to Mossadegh. The two men would not meet again, though Mossadegh continued to speak highly of the American. A few weeks later, McGhee took up his new ambassadorial post, in Turkey and his boss, Dean Acheson, left office after the victory of the Republican Dwight Eisenhower in the 1952 presidential election. They had worked hard to bring Mossadegh and the British together, and in the process they acquired, from different vantage points, valuable insights into the protagonists. McGhee had found himself in the uncomfortable position of telling America's greatest ally that it was digging itself a hole in the region. For all his pro-British sympathies, McGhee had observed with frustration Britain's attempts to prolong its imperial hold, and its inability to see that this was what made it so disliked. McGhee appreciated the strength and validity of the nationalist movements of Iran, Egypt and other places, seeing in them 'examples of a much wider movement in men's minds'. He urged his friends in the Foreign Office to set their relations with the Middle East 'on a basis of equality and do it in such a way that it is recognised by these countries that they are being treated as equals and partners'.[8]

No matter how perceptive and enlightened, a mid-ranking American official, a novice meddling in the British sphere, would get no more than a cursory hearing in Whitehall. McGhee would have stood more chance had Attlee won a third term, but now Churchill was back to power after six years in opposition. Here was a change from the 'long, dismal, drawling tides of drift and surrender' (Eden's words) that had constituted Labour's foreign policy. Tory imperialists were back in the saddle, and their stride was lengthening.

Churchill acknowledged the shift in power that had taken place since the end of World War II, but he saw British interests as being preserved through as close as possible an association with the source of that power, in Washington. Attlee's socialism, he had declared, marked 'the greatest fall in the rank and stature of Britain in the world which has occurred since the loss of the American colonies nearly 200 years ago'.

Churchill's determination to preserve Britain's position in the world cannot be attributed solely to pig-headedness and nostalgia. The country was afflicted by a palpable sense of economic crisis. It had gone from being the world's biggest creditor to its biggest debtor, and its gold and dollar reserves were enough to cover just a few months of imports. Dean Acheson, for one, saw the agony of a close ally. 'Britain', he wrote in a remarkable cable,

> stands on the verge of bankruptcy . . . despite the ravages of the wars and post-war periods, Britain still retained [sic] important overseas interests and the invisible items in her balance of payments are of overwhelming importance to her. Without them she cannot survive. Mossadegh's seizure of the [Anglo-Iranian] properties and concessions were a serious blow. But they were [sic] a loss which Britain can stand. Refining capacity can be built elsewhere. Iranian oil is not essential, and, with firm support from her friends, Britain can recover from this blow.
>
> But Britain cannot recover from the course of action which would destroy the last vestige of confidence in British power and in the pound. If it should be believed abroad that Britain would acquiesce in the despoliation of Iran and even cooperate to make that despoliation profitable to the Iranians, she would have no properties left within a few months – and, indeed, the same would happen to all Western investments.
>
> Therefore, in my judgement, the cardinal purpose of British policy is not to prevent Iran from going Commie; the cardinal

point is to preserve what they believe to be the last remaining
bulwark of British solvency; that is, their overseas investment
and property position. As one of the British said to me . . .
'the choice before you is whether Iran goes Commie, or Britain
goes bankrupt. I hope you would agree that the former is the
lesser evil.'[9]

On his way home, Mossadegh received an invitation he could
not refuse. The world watched his entrance to Cairo, which was
aflame with anti-British feeling and where he was greeted like a
conquering hero. 'From early morning,' the correspondent of *The
Times* reported, 'crowds blocked the streets around Shepheards
Hotel where he is staying, and when he entered, in a bath chair,
the crowd broke through a double police cordon into the hotel
lounge.'[10] There were banquets and a radio address, in which
Mossadegh promised Iran's full support for the Egyptians' 'sacred
struggle' for freedom.

He was received graciously by King Farouk, the Shah's sybaritic
former brother-in-law. The Crown Prince came calling when
Mossadegh was resting, and went away again insisting that he
should not be disturbed. Mossadegh urged the Egyptians to reclaim
their 'property' – an allusion to the Suez Canal.*

He returned home to Tehran to massive crowds in the streets,
shuffling into parliament and bowing, with his hand on his chest,
just like the old days.

---

* A few weeks later, with British troops and government-backed 'liberation battalions'
effectively at war, the Shepheards Hotel and other symbols of the European presence
were burned to the ground.

# 12

# Riding Satan's Donkey

Mossadegh's premiership lasted almost two and a half years, with a short *entr'acte* for the people to rush out and holler for his return. In other less dramatic circumstances that might have been long enough for the country's first fully legitimate prime minister in decades to carry out reforms and leave his mark for ever. But Mossadegh's time in power was like a flood, with the waters rising inexorably and the people moving their belongings onto the roof – and then receding with appalling suddenness, leaving debris and acrimony in their wake. Within a few years, the shop-fronts repaired, the drama no longer discussed, Mossadegh would be effaced from Iran's official past. And then, like a great and noble pain, his memory would sear the people and they would realise what they had lost.

His enemies called him a malignant, negative personality, but his vision was broad and progressive and had ripened over a lifetime. From his actions as prime minister and his long-established beliefs, it is possible to conjecture the Iran he might have made.

Mossadegh's Iran would have tilted to the West in foreign affairs, bound by oil to the free world and by wary friendship to the US, but remaining polite to the big neighbour to the north. In home affairs, it would have been democratic to a degree unthinkable in any Middle Eastern country of the time except Israel – a constitutional monarchy in a world of dictatorships, dependencies and uniformed neo-democracies. The broad strokes of his government would have been egalitarian and redistributive, with a planned economy eroding the power of the 'thousand families', but dappled with elitism (a literacy condition for voters; a penchant for

French-educated cabinet ministers). In social affairs, secularism and personal liberty would have been the lodestones, and the hejab and alcohol a matter for personal conscience. Sooner or later, women would have got the vote.

He triumphantly upheld Voltaire's aphorism, 'I may disagree with what you say, but I would defend to the death your right to say it.' One of his first acts on coming to power was to order the police chief not to pursue any newspaper editor for insulting the prime minister. 'Let them write what they want!' This was unprecedented and there followed a cascade of press abuse such as no other Iranian head of government has faced, before or since. Later on, he agreed to the opposition's demand that majles sessions be broadcast live on the radio, even though these sessions were dominated by vitriolic attacks on himself and his government. He lambasted some well-meaning fools who proposed to erect a statue of him, inviting 'the curses of God and of the Prophet' onto anyone 'wishing to raise an icon in my name in my lifetime or after my death'.[1]

His probity and civic sense were exceptional for a national leader, anywhere. One of his first acts as prime minister was to ask for his elder son Ahmad's resignation as deputy minister of roads. His eldest grandson, Majid, who was studying in Geneva, was told that he would no longer receive the help to which he was entitled as an Iranian student abroad. Mossadegh drew no salary and would pay his own and his children's passage when representing Iran abroad.

On one memorable occasion the prime minister's wife and her driver were stopped by a traffic policeman after they entered a street with a no-entry sign. Upon being informed who was in the back of the car, the policeman said, 'I don't care who it is,' and demanded that a fine be paid. Zahra was cross and when she got home she gave Mossadegh the policeman's name. Mossadegh immediately phoned the chief of police and had the officer in question promoted to head of the traffic police.[2]

Shortly after coming to power, he made an impromptu visit to the police jail, where he was so disgusted by conditions, and especially by the broth the prisoners were given for lunch (he insisted on tasting it), that he delivered a moving speech to parliament asking MPs to visit this 'madhouse' and legislate to 'get these people out of jail'.[3] The visit must have brought back disagreeable memories of his own incarceration, but his reference to a 'madhouse' suggests that Khadijeh, in her Swiss clinic, may have still been on his mind.

Mossadegh had ended his stay in the majles but he would not occupy the prime ministry in the Golestan Palace in central Tehran. Instead, 109 Palace Street became his office. He maintained his secretariat in the prime ministry, from where staff brought him correspondence, but Palace Street was the nerve centre of his premiership. It was here that the cabinet usually met, in the first-floor meeting room when he was well enough, around the famous bed when he was not, and spilling onto the balcony if necessary.

Mossadegh would be criticised for rarely showing his face but his premiership turned on a single great question and was not a ribbon-cutting exercise – such frivolities he happily left to the Shah. From Palace Street he deployed his forces in pursuit of the ultimate prizes, oil and honour, emerging for a speech and then ducking back inside for more brainstorming and negotiations. He gave rousing radio speeches and addressed both houses of parliament in epoch-making terms, challenging his opponents to bring him down in a vote. They did not dare.

He saw everything through the prism of oil and the struggle and neglected peripheral issues.[4] Even the appointment of an important official might not hold his attention, or he would end up asking someone else to choose for him. At least he knew what sort of man he did *not* want. He turned down one candidate for a provincial governorship on the grounds that he 'opposes oil'.

He expected similar dedication from his colleagues. Any cabinet minister who happened to be a European-trained lawyer was liable to be called away from his office for days at a time to labour over a legal document or fly to The Hague to prepare Iran's defence. On the eve of the repossession of the southern oil facilities, he personally telephoned members of the cabinet to remind them to be at the airport to see off the government's emissaries.

As a boss he could be mercurial, tolerating insubordination from some ministers while in other cases taking exception to the slightest deviation from his wishes. He wavered between his desire to see the struggle through to the bitter end and his instinct to crawl away. When negotiations failed at the end of the summer of 1951, he confessed to longing for parliament to bring him down. Then, the next morning, he would be up as usual before dawn, thinking of new ways.

Over the course of the second half of 1951, parliament gradually fell from his affections as it became a centre of opposition and deputies were cultivated by the British and the Court. He approached his office as a war premiership, but he had not sat with his generals and worked out that he could win. He was unable to strike that balance, between interests and ideals, of which a true politician is made. But Mossadegh was not a conventional politician. He was a moral force, and in no time he had offended almost every institution in the country.

Arriving at the majles to brief deputies before his trip to America, he had been infuriated to find that the opposition had stayed away and were operating a quorum veto. Leaving the building with the intention of going home, he had a change of heart and asked for a stool. Reverting to the opposition role he so relished, he went up on the stool and addressed the crowd that had gathered in Baharestan Square, explaining how he had tried to reach an honourable agreement but had been thwarted by that 'merciless butcher', Britain. He burst into tears and the people also wept. He was handed flowers and raised the bouquet to his forehead before handing it back. 'People,' he declared, 'benevolent and patriotic, who are gathered here! You are the majles and that place' – he indicated the parliament building behind him – 'that handful who do not want the best for their country, are not parliament at all!'

Another leader – Qavam, for instance – might have seized the opportunity to step back from the maximalist position and accept massively enhanced revenues and the appreciative friendship of a new superpower, then bend his propaganda arm to sell the deal to the public. Mossadegh had no propaganda arm except for his

patriotism and integrity, and these could not be repaired if he tried
to strike a dishonourable peace. The Tudeh screamed that he
pursued a relationship of subservience to the United States – a
more sinister enemy, in their eyes, than the British. The radicals in
his own entourage watched for any chink in his resolve, heaping
odium on the 'ill-omened owl of London', as Hossein Fatemi, the
government spokesman and editor of *Bakhtar-e Emrooz*, put it.
Beyond legality, other fanatics circled menacingly, and in February
1952 Fatemi was shot and almost killed by the Warriors of Islam.

Many people, including members of the cabinet, deplored his
indulgent attitude towards the Tudeh. The party remained banned
and many of its leaders were abroad, but it boasted front organisations and a powerful network in the factories and schools. In the
prime minister's view, the freedom being exploited by the Tudeh
could not be separated from the freedom that the country as a
whole was in the process of attaining. Only with great reluctance
did he impose martial law in the capital, in March 1952, after violent
street clashes between the Tudeh and a right-wing group supportive
of the government. But Mossadegh never believed that Iran was
close to falling under Moscow's thumb, and events would prove
him right.

There had been violence when he was in the United States, with
Tudeh students and factory workers battling Baghai's thugs and
the police. A Tudeh newspaper excoriated the 'murderous and
marauding regime of Mossadegh al-Saltaneh', and the opposition's
goons shouted 'Death to Mossadegh!' from the public gallery in
the majles. The government was helped by Ayatollah Kashani, ever
ready to summon the people for another huge, anti-imperialist,
anti-communist rally. 'Nothing but rallies happens in our country,'
lamented one opposition stalwart. 'One day this lot have a meeting,
and the next day the other lot . . . our oil is beneath the ground
and hidden away like the other sources of our wealth . . . enough!'

The impression was sometimes of a government that did not
know how to take charge, but Mossadegh was proving far more
durable than Shepherd and many others had expected. He was a
daring improviser and some of his tactics, such as taking the cause

abroad to shore up his position at home, and his later promotion of an economy that was not reliant on oil receipts, succeeded well. Even Loy Henderson acknowledged his 'masterly' dominance of the domestic arena. Above all, he was helped by Britain's unabashed hostility. By hating Mossadegh, the British made him even more loved.

The Tehran which Mossadegh found on his return from the US was saturated in threats, disinformation and paranoia. The economy had been sapped by the international embargo and severe austerity measures were in place. An internal loan did not raise much and the armed forces could not afford to buy spare parts. Parliamentary life had sunk to new depths with the galleries groaning under the weight of brawling spectators, while the street corners saw vicious skirmishes between pro- and anti-government groups brandishing crowbars and knuckledusters.

The hazards of domestic politics made it all the harder for him to continue with oil negotiations. The prime minister felt safest while engaged in negotiations, a position from which attempts to topple him could be denounced as unpatriotic, but he was distracted by his chronic mistrust of the British, and now he was reliant on a tiny number of advisers around him, the most influential of whom, Kazem Hassibi, revelled in his ability to scupper a deal. Mossadegh had earned the trust of the Iranian people with his pursuit of nationalisation, and the great mass of them would have accepted whatever concessions he deemed necessary for an honourable resolution. The tragedy is that he never asked them to do so.

Mossadegh accused the British of negotiating in bad faith, but after his failure in America his preference was not for an oil deal but for short-term finance to tide the country over, and to this end he engaged in reckless brinkmanship. He was spending emergency funds and it was feared that soon the government would be unable to pay salaries or bills for services and supplies. Mossadegh told Henderson that if the United States did not step in immediately to cover Iran's monthly budget deficit of $10m, he would have no choice but to seek help from the Soviet Union, and the Tudeh would take over the government. This plunged the Americans into panic, with the CIA predicting that Iran would start selling oil to the communist bloc and Henderson hinting that if aid was not promised within twenty-four hours the country would be overtaken by revolution or bankruptcy. The risk of 'sitting tight and letting events take their course', he said, was 'too great'.[5]

In trying to thwart British designs with the help of Britain's greatest ally, Mossadegh showed more chutzpah than wisdom. He had gone too far with his dire predictions and the State Department recoiled from his 'extortion' and 'blackmail'.[6] London assured Washington that Mossadegh had no intention of getting into bed with the Soviets, and that the communist bloc had neither the wherewithal, nor the need, to buy Iranian oil in big quantities. The British knew from historical experience that no Iranian statesman could ally himself with the Soviet Union and hope to survive.

In the end, the Americans called Mossadegh's bluff. They would offer aid only if Iran and Britain reached an agreement. Mossadegh shrugged his shoulders but his games would have a baleful, longer-term effect. They contributed to the erosion of his credibility in American eyes.

Also at the beginning of 1952, Mossadegh was supposedly engaged in serious negotiations with officials from the World Bank. A scheme had been proposed whereby the bank would take over the oil industry as a neutral trustee, allowing Iran to receive income and Anglo-Iranian to sell part of the oil. Mossadegh was receptive at first, but negotiations snagged on disagreements over price, the question of whether or not British technicians could be engaged, and Mossadegh's insistence that the bank should state that it was acting on behalf of the Iranian government – anathema to the bank, whose guiding principle, in public at least, was its neutrality.

In rejecting the deal, Mossadegh was influenced by the extreme positions of Hassibi, and the poisonous atmosphere in Tehran. There were certainly grounds to doubt the sincerity of the British, but Mossadegh's diplomatic strategy had been based on driving a wedge between London and Washington, and, by playing spoiler, he inadvertently facilitated a rapprochement between the two. Later, he would denounce the World Bank proposals as a 'black stain' and a 'road to hell'. They were nothing of the sort. The bank's terms would not have undermined the principle of nation-alisation, nor would the return of a number of British technicians under the bank's aegis. Mossadegh rejected the deal partly on the basis of Hassibi's computation of a fair price, but Hassibi's sums have been shown to be badly out.[7] They were no grounds for a landmark decision of state.

Mossadegh could not forever carry on riding 'Satan's donkey', as the Persian phrase goes. How on earth was he going to get off?

Twelve acres in the heart of Tehran, teeming with political and consular officers, military attachés, ciphers and gardeners, a walled city graced by a clock tower, lily pool and a crescent of residential cottages, the British Embassy on Ferdowsi Street belied an England in decline. In early 1952, on this venerable plot in the diplomatic quarter, the air cooled by miraculous subterranean water courses and sweetened by the ambassador's wisteria, a British scholar of Iran laboured, conniving to bring about Mossadegh's fall.

Robin Zaehner had been recommended by Britain's doyenne of Iranian studies, Nancy Lambton. An austere bluestocking with a somewhat surprising penchant for roller-skating, Lambton had run British propaganda in Tehran during World War II, and Zaehner had been her declared deputy – while working in fact as an agent for Special Operations Executive, countering the spread of Soviet propaganda. After the war Lambton had returned to London to teach at the School of Oriental and African Studies, the newest of Britain's great orientalist institutions, where she put her students through courses of legendary severity. In 1951 the Foreign Office asked her what should be done about Mossadegh.

Lambton believed that negotiating with Mossadegh was futile since he had built his public position on Anglophobia, and she made the fateful recommendation that he should be overthrown using covert means. Zaehner, who had returned to Oxford as lecturer in

Persian, liberated himself from his teaching duties and was dispatched to the embassy in Tehran as an 'acting counsellor'. He would answer to the Foreign Office, and not MI6 – a stroke of luck for the historian, for the cables relating to his work are now in the public domain.

Zaehner was a Catholic convert with a taste for gin, opium and the homoerotic verses of Rimbaud – his first reading of *O Saisons, O Châteaux* had tipped him into a mystical ecstasy. Bespectacled and giggly, he was a born networker who knew everyone who mattered in Tehran. Soon he had re-established his old links with the majles, the armed forces and the Court, distributing bribes in empty biscuit tins and shocking professional spies with his amateurism. Zaehner paid a substantial retainer to a wealthy trio of Anglophile brothers, the Rashidians, which they spent on bribing bazaaris, parliamentarians, mullahs and newspaper editors. Hossein Ala, the Shah's court minister, was acting as a discreet conduit for royal frustrations, though he too was driven almost to his wits' end by the monarch's chronic indecision. The Shah's Swiss friend Ernest Perron beetled about dropping names and bits of information, and feuded with members of the royal family for influence over the Shah. A senior civil servant volunteered detailed reports about the latest cabinet meetings. Might Ayatollah Kashani be turned against Mossadegh? What of those ambitious younger radicals, Makki and Baghai? Feelers were put out, ambiguous answers received.

Into this world, murky but glinting, outsiders dropped at their peril. When Kingsley Martin, the editor of the *New Statesman*, asked Zaehner at a cocktail party in Tehran what book he might read to enlarge his understanding of Iran, Zaehner suggested *Alice Through the Looking Glass*.

Zaehner was brilliant and had a dazzling command of languages and world literature, but his commission was ugly: to sow chaos in the heart of a sovereign government. As Zaehner saw it, his mission ended in defeat, for when he returned to Oxford in the summer of 1952 he was disillusioned by his failure to dislodge Mossadegh and gloomy about future prospects. Events of the following year would confute this modest self-assessment; it was he who had paved the way for the coup, probing the nationalists for divisions and cultivating key assets. The Americans would carry the principle of overthrow to its violent conclusion. But it was Lambton's and Zaehner's in conception.

Bribed by Zaehner and his MI6 colleagues (of which there were at least four in the embassy), abetted by the Court's different cliques, Mossadegh's opponents subverted the country's fragile democratic institutions. British spooks worked the tribes and the Rashidians drummed up a parliamentary vote of no-confidence. Mossadegh was powerless to stop the army and pro-Shah provincial governors from manipulating the polling for the seventeenth majles, when, among other outrages, a Shia cleric was elected to represent a Sunni-dominated constituency he had not set foot in. While he was dealing with these crises, the prime minister was also negotiating with the World Bank and the Americans, and in May 1952 he made another foreign sortie to defend the country's honour at The Hague. No wonder he might nowadays be found smoking – a local brand, without inhaling – to soothe his nerves. (The Shah, by contrast, smoked American Camel.)

An opposition newspaper which enjoyed friendly relations with the British Embassy printed the following ditty:

Sleep, child, a thief's in the house; hush, it's that infernal lunatic;
Sleep, child, for the ogre has come. It's Mossadegh with a blanket over his shoulders;
My child, if this is a national government, it'll shit over the country even more;
He's burrowed so far under his blanket, he's bloody well dropped the country in it.[8]

Mossadegh's response to the threats and abuse was in keeping with his idea of himself as a wartime prime minister fighting desperately to stave off national collapse. He would not give the order for brutality, but he would use every other weapon at his disposal, even if that meant abandoning his political scruples. He began to imagine that he could run the country solely on the basis of his rapport with the people, bypassing those institutions which he considered corrupt. It was pure demagogy when he announced, 'However much the deputies curse and insult me, my prominence in society rises proportionately.'

Increasingly he addressed the people by radio, and his appearances in parliament grew rarer – though this was also connected to his fear of assassination. He accused anyone doubting him of lacking patriotism; he did not care 'a farthing' for their opposition. He saw off the parliamentary no-confidence motion with an appeal to jingoism, announcing the closure of all provincial British consulates on the day that the motion was to be debated, and prompting anti-British demonstrations around the country. Events abroad only served to jangle the Shah's nerves.[9]

When it was clear that the elections to the seventeenth majles were being perverted in the regions, Mossadegh waited until results had been declared in the urban constituencies where his supporters were strongest, and then had the poll suspended in the remainder of the constituencies. (The seventeenth majles met for the first time in May 1952, with only two thirds of the seats occupied.) Finally, and most controversial of all, realising that the majles would oppose his government on many issues, he gave the deputies an ultimatum: grant him plenary powers to rule by decree for six months, or he would resign.

Here was Mossadegh turning away from the institution he had once so loved, and where he had enjoyed his finest triumphs. It was a scandal. The prime minister proposed to bulldoze the principle of the separation of powers on the grounds of national expediency, in the full knowledge that it was against the constitution. He had arrogated to himself the authority to judge when and how the constitution should be applied. 'When unconventional warfare is being waged,' he would write later, 'the granting of [plenary] powers is in harmony with the spirit of the constitution, for the constitution is there for the country, not the country for the constitution.'

Mossadegh's obsession with complete and unconditional victory over the British and the Shah was leading him to dismantle the very institution he had spent his life trying to build, and which he now regarded as corrupt beyond redemption. With the Court, uneasy cooperation had given way to open breach. That left just himself and the people. Mossadegh was a master at manipulating the popular mood, but he was only one man against a legion of enemies. The people were only just being tested. Building a national strategy between the two was like treading a wire strung between two poplars in a gale.

By the summer of 1952, Zaehner and his colleagues were preparing for the moment when the Shah would have no option but to support a scheme to dump Mossadegh and replace him with someone to cut an oil deal that would be satisfactory to the British. The government in London continued to regard their old favourite Seyyed Zia as the best candidate. Since his return from exile at the end of Reza Shah's rule, Zia had wormed his way into the Shah's confidence; his Anglophilia burned as brightly as ever. Eventually, the British and the Shah were persuaded by the Americans that Zia's pro-British reputation would make it impossible for the people to accept him. Their thoughts turned to Qavam.

Even before Mossadegh's ascent to power, Qavam had solicited British support for another bid for the premiership, in return for which he promised to engineer a favourable oil deal. The grand old man was not idle as he convalesced in Europe in the spring of 1952, following an operation. He assured establishment figures in London that the Shah was not up to the job and that they should consider a Qajar restoration. But Qavam's ill-health made backing him a gamble. He was even older than Mossadegh and his doctors had ordered him to restrict himself to two hours' work a day. His left eye twitched disconcertingly whenever he took off his dark glasses.

Four decades after Mossadegh first bowed to his nagging mother and accepted the post of deputy finance minister under Qavam, the cousins faced each other as adversaries. The Shah was torn between his hatred for Qavam, who had never concealed his contempt for the young monarch, and his hatred of Mossadegh. He fretted particularly about the mechanics of Mossadegh's exit, and the popular explosion that would follow if the affair was badly handled. Then, quite unexpectedly, Mossadegh thrust an opportunity into his hands.

Mossadegh's entourage had seen the danger in letting relations between him and the Shah deteriorate further, urging the prime minister not to nurture his grievances but to take them to the monarch. The Shah had given Mossadegh assurances of non-interference, and Princess Ashraf's long sojourn abroad was one of several camouflaged banishments of royal intriguers in this period. But the plots continued, particularly during elections to the seventeenth majles, and whatever mutual trust remained between the two men had evaporated long before they met on July 16, 1952, when Mossadegh went, as convention demanded, to seek royal approval for his new cabinet. In fact, Mossadegh harboured bigger ambitions as his car entered the park at Saadabad, the Shah's summer palace. Here, among the oriental planes that Reza Shah had planted, Mossadegh would avenge himself on the defunct founder of the Pahlavis. He would demand that the Shah reign, not rule.[10]

Mossadegh was helped up the steps of the palace by a guard, and was shown into a reception room. The Shah came in and the conversation began decorously enough, with inquiries into health and a wary *tour d'horizon* of the nation and its affairs. Finally, Mossadegh handed the Shah his cabinet list. The Shah lingered over the list, and it cannot have escaped his notice that its composition was markedly less royalist than its predecessor. Furthermore, there was one significant omission.

'Who', he asked, 'is to be war minister?'

On this question much more rested than a seat around the cabinet table. Constitutionally, the Shah was nominally the commander-in-chief of the armed forces, but the war minister was a member of the government just like any other, and answerable to the prime minister. No past prime minister – even Qavam – had dared challenge the Shah's unwritten right to nominate the war minister. Any who did so would be reviving memories of Reza himself, who had seized control of the army and used that as a springboard to power.

Such a prime minister could but harbour hostile designs towards the monarch. So, it did not please the Shah when Mossadegh replied, 'Your humble servant is to assume that burden.'

There followed a rambling conversation in which Mossadegh expressed his devotion to the throne and the Shah recalled the circumstances of Reza's political rise. Mossadegh lost patience. 'At present,' he said bluntly, 'the War Ministry acts as a government within the government and does not carry out my wishes. The Ministry did not execute my orders during the elections. I repeatedly informed you and you even issued orders to this purpose, but they were not carried out.'

Now the Shah grew angry. If he yielded up the War Ministry, he snapped, he 'might as well pack [his] bags and go'. Mossadegh answered that he would sooner resign, and made for the door. But the Shah was there in a flash and put one arm around Mossadegh while keeping the door shut with the other. There followed another of those wrestling scenes that cropped up from time to time during Mossadegh's life. Mossadegh tugged at the door handle. The Shah pushed, the servants came running, and Mossadegh got out of an awkward situation with his usual expedient. He swooned.

When he came to, he was on a sofa with the Shah sitting next to him and Hossein Ala also present. The prime minister accepted a glass of water but declined the Shah's invitation to stay for lunch. The two men reached agreement. If Mossadegh did not hear from the Shah before eight o'clock that evening, he was to consider his resignation accepted.

Back at Palace Street Mossadegh gave orders for the main gate to be shut. He admitted only Makki, who found him sitting in his dressing gown on his bed on the balcony, drafting his resignation letter. Eight o'clock passed without word from the palace, and the letter was dispatched. The doors shut once more, and Mossadegh waited. He had picked up the deck and hurled it into the air. Now he would see where the cards landed.

The following afternoon, that other gambler Qavam was playing poker at the house of a crony when he was told that parliament had given him its vote of confidence. Qavam showed no emotion

– this unreconstructed grandee, who had, in Makki's words, 'come into this world as prime minister', insisted on finishing the game before taking up his functions.

In fact he would never truly take them up, for as the country went to pieces over the next few days, the new prime minister, partially bed-ridden, unable at times even to open his eyes, was overtaken by events and eventually swept away by a popular uprising that no one – not himself; not the British; perhaps not Mossadegh himself – had anticipated. Qavam's infirmities were not old friends as Mossadegh's were, for hamming up as the performance demanded, but genuine physical crises. Qavam spent the whole of his last, ill-starred premiership in one such crisis, his doctors hovering with their syringes and warning of his imminent demise if he did not rest, and his judgement much impaired. Mossadegh, by contrast, found strength and lucidity in the iron bed.

On Friday morning Qavam accepted office from the Shah – having kept him waiting, of course. He returned to his Tehran mansion in the prime-ministerial Cadillac that his predecessor had disdained to use. Over lunch he sprang an unpleasant surprise on his allies and the nation. He ordered the radio brought in and, as the presenter read out the new prime minister's first official declaration, his advisers looked at each other in horror. Qavam's words showed neither the compassion nor the eloquence that his new position required – only wrath.

Around the country, in homes and tea shops, Iranians listened as Qavam trashed all they held precious. His promise to solve the oil crisis was delivered so ambiguously, the people thought he meant to reverse nationalisation. He opened fire recklessly on Ayatollah Kashani, lambasting the 'black reaction' that had been manufactured to fight 'red extremists', and vowed to set up 'revolutionary tribunals' to punish 'criminals of all classes'. He even promised to keep politics and religion far apart – as if Iran were France! Mossadegh, despite being as much of a secularist as Qavam, would never have made such a reckless suggestion.

Qavam's final words were the threat of a dictator: 'Woe betide those who disrupt the expedient actions I take,' for they would suffer 'the dry and unforgiving judgement of the law. I warn the public that the days of rebellion have come to an end and that those of obedience to the orders and proscriptions of the government have arrived. The captain is taking a new course.'

How many Iranians who heard this declaration were reminded of the despotic caliph who had martyred their beloved Imam Hossein? Mossadegh, the old man biding his time at home, was being martyred, and the country was quickly inflamed. Qavam's only chance of survival, one of his supporters now suggested, was to waste no time in establishing the despotism that was implicit in his radio address – to dissolve the majles and arrest his opponents. This is what the US and British envoys urged him to do. But only the Shah could dissolve the majles, and already he was putting obstacles in Qavam's way, advising patience when haste was required, and receiving a delegation of nationalist deputies. The Shah had only reluctantly acquiesced to Qavam's premiership and would not spend political capital helping him to a position from which he could challenge the throne.

Events leaped forward, with Kashani as the spur. On July 19 the ayatollah declared a jihad against Qavam's government, by whose pernicious agency 'the foreigners are resolved to take an axe to religion and freedom and independence'. Tehran was filling with soldiers and tanks, but also with groups of Mossadegh supporters, shouting 'Death to Qavam!' and 'Long Live Mossadegh!' They also tore down copies of the infamous Qavam declaration, which the authorities had pasted to the walls, and many were injured by the security forces.

If he had enjoyed the Shah's support, Qavam might have stood a chance. Secret negotiations were going on with Kashani, but Qavam had exiled the ayatollah during his previous government and there was bad blood between them. Furthermore, Qavam knew that the price of Kashani's support would be nothing less than control over the government. 'The enmity of such people', he said, 'is less harmful than their friendship.' Meanwhile, Henderson, the American ambassador, was promising aid and other assistance on condition that Qavam strike an oil deal with the British. Then news got out that Qavam had ordered Kashani's arrest. Fearing revolution, the Shah withheld his blessing, and Qavam became an ogre made of straw. As the new British *chargé d'affaires*, George Middleton wrote, in a fury of frustration, 'We had long known that he [the Shah] was indecisive and timid, but we had not thought that his fear would so overcome his reason.' Now, the ayatollah was boiling. In a warning to the army not to set itself against 'the clarion of conscience and patriotism', he called on all to join the 'struggle between good and evil'.

The following day, the capital slid into disorder, while the news from the provinces was dire. The workers at Abadan had shut down the refinery, which had been operating at reduced capacity to meet domestic needs, and from the western provinces processions of men wearing martyrs' mantles set out for Tehran. Kashani declared his readiness to die in order to be rid of 'this murderous magnate'. In a letter to Ala, he threatened his sovereign in no uncertain terms. 'Inform his Majesty', he wrote, 'that if he does not take steps tomorrow to restore Dr Mossadegh, I will personally direct the sharp teeth of revolution against the court.'

It is tantalising to imagine what Mossadegh was thinking on the eve of July 21. By the simple device of resigning he had brought the country to the brink of revolution. He was certainly aware of what was going on, but he spent most of the time resting. That night, also, Mossadegh spent at Palace Street, and not, as many of the reports stated, at Ahmadabad. In Makki's words, Mossadegh 'has no need to go to Ahmadabad. Today for Dr Mossadegh all of Iran has become Ahmadabad.'

A general strike was held on July 21. There were no buses and the bazaar and all petrol stations were closed. Only military vehicles roared around, and there was a build-up of security forces in the vicinity of Baharestan Square. But the people stood firm. Rallied by Kashani's network and the pro-Mossadegh parties, swelled by the Tudeh, which had belatedly thrown its weight behind the uprising, shopkeepers, bazaaris, students and factory workers came out to show their hatred for the government of Qavam al-Saltaneh.

At nine in the morning a few people were seen carrying a funeral bier at speed away from the bazaar, and the crowd following swelled to several hundred by the time they reached the parliament building, where the police fired over their heads and the corpse got up and ran. There was pandemonium. The security forces had been given authority to fire into the crowds and the shirts of the dead were raised on sticks as standards, their blood being used to daub slogans on the walls. In Ekbatan Street, leading into Baharestan Square, a policeman shot a child and was lynched by the crowd.[11] A tank made as if to roll over the people but they stood their ground. The tank stopped dead and its occupants emerged weeping and were embraced by the crowd. The Shah's brother Ali-Reza narrowly escaped death as his car was pelted with stones. He fired back using his revolver. Six hundred detainees from earlier demonstrations escaped from jail after the police abandoned their posts.

The majles was aghast. Parliament employees yelled, 'Death to Qavam!' A woman whose child had been shot ambushed the speaker as he tried to set off for the palace, thrusting the little corpse before him and screaming, 'You are not your father's son!' The Shah promised to rein in the violence but still it went on, and one of the deputies yelled at him over the telephone, 'Under what authority did you hand control of the country to that decrepit old bird whose record shows nothing but treachery?' Later that afternoon, large crowds gathered with the intent of pulling down statues of the Shah and attacking the royal palaces; nationalist deputies helped disperse them.

Qavam al-Saltaneh had become what he had never expected to become: an irrelevance. His heartbeat was irregular and he chafed because he knew so little of what was going on. He requested an audience but now it was the Shah's turn to keep him waiting. The Shah received more nationalist deputies, who warned him that the people would no longer tolerate a government that was imposed on them on the basis of consultations behind closed doors. Hours passed before Qavam was finally granted the audience he craved, late on the afternoon of July 30, when the Shah once again disregarded his demand for the dissolution of the majles and Kashani's arrest.

After leaving the palace around the time the radio announced his resignation, Qavam took sanctuary in the house of a friend, where the shouts of the mob, calling, 'Death to Qavam!' brought home to him the depth of his failure. His reaction was perfunctory and defiant. Even in defeat, he would not show fear. He consulted his host's copy of Hafez to see what was in store. Then he asked, 'Got any cards?'

After five decades of sharing the political field, the two Qajar grandees had faced each other, and Mossadegh's masterly inaction had won the day. Hauteur and cunning had brought Qavam to the pinnacle but his radio declaration told of a titanic arrogance and a disassociation from the people he was meant to serve. The old qualities were less useful now that Mossadegh had moved politics out of the mirrored halls, and into the street. It was there, in the street, that Qavam's fate had been decided.

That evening, after a self-imposed purgatory lasting five days, Mossadegh responded to the crowds that had gathered outside 109 Palace Street. Appearing on the balcony, he declared to the adoring people, 'The independence of Iran was going but you have won it back with your bravery.'

On July 22, the majles voted him back into power. The previous night, the International Court at The Hague had ruled that it had no jurisdiction in the dispute between Anglo-Iranian and Iran.* It was nothing more than Mossadegh had argued all along. He seemed invincible.

These were great victories, achieved in the teeth of immense pressure, but they did not make Mossadegh reflect on his debts and obligations. On the contrary, they spurred him to a new level – one of total leadership, alone with his people.

Between July 1952 and the coup thirteen months later, hardly a

---

* Mossadegh's grandson Hedayat Matine-Daftary was at boarding school in England when he heard the news. He told his housemaster, a retired colonel with thespian pretentions, 'Sir, the Hague has decided in Iran's favour. They have declared they have no jurisdiction.' The colonel snorted, 'Of course they have no jurisdiction! This case should be heard in the criminal courts!'[12]

week passed without some urgent challenge rattling his position or threatening his safety. Plots, assassinations and public disorder became almost banal occurrences. Tehran was under martial law, generals and businessmen were arrested for plotting, and Iran severed its relations with Great Britain. The senate was dissolved by a combination of pro-Kashani and pro-Mossadegh forces, a referendum was held, and there was a revolt in the Bakhtiari hills. Even for Iran, the situation was combustible.

Mossadegh's reaction to the threats against him was not to seek protection in a huddle. The only person the prime minister trusted completely was himself. His solitude was his strength; everyone knew that he had sunk Qavam simply by going home and shutting the door. Mossadegh, in his second, abbreviated term of office, became a radical prime minister who insisted on complete freedom of manoeuvre. He resisted the advice of men who had formerly had his ear, which hurt and angered them. Those comrades in the majles who had been at the forefront of the nationalisation campaign, Hossein Makki, Muzaffar Baghai and Abolhassan Haerizadeh, regarded themselves less as his disciples than as co-founders of a movement. Ayatollah Kashani's ambitions observed no national boundaries. All were convinced that they had rescued Mossadegh on July 21, and all expected rewards. The prime minister did not hesitate to disabuse them.

Mossadegh's vision of his immediate task was clearer than it had been for some time. The oil negotiations went on with American brokerage but he did not expect them to succeed, for he saw with dismay the success that Churchill was now enjoying in closing the gap between the British and US positions, and that there was no longer any realistic hope of a loan from Washington.* At home, Mossadegh was hemmed in by rivals who would howl that any

---

* The first fruits of this success came with the joint proposals that Truman and Churchill submitted to Mossadegh in August 1952. Churchill had been at his most meretricious when proposing this diplomatic 'gallop' to Truman, 'such as I often had with FDR'. Having invoked tradition, Churchill went on reasonably, 'I do not myself see why two good men asking only what is right and good should not gang up against a third who is doing wrong. In fact I thought and think that this is the way things ought to be done.' Mossadegh reacted with hostility to the démarche.

deal, no matter how beneficial, was a sell-out. His secretive, mercurial conduct of negotiations in late 1952 and early 1953 on the question of international arbitration betrayed his terror that his critics (and even so-called friends) would maliciously misinterpret any deal he made. Absorbed in the domestic maelstrom, he may not have appreciated fully the distance that the British government had travelled to meet his demands.

In the spring of 1953 Mossadegh was offered an arrangement whereby the Iranians would retain charge of the oil industry and Anglo-Iranian would be reduced to the status of a participant in an international consortium that would market Iranian oil exports. The essence of privatisation, not merely its form, would be preserved. This would be the last serious deal Mossadegh was offered, and his rejection of it was as grave a failure of leadership as any in his premiership. He continued to declare that a negotiated settlement was within reach so long as the people continued to support him and his enemies stopped their conspiracies, but he probably did not believe his own propaganda.

He had been more frank in his announcement of the severance of relations with Britain, the previous autumn, when he described the strategy of his foes as one of 'wasting time until our country is in such a state that the economy has breathed its last and surrenders to [British] demands'. Mossadegh's belief that the British were bent on toppling him through skulduggery was only partially correct, for some senior British officials were opposed to covert action, and for a while, at the beginning of 1953, these sceptics were in the ascendant.[13] But it was Mossadegh's nature to simplify the challenges he faced, and to regard his many foes as implacably united in his pursuit. In the end, his suspicion became self-fulfilling.

The response could only be resistance, and he had a plan. The Iranians would modify their economy so that it could withstand an indefinite oil embargo. Soon after coming to power, Mossadegh had laid the foundations for a pared down, 'non-oil' economy. The government had depreciated the riyal, promoted non-oil exports (there was a helpful boom in the international commodities market), and penalised non-essential imports. The new economy was not without pain. Inflation rose, growth stalled and there were factory closures and unemployment, but the country did not buckle as so many had expected – and as Mossadegh, angling for his US loan, had said it would. There was neither famine nor major industrial unrest. Between 1951 and 1953, when oil all but ceased to contribute to state revenues, the current-account deficit actually came down.

To an economic policy of austerity and self-reliance, Mossadegh's second government hitched a much broader reform agenda. The prime minister was no longer content to react to events; his instincts told him that in this moment of peril lay a unique opportunity. His old coterie had been superseded by a new one, bolstered by progressive, left-leaning intellectuals in the cabinet and parliament – men like the law dean Ali Shayegan, and the cabinet minister and newspaper editor Hossein Fatemi. In league with men such as these, Mossadegh showed himself to be a bold reformist.

Many of the policies which Mossadegh unveiled after the uprising of July 1952 were not implemented, or were reversed after the coup. Had they survived, Mossadegh would now be remembered as an agent of extraordinary change. Exempt from parliamentary scrutiny, the prime minister passed pro-poor land reforms and introduced social security and rent controls to help the working class. He retired corrupt and hostile senior army officers and strengthened the separation of powers by removing responsibility for judicial appointments from the government and handing it over to the judiciary. Laws were prepared for the holding of the country's first provincial elections in which women would have the vote.

Wealth distribution; a military under civilian control; modestly enhanced rights for women in the face of clerical unease; these were the most visible parts of a modernisation programme that would have brought Iran substantially closer to a secular, constitutional regime. The final year of Mossadegh's premiership is a salutary episode in modern Middle Eastern history – an opportunity spurned because of the British obsession with lost prestige and the American obsession with communism.

One of the remarkable things about Mossadegh during his second government was his readiness to abandon former allies. Smarting at their rebuffal, Baghai, Makki and Haerizadeh gradually made common cause with the government's enemies at Court and among the purged army officers. They spoke out against Mossadegh's plenary powers and excoriated some eccentric appointments. Baghai was exercised by Mossadegh's refusal to pursue the fallen Qavam, who after a period in hiding was allowed to go home to live out his final years. Baghai and the others particularly loathed the anti-Court secularists, who included suspected Tudeh-sympathisers, and who now had the prime minister's ear.

Above all, the malcontents fretted for their lost influence and prestige. Makki and Baghai would surely have laid down their lives for Mossadegh early in the struggle. Now, their trouble was thwarted ambition; they had been touted as possible heirs to Mossadegh and it hurt to be frozen out.

Mossadegh's rift with Kashani widened less rapidly, but to even greater effect. The ayatollah and his network had enjoyed much influence over Mossadegh's first government. Few were the departments that had not been bombarded with letters from Kashani, requesting special consideration for a client, or advising on appointments. The ayatollah had even interfered in the manufacture of salt.

Kashani had always had delusions of grandeur, announcing that 'all the Muslims of the world acknowledge me as their leader'. His alliance with Mossadegh had been – for them both – one of convenience. The prime minister's triumph in July 1952 had emboldened him to try to eject the meddling mullah from politics. Mossadegh ordered government departments to ignore the ayatollah's missives, and, when Kashani fell ill, he stopped prayers for his recovery from being read out on the radio.[14] Kashani was not a great religious scholar; to ignore him politically was to put him in the shade. So, while the outward professions of mutual respect continued, the ayatollah's opposition hardened.

Now the accusations came thick and fast. Haerizadeh compared Mossadegh unfavourably to Reza Shah. Makki claimed to see something of Hitler in him. Mossadegh accused his detractors of using the law to advance along a crooked path. Amid the chaos and recrimination and the shuffle of men switching sides, Mossadegh's was the only voice which rang clear and unambiguous. He was not a dictator in the sense of a tyrant lusting after power, but he shared the dictator's sense of his own indispensability. There is no reason to assume that this sense would have diminished had he not been toppled.

He was an unrivalled moral manipulator, addressing the nation through the radio and hurling all-comers from his high ground of patriotism and purity of intent. He accused those who opposed him of wielding 'a dagger, from behind'. From the majles he wrung his plenary powers and an almost unanimous vote of confidence. The reason for his success in a chamber he had come to loathe and revile was his opponents' fear that they would be accused of martyring Iran's saviour, bringing the wrath of the people crashing over their heads. And when their plans were defeated, these opponents scuttled back and adopted pained, wronged expressions. Baghai protested that it was not Mossadegh he opposed, but his extra powers. 'Hypocrite!' snarled a prime-ministerial loyalist.

One of these loyalists, Ahmad Razavi, described the moral authority wielded by Mossadegh as 'unparalleled in the history of Iran. No prime minister in the constitutional era and no chief minister during the period of despotism has ever enjoyed this degree of popular trust and faith . . . from the farthest point on the Gulf of Oman to the Caspian, all the people of this country have fixed their eyes on him so that he may heal their wounds.'[15]

His new adversaries had to go cautiously. Over the second half of 1952, Ayatollah Kashani renounced the anti-Court ideals on which his politics had been founded. He was looking for a candidate to replace Mossadegh, and his eye fell on a military man. General Fazlullah Zahedi was a retired general whom the Shah had raised to the senate – though the Shah, typically, did not trust him. The general had been Mossadegh's interior minister but had lost his post following the violence that had greeted Averell Harriman's arrival in Tehran in August 1951, and he had gone on to become one of the government's most effective critics. Plausible, well-connected and good-looking (he bore a passing resemblance to Ataturk), Zahedi had been arrested for pro-German proclivities during the British occupation, a search of his bedroom yielding a small arsenal, some opium and a register of local prostitutes.[16] The British had interned him but there were no hard feelings and he let himself be courted by British spies and diplomats following the Qavam débâcle. Both the British and the Americans regarded him as the best candidate to replace Mossadegh.

George Middleton had become British *chargé d'affaires* after Shepherd's departure in November 1951. The Iranians had refused to admit Shepherd's successor as ambassador on the pretext that he had served in a British colony, so Middleton remained as Britain's top diplomat in the country. The following summer, Middleton reported that Zahedi was in touch with Kashani and ex-Mossadeghists such as Makki and Baghai, but in October another retired general and two of the Rashidian brothers were arrested for what the government called 'plotting and incitement in favour of a foreign embassy'. In the words of a British diplomatic report, 'This in no way disconcerted the brothers, who continued to operate from jail, where they also obtained all the good food they desired.' Soon they were freed for lack of evidence.

General Zahedi had also been publicly accused of involvement in the plot, but he could not be arrested because he was a senator and enjoyed immunity. The British denied any role, but Mossadegh had been looking for excuses to close down a mission which he regarded, with perfect justification, as a hotbed of intrigue against him, and on October 17 he announced the final rupture. A few days later, Middleton and his colleagues were on their way back to London.*

---

* The British left Iran at dawn to avoid unpleasantness. There was a farewell picnic on the road west, towards the Iraqi border, with friends from the Belgian Embassy providing bacon and eggs and the Americans dry martinis. A government car caught up with the party and Middleton was asked to deliver a letter to the British people. He refused on the grounds that he was no longer an accredited representative. The Iranian official thrust the letter into Middleton's hand. Middleton dropped it. The official tried again, and this went on, in Middleton's words, until 'finally, I think about the nineteenth time, I let the envelope drop . . . and that was the end of that one, and off we went. Having drunk about two gallons of American dry martinis.' [17]

In January 1953 Mossadegh's delegated powers expired and he caused uproar by demanding a year's extension. Makki resigned his majles seat in protest and Kashani vowed in a letter to parliament to use his powers as speaker – to which post he had been elected in the summer of 1952 – to prevent discussion of the bill, 'which is in clear contravention of the constitution'.

Kashani's mistake was to assume that Mossadegh's popularity was a reflection of his own; while the reverse was true. Barely had the ink dried on the ayatollah's letter than pro-Mossadegh strikes broke out in the oil region and men in funeral shrouds gathered to march on Tehran. Telegrams flooded in from small towns the length and breadth of the country, and the slogan 'Death or Mossadegh!' crackled down the telephone wires. The following day the Tehran bazaar was shuttered and Baharestan Square filled with people holding the prime minister's picture aloft. All this was in support of Mossadegh's renewed powers, and Kashani and the others beat a hasty retreat. The ayatollah issued an emollient statement, Makki retracted his resignation, and 59 out of 67 deputies present in the chamber voted in favour of the extension.

In a game of chicken Mossadegh was supreme, but the strains of incessant combat had left their mark. Ghollamhossein was on hand every morning to test his father's blood pressure and inject him with vitamin supplements. Mossadegh's habitual sleeplessness had been exacerbated by the demands of office. His staff went home at 10 p.m., but he would answer the phone late into the night, dealing with such trivialities as the arrest of someone who had been out after the 11 p.m. curfew. He scarcely set foot in Ahmadabad during his premiership, let alone took a proper holiday.

He was seventy years old and there were rumours that he was suffering from a 'nervous disorder'.[18] Henderson took account of the prime minister's 'mental instability' when analysing their interminable, sometimes fractious conversations. By the time the British were expelled, even Middleton, who had some sympathy for Mossadegh, was noting a deterioration in the prime minister's mental state. Mossadegh was becoming 'more and more Messianic', believing that he was 'the only person who could handle the situation', and 'obsessive' about the wickedness of the AIOC. Wherever there was trouble, Mossadegh saw the hand of traitors and patsies. Middleton likened his attitude to a tendency that he had noted in the French (Middleton had grown up in France, and had a French wife), to say, '"We are betrayed!" when everything goes wrong. "Nous sommes trahis. Not us! Someone else has betrayed us".' He summed up Mossadegh's attitude as 'everyone go away, and we'll be very happy growing melons.'[19]

It would be remarkable if the struggle Mossadegh had been waging since 1949 had not taken a toll on such a taut, emotional personality, particularly since his distrustful nature led him to take vital decisions on his own. And now, in the winter of 1952–53, the challenges came in swarms. Civil servants were not being paid, the Tudeh was resurgent, the National Front was collapsing as a consequence of defections, and finally General Zahedi was suspected of stirring up the Bakhtiari rebellion that flared in February.

The senate had been dissolved and the general no longer enjoyed parliamentary immunity. He was arrested, along with the Rashidians (again) and some other troublemakers. But Mossadegh's government had never been any good at crackdowns. The prime minister had too much respect for the law to be a despot, and many senior men in the army and the police were of doubtful loyalty. Within days, Zahedi and the Rashidians walked free.

For Mossadegh, the 'someone else' who had betrayed him was the Shah. There is irony in this, for by this time the Shah had become the least threatening of his adversaries. Ignored by the government, spending his time playing canasta and reading detective novels, the Shah had lost his bravest ally, Princess Ashraf, to foreign exile. He had been slapped down so effectively that he had become the ideal constitutional monarch: quiet, shiny and denuded of authority. And yet there was an ominous sense that this state of affairs could not continue, what Middleton called a 'very insecure feeling of the end of an era . . . like being in a quicksand – you don't know where you're going . . . I imagine it felt like this in the French Revolution.'[20]

On February 19, 1953 Mossadegh went on the offensive,

complaining that the Court was fomenting unrest to destabilise him and threatening to resign . The Shah was suffering from psychological problems of his own, and Hossein Ala feared that he might have a 'complete nervous breakdown' in the face of this fresh attempt to bring him to a state of 'servile dependence'.[21] Thrown into a panic by the prime minister's threat, the Shah took the extraordinary step of offering to go abroad.

He and Sorayya had been planning a trip to consult European doctors on their inability to have children. Now that preparations were advanced, their absence could be passed off as innocuous and temporary – although Iranians' experience of monarchs going abroad under pressure was that they rarely came back. An ill, republican wind was blowing in from the West. In July 1952 Egypt's King Farouk had been sent into exile and the country declared a republic, dominated – as it would become clear – by an ambitious colonel, Gamal Abdel Nasser. Soon, Farouk remarked, there would only be five kings left in the world: the British and those belonging to a deck of cards. Was Mossadegh complicit in this scheme?

There is no evidence that he was. Had Mossadegh been a closet republican, he would now have done all he could to get the Shah out of the country. Instead, he advised him to stay, and it was the monarch himself who insisted on travel preparations continuing. They did not remain secret and, with the Shah's fate in the balance, Mossadegh's opponents sensed an opportunity.

On the morning of February 28, the date that had been set for the royal departure, rumours spread that Mossadegh was running the Shah out of the country. Kashani and a royalist ayatollah, Muhammad Behbehani, joined forces with the network of retired officers to generate a big loyalist crowd to encircle the palace and beg the Shah to stay. 'People, be warned!' Kashani declared. 'If the Shah goes, whatever we have will go with him. Rise up and stop him, and make him change his mind!' Groups yielding sticks patrolled the bazaar, shouting to the shopkeepers, 'Close up! Close up! The Shah has abdicated!'

Mossadegh had been summoned to the palace to wish the Shah godspeed. He came out again with the intention of hurrying home to receive Loy Henderson, who had unexpectedly requested an appointment, but found his way blocked by a large, hostile crowd. Helped by a royal employee, Mossadegh escaped by a side entrance and was driven home in time to receive the US ambassador.

By the early afternoon it was clear that the Shah would find it physically impossible to leave the Marble Palace. The loyal delegations threw themselves at his feet, the demonstrators grew more vociferous, and the royal resolve faltered. First the Shah sent Ala to tell the crowd that he had postponed his departure, but Ala was booed away and the Shah himself appeared to announce the news. Still the crowd was not satisfied, and, after more distraught visitors and loyal indignation in the street, the Shah informed his subjects through a radio broadcast that their 'pure and stainless emotions' had moved him to cancel his trip altogether.

Mossadegh had also been confined – but less benignly. Following Henderson's departure, 109 Palace Street was attacked by thicknecks and retired officers and their followers, who screamed for Mossadegh's death and tried to break into the compound through the iron entrance gate. Shinning up a plane tree overlooking the compound, one cut-throat showed his knife to a terrified servant inside, vowing, 'With this knife I'll finish you off and Dr Mossadegh!' Later the notorious thick-neck Brainless Shaban, an acolyte of Kashani, succeeded in breaking down the gate by ramming it with a jeep. Shaban had vowed to send Mossadegh's severed ear to the Shah, but nationalist students rushed to the scene, and they and the prime-ministerial guards were able to repulse the attackers.

By that time, Mossadegh was gone. Using a ladder, he had climbed over the wall with his son Ahmad and escaped to the army headquarters. Later that evening, deputies in the majles were astonished when the prime minister entered the chamber in pyjamas and dressing gown, the head of the army supporting his right arm, a retainer his left.[22] The account he gave to parliament of what had transpired showed that he regarded the events of that day as an orchestrated plot.

For the rest of his life, Mossadegh would insist that the Shah and Henderson had been in cahoots to bring him to the royal

palace, and then out again, in such a way that he would meet a
hostile crowd which would kill him. No doubt Mossadegh would
have been lynched had the crowd got to him, or if 109 Palace Street
had fallen with him inside, but this would have been the consequence not of a premeditated murder plot but of the rabble-rousing
of the ayatollahs. Mossadegh's insistence on a plot is of a piece
with Middleton's depiction of an exhausted, highly-strung prime
minister who saw no way out of the hole he had dug for himself
but to dig through to the other side.

Nothing we know about the Shah during this period suggests
that he would have dared condone a plot to kill Mossadegh, let
alone take part in one, and he was reported to have been shaken
by the sound of firing from the direction of Palace Street, and gave
orders for Mossadegh's house to be made secure. The Shah was
not an instigator of the events of February 28, but was caught up
in them to the extent that he was obliged to foreswear his plans
to depart. It is highly unlikely that Henderson would have connived
so directly in the skulduggery, and Mossadegh's later claim that the
ambassador had called him away from the palace on a matter of
trifling importance is not convincing. Henderson wanted to let
Mossadegh know how concerned he was by reports of the Shah's
imminent departure, and begged the prime minister to prevail on
him not to go.

Mossadegh got home at eleven o'clock that night to find his
family waiting up for him. Ghollamhossein recalled that

> he came up the stairs with difficulty and with the help of
> myself and [Ahmad]. He had not rested from five in the
> morning until that moment – around sixteen hours . . . he
> was not strong enough to stand. I had never seen my father
> so broken and shattered. As soon as he had entered his room,
> he sat on his bed and started crying.
>
> He said: 'Today I lost all hope. No longer do I trust that
> man. I swore allegiance to him in a way I did not do to his
> father . . . I thought that this young man, with all that
> happened to his father, would serve the people and the

country. How I counselled him, and told him to be with the people and not to lean on foreigners. In times of hardship it's the people who will support you . . . today, I realised what kind of a man he is! He lied to me. He deceived me and he wanted me killed . . .'[23]

# 13

# A Coup of his Own

The coup of August 19, 1953 challenges the axiom that history is about irresistible social movements and not the characters of individual men and women. An unlikely assortment of people commanded events, and were commanded by them, from the Shah to the CIA's agents on the ground, not forgetting the thick-necks, agitators and charlatans on the streets of the Persian capital. Their qualities left as deep an impression as any current running through Persian society. Above all, the coup was Mossadegh's coup, for it found its form according to his own personality, and it was defeated, and then resurrected, on the pitching, lunging foredeck of his conscience.

Whether it was true or not, the dominating belief for Mossadegh in the aftermath of February 28 was that the Shah wanted him and his government out of the way, even if it meant killing him, and that to concede would be to condemn nationalisation and the patriotic movement – indeed, Iran itself. In fact the monarch, however much associates like Ala conspired at the fringes, was more reluctant than ever to endorse an alternative candidate for prime minister, and he tried desperately to patch things up with Mossadegh. Well into the summer, the Shah refused to allow himself to become the figurehead for any attempt to remove the prime minister, and he was minded to accept a majles report interpreting the royal prerogatives in such a way as to emasculate himself politically. Time and again, the Shah showed Mossadegh that he wished to cooperate in his own disarmament. Time and again, he was snubbed and humiliated.

Mossadegh had not allowed the abolition of the Qajars or the fate of his daughter Khadijeh to dictate his attitude towards the Pahlavi dynasty. His politics had been blessedly free of personal resentment, to the extent that he had defended his great rival Seyyed Zia when the latter had been unfairly jailed, and he had been heavily criticised for not pursuing Qavam vigorously after the July uprising. Now, though, he believed that the Shah had crossed a line and become a traitor to his country and an ally of its foes. Inevitably, the prime minister turned against his sovereign.

Mossadegh now refused to see the Shah and it was a scandal. His failure to visit the Shah on the occasion of the Persian New Year was a grotesque breach of convention. A few weeks later Mossadegh sent Hossein Fatemi – who had recovered sufficiently from the assassination attempt against him to be named foreign minister as well as government spokesman – to see the monarch. Fatemi demanded the dismissal of Ala, whose conversations with anti-government plotters had come to light, and Ala was duly replaced with a Mossadeghist who issued a statement associating the Shah with the nationalist movement – itself a breach of the principle of royal impartiality.

'Now that the disagreement has been solved,' one newspaper asked hopefully, 'will the prime minister have an audience with the Shah, or not?'[1] The answer was negative, and rumours of a rift went around again. Mossadegh claimed that by visiting the Shah he would put himself in danger of assassination by the royal guard. But he also refused the Shah's offer to come and see him at Palace Street. Such a visit would 'damage his majesty's prestige'.[2]

Barely two years before, Muhammad-Reza Pahlavi had bullied a constituent assembly into giving him the power to sack govern-ments and prorogue parliament. Having got these powers, he was terrified to use them. The leftists surrounding Mossadegh did not hide their contempt for the throne. Queen Sorayya felt like a thief whenever she wanted to wear jewels, having to sign a chit and return them to an official after use. Ahmad Razavi warned that 'we cannot accept interference by the holders of ceremonial office, which is in clear contravention of the constitution.' Only one man answered this description, driven from the centre of politics to what Sorayya called his 'palace of solitude'. Trusting no one, sleeping with a revolver under his pillow, the Shah flew up to Ramsar, on the Caspian coast, or to the hill station of Kelardasht, where he refused to read the newspapers or listen to the radio, occupying himself with swimming and riding. In Tehran, all the while, the conflict hurtled on.

The Shah's isolation may have given Mossadegh grim satisfaction and pleased his radicals, but it was a heaven-sent opportunity for those who wanted to paint the prime minister as a closet republican driving the country into the arms of the communists. Although the people continued to adore Mossadegh, the idea that the monarchy might be abolished filled many with unease. The last serious effort in this direction, by Reza Khan, had provoked a popular reaction because people believed that the end of the Crown would signal the end of Islam and the beginning of Bolshevism. Mossadegh assured the Shah that he harboured no republican designs. Had he not sent the Shah the very Qoran upon which he had sworn fealty?

Violence in all its forms overwhelmed Iran during the spring and early summer of 1953. The bound and mutilated body of Mossadegh's chief of police, Brigadier Mahmud Afshartus, was found in the mountains outside Tehran, and two of the main suspects in the case, Baghai and Zahedi, were welcomed by Ayatollah Kashani into the majles, where they took sanctuary. Parliament was now the centre of an epic struggle to decide the country's fate, with obstructions to prevent a quorum, fisticuffs on the floor and the anti-government deputies requesting arms to protect themselves.

The accusations and counter-accusations grew more and more extreme: the 'diabolical' Mossadegh, as bad as Genghis Khan, was planning to close down the majles and end the dynasty; he should be committed to an asylum; the government intended to massacre its opponents; a bloodbath was in store.

Into these turbid waters waded another competitor, sensing an opportunity – the banned Tudeh Party. The communists had profited from Mossadegh's democratic indulgence over the past two years, building up front organisations and impressing the CIA with their discipline and size. This may not have displeased Mossadegh, for by depicting himself as a bulwark against an ever-present communist threat, he had hoped to retain American support. Now, though, he had lost key anti-communist allies, such as Kashani and Baghai, whose supporters had battled the Tudeh in the streets.

Some of the prime minister's left-leaning allies may have secretly favoured a tacit alliance with the Tudeh against the army and the Court. To such an alliance, the Tudeh could bring huge manpower, discipline and an invaluable network of agents in the army. On the other hand, the danger of shackling the government to an illegal party following orders from Moscow was obvious. The Tudeh had made inroads in factories, schools and government offices. Its military network boasted some 600 officers in the police and armed forces. Its newspapers had attacked Mossadegh from the first day of his premiership. What if the Tudeh overtures were a trap?

The limited and wary cooperation that the nationalists and the Tudeh now embarked upon would have a decisive effect on Mossadegh's relations with the US. In November 1952, American voters had ejected Truman's Democrats in favour of the Republican Dwight Eisenhower. The new president was a gloves-off cold warrior who believed that America was pitted against 'an implacable enemy whose avowed objective is world domination', and that 'long-standing American concepts of fair play must be reconsidered'.[3] Fair play had gone by the board at home, where Senator Joe McCarthy was directing a persecution of suspected communists in the State Department and across national life. It was a good moment for a muscular assertion of American values abroad.

The incoming secretary of state was John Foster Dulles. At the same time his younger brother Allen was named director of the CIA. Grandsons of one secretary of state, nephews of another, these Washington insiders had been wartime spies and had more than a passing interest in Iran. Foster feared that the country was a prime target for communist expansion, and Allen knew the Shah through his business contacts in the Middle East. Neither brother needed much persuasion that Mossadegh was a dangerous madman tipping his country into the abyss, and that he needed to go.

The change in US administration was also significant for those British officials hoping for decisive action against Mossadegh. With the expulsion of British diplomats and spies from Tehran, America's enthusiastic participation was now essential if a covert operation was to succeed. Travelling to Washington to put the case for intervention, the MI6 officer Monty Woodhouse played to the American gallery, downplaying the importance of Britain's oil interests and dwelling on the dangers of communism.[4] In fact, most British officials took a much less dramatic view of the Tudeh than the Americans, and Churchill would soon tire of what he regarded as Foster Dulles' 'obsession' with communism in Persia to the detriment of British interests. 'Mossadegh had done all he could to ruin his country,' Churchill's private secretary would recall, 'but there were no signs that Persia was nearer Communism.'[5] The irony was that Mossadegh had done as much as anyone to fix American attention on the communist bogey, even though he, like the British, believed it to be exaggerated.

Building that bogey into a terrifying monster would be a key part of the coup, as it now began to be conceived by the CIA and MI6. From their earlier operations to counter Soviet influence, the CIA had a network of assets in Iran, who were being used to organise attacks on Tudeh rallies and to blacken the party's name by showing that it was a creature of the Soviets. To these agents would now be added Britain's assets, notably the Rashidian brothers. Using a massive campaign of alarmist propaganda, and fomenting chaos to demonstrate that Mossadegh was no longer in control, the coup planners aimed to instil panic that the country was sliding towards a communist takeover.

There was a parallel, overt campaign: to impress on Mossadegh as well as his enemies that the Iranian government no longer enjoyed American goodwill. Eisenhower took a month to reply to Mossadegh's plea for 'prompt and effective aid' to stave off 'great economic and political difficulties', and the terms he used were cold and unsympathetic. The release of the exchange into the public domain caused Mossadegh much embarrassment. Loy Henderson signalled that he was washing his hands of Mossadegh by going abroad indefinitely, while Iranian officials of all kinds found that the US government representatives they were used to dealing with had become much less friendly. It was all part of a campaign to unnerve the government, and it worked.

Mossadegh had never believed that the communists would be able to challenge him, and he boasted that it was he who manipulated the Tudeh, not the other way around. He was right, but events in Tehran were being manipulated to give a different impression.

To mark the anniversary of the July uprising against Qavam, pro-government nationalists planned a rally in Baharestan Square, but the Tudeh also wanted to take part. Mixing the two groups was considered risky, so Mossadegh agreed that separate rallies should be held, one in the morning for the nationalists, and a second one after lunch for 'other groups' – meaning the Tudeh.

These arrangements only strengthened the impression that the Tudeh had gone from being an enemy of the prime minister to an ominous and threatening element of his support base. The Tudeh rally was by far the better organised and attended. In the words of Kennett Love, a correspondent for the *New York Times*, the nationalist rally mustered a 'straggling assembly of a few thousand demonstrators and idlers' which broke up an hour ahead of schedule. The Tudeh, on the other hand, 'turned out a vibrantly disciplined throng . . . the capacious square and the approaching avenues appeared to be paved with faces as far as the eye could see.' Observing the discipline and size of the Tudeh rally, one of the party leaders asked Love, '"Do you think they can refuse our support much longer? You have seen for yourself how small they are and how big we are."'[6]

'The Tudeh have put us to shame,' agreed one of Mossadegh's most astute supporters, Khalil Maleki, himself a former communist, and the effect of the anniversary on public opinion outside Iran was as he feared.[7] In Washington, Foster Dulles publicly deplored 'the growing activity of the illegal communist party', which appeared to be 'tolerated by the Iranian Government'.[8] Tolerated it was, for Mossadegh refused to 'wage war on the beliefs of the people', and although Soviet foreign policy had been in limbo since Stalin's death in March, the two countries were now negotiating Iranian financial claims which had been outstanding since the war.

All this was useful for the CIA propaganda operation, which was now working with impressive precision. The man in charge was Donald Wilber, a Princeton scholar who had a background in the Office of Strategic Studies, the forerunner of the CIA, and would go on to write a hagiography of Reza Shah.[9] Articles commissioned by Wilber appeared with miraculous rapidity in the Tehran papers, and several new publications appeared in the spring and summer of 1953, all harping on an anti-government theme. One newspaper proprietor was extended what Wilber described as a 'personal loan' of $45,000, while a stream of 'black' propaganda emanated from local stooges posing as Tudeh enforcers, who threatened mullahs with 'savage punishment' if they stood against Mossadegh. There were attacks on mosques and rumours that the prime minister was secretly a Jew.[10] It was not pretty.

By now Zahedi had begun to receive the $60,000 which he had been allocated in order to build up the military and tribal network that would propel him to power. (This sum would be doubled as the coup approached.) In an astonishing act of negligence, Mossadegh had allowed the general to be escorted safely out of the majles in July, upon which he went into hiding in preparation for the coup. But Zahedi proved a less accomplished networker than his CIA contacts had anticipated, and they ended up having to build a military support base for him. This was difficult, for the armed forces were split between the Mossadeghists – notably the head of the army, General Taqi Riyahi, and most of the Tehran commanders – and the royalists, including the Royal Guard and some forty officers commanding units in the capital. These officers would in the end provide the military firepower for the coup.

That still left the key man: the Shah himself, who would be a figurehead for the plotters and provide the legal basis for Zahedi to be appointed prime minister. But the only constant thing about the Shah was his inconstancy. He would not lend his support to a coup until he was convinced that it had the personal support of Eisenhower and Churchill – his terror of the old 'hidden hand' still induced palpitations that the British sought his removal. The Shah needed to be chivvied into supporting an operation that could, if it failed, cost him his throne or his life. He was an 'unaccountable character', mused Allen Dulles, capable of pulling out 'at the last minute'.[11]

The exiled Princess Ashraf, kicking her heels in France, might be able to goad her brother into action, and agents were dispatched to convince her to return to Iran and speak to him. This too was risky, for Ashraf had been driven out of the country at Mossadegh's insistence and was under suspicion of siphoning money from a public bank. But the princess more than made up for her brother's lack of spunk. Besides, the MI6 agent who met her in Paris was brandishing a mink coat – at which 'her eyes lit up'.

Two days later, Ashraf was on a flight to Tehran, where she was met by a friend and whisked off to Saadabad. The nationalist and Tudeh press reacted violently to the news that she was home without permission, and Mossadegh forced the Shah to call for the 'severest measures' in case she transgressed against 'court rules' again. During her ten-day stay in the royal compound, after which she returned to Paris, Ashraf managed to get a morale-stiffening letter to the Shah, and even to see him, though the siblings feared eavesdroppers and spoke in guarded platitudes.[13]

Still the Shah wrung his hands; rarely can a monarch have been so resigned to his own extinction. The CIA arranged another envoy, General Norman Schwarzkopf, who had commanded the Iranian gendarmerie and who knew the Shah (and whose son, of the same name, would expel Saddam Hussein from Kuwait in 1991). But there was uproar in Tehran when the general arrived, and his conversation with the Shah was nerve-wracking and inconclusive. Other methods were employed to stiffen the monarch. A message came from Churchill: 'We should be very sorry to see the Shah lose his powers or leave his post or be driven out.' To avoid bugging devices and eavesdroppers, the Shah held covert conversations in the palace gardens (not too near the trees), or in the middle of a ballroom. Even now he wavered. Finally, on August 1, he agreed to receive in secret an American claiming to speak for both Eisenhower and Churchill: the coup-master himself, Kermit 'Kim' Roosevelt.

Bespectacled, balding and somewhat cherubic, Roosevelt was the grandson of the 'rough rider' president, Theodore. Born in Argentina, where his father had business interests, he had left a junior position in the Harvard History Department to join the Office of Strategic Studies, and ran its Arab operations in the war. Roosevelt had disapproved of British policy in the region, accusing his MI6 counterparts of 'shoddy cynical intrigues' and of cultivating mediocre local allies.[14] Not that Roosevelt disapproved in principle of the dark arts; his PhD was entitled 'Propaganda Techniques in the English Civil War' and he was known in the CIA as a 'bold Easterner' – an Ivy Leaguer of private means urging cloak-and-dagger operations while the policy wonks churned out learned papers. The British double agent Kim Philby described Roosevelt as 'well-educated rather than intellectual . . . the last person you would expect to be up to the neck in dirty tricks'.[15]

Now thirty-seven, Roosevelt was the head of the CIA's Middle East Department, and charged with carrying out the coup plan. He entered Iran on July 19 under an assumed name and began his activities in leisurely fashion from the house of another agent in the foothills. In between meetings with CIA and SIS contacts, Roosevelt drank Johnnie Walker, sunned himself by the pool and worked up a sweat on the diplomatic tennis circuit, almost giving himself away with the cry, 'Oh, *Roosevelt!*' whenever he missed an easy shot. To undo the damage, he recalled later, 'I did my best to pass myself off as a black-hearted reactionary Republican to whom 'Roosevelt', meaning FDR, was a heartfelt obscenity.'[16]

Shortly after midnight on August 2, Roosevelt was admitted in great secrecy to the compound at Saadabad. The Shah was friendly but wary. Roosevelt would exert himself over several meetings to persuade his host that the US government would not sit idly by while Iran turned communist, and that if he, the Shah, did not participate in the plan to save his country, he would be overtaken by events. The Shah was already being strong-armed by other secret assignees, including Assadollah Rashidian and Zahedi's swashbuckling son, Ardeshir. Arguably, though, it was Mossadegh himself who did more than anyone to convince him to act.

The prime minister was a mixture of visionary and fusspot. He had failed to solve the oil problem because he had not identified the best deal that was available to Iran, far less pursued it. After the failure of his talks in Washington he had blustered and time-wasted and hoped against hope, squandering America's goodwill, and as the dismal process went on so the discomfort of his own position increased until there was no deal, however beneficial, to which he could put his name.

By contrast, in choppy domestic waters, Mossadegh was accustomed to taking decisions on a basis of complete self-reliance before unveiling them to an astonished public. This formula had brought him remarkable success. His tenure (if one discounts the brief Qavam interregnum) was already the longest-lasting since the fall of Reza Shah. It had survived extraordinarily determined opposition. Only Mossadegh's genius as a popular leader explains his longevity.

Now, in the early summer of 1953, he sensed the majles falling to the enemy and his solution, as ever, was to take succour from the people whose exclusive representative he had become. He had raised a storm by demanding plenary powers and then insisting they be renewed. Now he would deal with the chamber.

It started on July 14, when twenty-seven deputies professing their loyalty to Mossadegh resigned their seats at his behest; by July 28, the number had risen to fifty-six. This was more than enough to stop the majles from convening, but Mossadegh also wanted to end the parliamentary immunity of those opposition deputies, like Baghai, who carried on plotting against him. 'In a democratic and constitutional country', he told a radio audience, 'there is no law that is higher than the will of the people.'

Mossadegh's plan was brutal. He would ask the people, through a plebiscite, to dissolve parliament. If the answer was yes, elections to the eighteenth majles would take place. If it was no, the prime minister would walk away and the nation would have to get itself out of the mess he had made for it.

Mossadegh's spoliation of the majles is presented as a blot on his character and career, and needs examination. The referendum was won, of course, by a landslide and with an unprecedented turnout. But the prime minister was exploiting his personal magnetism at the expense of democracy. With the opposition boycotting the vote, it was more reverential bow than referendum. Like an alchemist Mossadegh converted the national will into law, but it would not have occurred to his constituents to dissolve the majles; the people's 'will' had been concocted by Mossadegh himself. What if 'the people' had demanded war with Russia or that the Bahais be herded into camps? Would that too have been the highest law?

In a democracy, the legislature is the place where the urges of the nation are consummated or rejected according to propriety and the constitution. Now there was no legislature: just the leader and the people, covering each other in kisses. It was possible that Mossadegh would take exception to the next chamber and get the people to close that one too. An ominous circle was being formed.

The Mossadeghist hard kernel – the oil-adviser Kazem Hassibi, along with the prime minister's legal experts, Karim Sanjabi and Ali Shayegan – came to 109 Palace Street to protest. His support in the majles was stronger than he supposed, they said. Referendums were not recognised by the constitution. How could he circumvent the Shah, who alone was empowered to dissolve parliament? But the prime minister was impervious to their arguments. When Sanjabi proposed that he ask the Shah to dissolve parliament, Mossadegh snapped, 'It looks as though you have smoked hashish this morning.'[17]

By shutting the majles he tied one of his own hands behind his back, and put his supporters in a terrible bind. A second delegation had come to 109 Palace Street, this one led by Khalil Maleki, and was similarly rebuffed. Seeing that further discussion was useless,

Maleki rose to his feet and exclaimed, 'Dr Mossadegh! This road that you are on leads to hell, but we will follow you there!'[18]

There is a shelf-full of arguments against Mossadegh's assault on the seventeenth majles. Crucially, there is one even stronger argument in its favour, which can be made with some assurance from our distant, historical perspective. Looking at the records – the official CIA history of the coup; the Foreign Office files in south-west London; the valuable work done by American scholars such as Mark Gasiorowski – it is clear that Mossadegh's government was by now the object of pitiless acts of war by two hostile powers. The crippling embargo; the bombardment of disinformation; the conspiracies to riot, murder and abduct; it is not necessary to send armies in order to wage a war, and there is no glossing the ruthlessness of the Anglo-American campaign.

The majles was a crucial part of this. Two months earlier, in June, the CIA had been allotted a large weekly budget of $11,000 to purchase the cooperation of Iranian MPs. By the time of the dissolution, Mossadegh claimed that thirty deputies had been bought and that it was only a matter of time before ten more went over – enough to threaten the government. Sitting MPs plotted murders and kidnappings whilst hiding behind their parliamentary immunity.[19] In these circumstances, it is hard to argue that Mossadegh's pre-emptive action was disproportionate. It might be considered mild.

His foes screamed that he was a dictator. If so, he was a shockingly dilatory one. Faced with a choice between stability and freedom, he veered unerringly towards the latter. On the eve of the coup, most of those who had been arrested for trying to kill Mossadegh in his home the previous February were once again at liberty. Mossadegh continued to give most un-dictatorial latitude to the Tehran newspapers. The prime minister had been consumed by a 'syphilitic madness', said one paper.[20] Another published a call for armed insurrection. These and other outrages went unanswered.

There is not one sole reason for the government's failure to protect itself. The unreliability of the security forces, some of whom were in league with the coup-makers, is a partial explanation. The elimination of Brigadier Afshartus had deprived the government of a canny police chief. The torpor of the legal system was well known. The main factor, however, was Mossadegh himself. The prime minister had not stopped believing in the importance of an individual's freedom to the freedom of a nation. He never would. Liberty of expression could not be taken from a group of citizens, for the country had achieved independence under its shade-giving branches. Even as the Tudeh's activists flexed their muscles and Khalil Maleki implored Mossadegh to lock them up, he refused. 'You say they should be jailed, but who should jail them? It's the job of the law and the judiciary.' And the judiciary was not up to the task.

The main objection to Mossadegh's gambit in closing the majles is not moral, but practical. It turned out to be a grave miscalculation which helped bring the government down. Even allowing for Mossadegh's pessimistic assessment of the support he enjoyed in the chamber, at least half the seats were still occupied by his supporters and he could probably have hung on if a vote of confidence had been held. Even more important, supportive deputies would have been able to react to any coup attempt by turning the majles into a nationalist fortress. They had done so enough times in the past.

Now these loyalists were scattered, some of them to their constituencies outside Tehran, where they expected elections imminently. The opposition MPs, by contrast, had been encouraged by the CIA to dispute the legality of the referendum, and they continued to plot.

The referendum was held in Tehran on August 3, the day after Kim Roosevelt's first meeting with the Shah. On August 4, President Eisenhower declared acidly that Mossadegh had 'moved toward getting rid of his parliament, and of course he was in that move supported by the Communist party of Iran'. In Washington, the Iranian ambassador was denied access to senior US diplomats. America could hardly have made its position clearer.

On August 10 the referendum was held in provincial towns. Back in the United States, Donald Wilber and his team of propagandists had spent the intervening week in overdrive, producing dozens of articles and anti-Mossadegh cartoons for publication in Tehran. Kashani and the others raved. Finally, around the time of the provincial vote, the Shah came off the fence.

To Muhammad-Reza Pahlavi, subject to immense pressure from Roosevelt, Assadollah Rashidian and the army plotters who came to see him, it now seemed that Mossadegh would stop at nothing to obtain absolute power. Mossadegh gave every impression of mounting his final challenge, but in closing the majles he unwittingly offered the Shah an opportunity to get rid of him while staying within the law. In the absence of a majles the Shah would be acting within the constitution if he fired his prime minister. It was this, as much as the urging of Roosevelt and the others, that gave the Shah the courage to act.

On August 10, the Shah told Assadollah Rashidian that he would sign two royal orders, one sacking Mossadegh and the other appointing Zahedi, and that he would keep himself out of the way while the coup took place. There was elation in the plotters' camp. By the evening of August 13, Colonel Nematullah Nassiri of the royal guard was in possession of the two imperial orders bearing the Shah's signature. The Shah and his Queen were at Kelardasht. But there was now an inexplicable delay, and the CIA lost contact with Zahedi's people. In Wilber's recollection, 'No more news came in from Tehran on the fourteenth, and there was nothing that either the station or Headquarters could do except to wait for action to begin.'[21]

# 14

# *Mussy Duck Shoot*

Shortly before midnight on August 15, Hossein Fatemi was brushing his teeth when his wife let out a piercing scream. Rushing out of the bathroom, the foreign minister found that his home was full of soldiers, two of whom had trained their rifles on him. Fatemi was taken in an army truck to a guardhouse in the Saadabad compound, where he was joined by a second member of the cabinet and another senior Mossadeghist – both still in their pyjamas. Fatemi was told that he would be executed at dawn. He asked one of his jailers, 'Who could have put you up to this?' The answer came, 'Who else but the Shah?'[1]

The plotters had failed to arrest their principal target, General Riyahi, because he had got wind of what was happening, and had left his house shortly before a military jeep arrived to pick him up. Zahedi's men had cut telephone lines and occupied the exchange, but Riyahi was able to deploy more troops at strategic points. By the time Colonel Nassiri of the royal guard arrived at Palace Street, followed by a large force with which to arrest Mossadegh, the defenders were ready.

At around 1.30 a.m., standing at the door of the prime minister's house, Nassiri handed over the Shah's decree to be taken in to Mossadegh. Twenty minutes later, he was given a receipt in the prime minister's hand, but by that time Riyahi had been informed, and Nassiri was arrested. Nassiri's forces had also been surrounded. The royal guard was immediately disbanded.

Mossadegh had known about the coup before it happened. An army informant had been giving him regular information by phone, and he had strengthened the defences at 109 Palace Street. That same night he had been roused by a call from a concerned citizen telling him of suspicious troop movements.[2] Following Nassiri's arrest, the cabinet and other prime-ministerial allies were raised from their beds and converged on 109 Palace Street. Hossein Fatemi was freed at 5 a.m. and went home. Then he too came to the prime minister's house. At 7 a.m. it was announced on the radio that a coup attempt had been foiled. 'The government is in complete control of the situation,' ran the announcement, 'and a number of treacherous and misguided people have been arrested, and will shortly pay the price for their anti-national actions.'

In the US Embassy a few blocks away, Kermit Roosevelt heard the announcement and felt close to despair.[3] General Zahedi had spent a sleepless night monitoring events. Now, rather than take up the reins of government, as he had hoped to do, he watched as pro-government tanks rumbled through the streets. In a meeting with his son and other allies, he spoke of leaving Tehran and mounting a resistance in some distant part of the country.

The Shah was told by long-wave radio what had happened. He and Sorayya flew by small airplane to Ramsar, where a larger craft was standing by. Soon, the royal couple were in the air again, heading out of the country. In his haste to leave, the Shah had omitted to put on his socks. The Queen was distraught; her beloved Skye Terrier, Tony, had also been left behind.

In Tehran the night curfew ended and people tried to come to terms with what had happened. With amazing suddenness, the country had emerged from a dismal shaft of strife and confusion and the horizon seemed without limit. People gathered in the streets to discuss events and speculate about the future. They hung around the cafés so as not to miss the radio announcements. The putschists were being rounded up and rumours flew of their imminent execution. If the coup had been successful, the people reasoned, Mossadegh and his allies would now be up against a wall; justice must be meted out to the coup-makers commensurate to their crime. Around lunchtime, a new stir: the Shah had landed in Baghdad.

Mossadegh now faced the task of his life. The departure of the Shah had left a hole in Iran that he could fill as he saw fit. The country's system of government; its orientation in foreign affairs – all could be planned anew. But would it be wise, or right, to do so? Economically, the country was on its knees. The true statesman must keep his eye on the future. Iran would eventually have to find a market for its oil, and that market could only be in the West. The prime minister's job was to narrow the possibilities and take control. He must calm his excited supporters and prevent the Tudeh from manipulating events. He must guide the country to the next stage. Above all, he must beware any attempt to revive the coup.

A younger and fitter man might have felt liberated by the unexpected turn of events, and come forward with joy. But Mossadegh was exhausted by the cares of office, and the United States, his greatest hope of succour, had abandoned him. Furthermore, Mossadegh had not changed, even if the circumstances had. He had made his oath to preserve the Crown in all sincerity and could not lightly abandon it.

The first challenge came early on August 16 from those who were closest to him. When Hossein Fatemi arrived at Palace Street after being freed, his fury could not be assuaged. Fatemi had got home that morning to find his house ransacked and his wife inconsolable. She had been roughly handled by the soldiers and their eleven-month-old child had been woken and subjected to a bizarre interrogation. These were the images that Fatemi carried into the first confabulation of the new era. He and many of the other men in the prime minister's first-floor meeting room had not slept the previous night. They were tired and emotional.

Suddenly, voices were raised and Fatemi's carried through the clamour, down to the journalists below: 'It's all right for you sitting here to speak about observing the law! You didn't have the bitter experience of watching the Royal Guard invade my house . . . if you had only felt the villainy and lack of mercy in these coup-makers, you wouldn't react in this way!'[4]

Fatemi had been addressing Mossadegh. He was insisting that the detained coup-makers be executed. Others agreed. Anything less would be a dangerous indulgence. But Mossadegh was firm; the law must take its course. Later on Fatemi told Muhammad-Ali Safari, his correspondent at *Bakhtar-e Emrooz*, 'The old man bangs on about the law, and I am afraid he is going to get us all killed.'[5] Appalled at the invasion of his family life, desperate for revenge, Fatemi spent the next four days trying to force the prime minister's hand, and his goal went way beyond retributive justice. He wanted regime change. He wanted a republic.

Fatemi hated the Shah. He regarded the monarch as a lackey of the British, and the British, ultimately, as responsible for the attempt on his own life by the Warriors of Islam, which had left him in constant pain. On August 15, Fatemi had the satisfaction of ordering the staff of the Iranian Embassy in Baghdad to have no contact with the Shah when he landed there. Three days later, when the royal couple flew on to Rome, the Iranian ambassador refused to hand over the keys to a car that Queen Sorayya had left there on an earlier trip. These insults were designed to show Muhammad-Reza Pahlavi that he was no longer Shah of Iran. They would not be forgotten.

The August 16 edition of *Bakhtar-e Emrooz* was a vessel into which Fatemi poured every drop of venom. Addressing the Shah, he wrote, 'You looted the wealth of a nation . . . and now, like a thief or a whore, you use the black of night to launch a coup, before going to Kelardasht to take your ease.'[6] Late that afternoon came a victory rally reeking of republicanism. One after another, the Mossadeghists took the microphone, and Shayegan quipped, 'The delicacy that should have come to Tehran has gone to Baghdad.' The crowd shrieked, 'Death to the treacherous Shah!' and 'Let the infamous Pahlavi Court be obliterated!'

Then it was Fatemi's turn. The Shah, he thundered, had 'wanted to go to war with God. He wanted to go to war with the people and the society which are the embodiment of the will of God. But God slammed him to the floor . . .' The crowd raised their hands to approve 'motions' to punish swiftly those who had been behind the failed coup, and to convene a regency council to determine the country's future.

Now there was a kind of madness. There was no parliament.

The Shah was gone. The prime minister was in his bunker, holding meeting after meeting. Politics had one place to go: the street. That evening, Shayegan and Razavi came back to Mossadegh's house, where the prime minister and his interior minister, Ghollamhossein Sadiqi, had been informed about what had been said in Baharestan Square. Sadiqi was furious. What, he demanded, had they hoped to achieve with such inflammatory speeches? Sadiqi was in touch with the chief of police, and the news was of riot and disorder. Did that not play into the hands of the government's adversaries?[7] Now, more than ever, the people needed to stay calm and alert. Mossadegh was silent. Shayegan and Razavi went out to try to restore order. But control was already slipping away.

The crowd in Baharestan Square had been intoxicated by the speeches. Now they roamed in groups, shouting slogans against the Shah. The attacks began. The window of a photographer's studio was shattered because it had a big picture of the Shah. Then the studio was looted. Fearing the mob, shopkeepers tore down their own royal pictures and hurled them into the road. Groups with picks and shovels started hacking at statues of the Pahlavis.[8] Some arrests were made but in general the forces of law and order were conspicuous by their absence. Indeed, that evening, the security forces had no orders to suppress the demonstrations.

Now Mossadegh needed his crowd-managing heavyweights: Baghai, Haerizadeh and the network of Ayatollah Kashani. During the uprising against Qavam they had shown how to fill the streets with people, denying space to the opposition. The Tudeh had been elbowed aside and nationalists had protected the royal statuary. But now, in the flush of victory, crowd management was nowhere on the government's list of priorities. The battle was on to design the new Iran.

It was not Mossadegh's battle of choice. A de-fanged Shah had been useful. His continuing presence had been reassuring to the Americans and was a message to the Soviet Union that Iran would not go communist. Besides, Mossadegh continued to believe that a constitutional monarchy was the best system of government. But now the Shah had fled after conspiring against his own prime minister; it would be hard to put the case for his return. In the meeting room at 109 Palace Street, Fatemi and Razavi and some of the others demanded a republic. Others would be content with the abolition of the Pahlavi dynasty. The constitution provided for a regency council in the Shah's absence, but it was the Shah's job to appoint one. Should the government do his job for him – or the people, through a referendum?

Between August 15 and 19 these questions were examined minutely by the prime minister and his coterie, and the spectre of a republic would not fade away. Fatemi, no doubt on Mossadegh's orders, declared that a republic was not on the agenda.[9] No one believed him. A visit by the nation's Dr Johnson, Ali Akbar Dehkhoda, fuelled speculation that he was to be the republic's first president. The reporter Safari asked him the purpose of his visit. 'To enquire after [Dr Mossadegh's] health,' the ancient lexicographer replied, and shuffled away.

Each day brought fresh meetings that no one wanted to talk about. Sanjabi and Shayegan and the others came out of Palace Street and joked awkwardly with reporters. Agreement was imminent – on what, they would not say. Platitudes gushed forth. Sentences trailed off unfinished. On August 18, Safari reported discussions on the composition of a regency council but did not know what the council would deliberate. Hossein Fatemi went about with an expression of thunder. Safari begged his permission to write in favour of a republic in the pages of *Bakhtar-e Emrooz*, and Fatemi replied, 'Don't be so obstinate! I don't have the final say, and he who has the final say isn't satisfied yet.'[10]

Much legitimate criticism has been directed at Mossadegh for absorbing himself in legal niceties as the ground was laid for his overthrow, but it is worth recalling that he faced a constitutional crisis of the greatest magnitude, and he was convinced that its resolution would determine the future position of Iran in the world. In particular, Mossadegh was guided by his desire not to isolate himself completely from the Eisenhower administration. He only had one foreign policy, to lean on the United States, and even now he hoped to preserve it.

Loy Henderson flew in to set him right. On August 17, after an absence of almost three months, the US ambassador arrived in Tehran to help resurrect the coup, and Mossadegh's decision to receive him speaks volumes for his desperation. Military investigators had found proof of American involvement in the failed coup. The commander of the US military assistance mission had tried to persuade General Riyahi to defect. Kennett Love and a second American correspondent were acting as Zahedi's unofficial public-relations team. What more evidence did he need that America was trying to destroy him?

When he received Henderson at 6 p.m. on August 18, Mossadegh still regarded the US as the most likely saviour of his government. He was probably hoping for crumbs of comfort and some guidance on future constitutional arrangements. He got neither. The meeting came at the moment when, in American eyes, the capital seemed to be falling to the Tudeh, and Henderson made it clear that the United States regarded Zahedi as the country's lawful prime minister, and the Shah as the rightful head of state. Convinced, at last, that the US was implacably hostile to him, Mossadegh vowed that his government would resist to the last man, even if its members were 'run over by British and American tanks'.[11]

Everything now suggested that the Pahlavis were doomed. The Shah's brothers were under house arrest. His portrait had been removed from ministries and his name erased from the staff college oath. Mossadegh's later claim that he intended to urge the Shah to return is far-fetched. Any attempt to bring him back would have caused mutiny in the government. The Shah himself would certainly not have come. On August 18, the royal couple arrived in Rome, and the Shah was contemplating a new life in the United States.

At dawn the following morning, the prime minister summoned Sadiqi, the interior minister, and ordered preparations to be made for nationwide elections to a three-man regency council. It was the first step to a regime that Mossadegh did not want but which he was powerless to resist. Iran was a republic in all but name.

★　★　★

Friend and foe alike have recognised that Kim Roosevelt and his fellow agents engineered a remarkable reversal in fortunes between August 15 and August 19. They turned defeat into triumph and their methods would enter the training manuals. The Harvard tie and tennis-playing have bred the idea that Roosevelt was something of a 'gentleman spy', but his methods were anything but chivalrous. Roosevelt's initial plan to divest Iran of its government was relatively modest and would probably have led to a few salutary executions. His second was hideous. It called for havoc on a vast scale and maximum loss of life, and contained ample provision for civil war.

The plotters' military network had been damaged in the wake of August 15, but the main players were at large. Zahedi had kept copies of the Shah's edicts appointing him and dismissing Mossadegh, and herein lay an opportunity. The government had not mentioned the edicts in their version of events, but the plotters would use them to show that Mossadegh was a rebel against the constitution. Second, they would whip up public fears that the country was about to fall to the Tudeh – and Islam with it. Finally, the military network would be expanded to include the commanders of garrisons outside Tehran, who would prepare to march on the capital. Roosevelt disregarded orders that he should abandon the project and leave Iran. The project, he concluded, was 'not quite dead'.

Over the next three days it was brilliantly revived under a draconian regime of secrecy. This time, there would be no leaks. Publicity for the Shah's edicts was arranged in the American and the anti-government domestic press, and copies handed out among army units. A declaration in Zahedi's name called on all Iranian officers to be ready to sacrifice themselves for God and the Shah. The CIA had handed its hirelings tens of thousands of dollars to generate propaganda, and to ensure that crowds would riot through the capital. Some of this money found its way to the royalist Ayatollah Behbehani, and some, perhaps, to Kashani.*

---

* According to the American historian Mark Gasiorowski, the CIA gave $10,000 to an associate of the ayatollah, 'to give to Kashani to organise demonstrations. It is not clear whether Kashani . . . received this money and, if so, whether he used it for this purpose.'[13]

The coup-makers played on the perennial fear of chaos, and in this they received valuable aid from an unlikely source: the Tudeh Party. Thanks to its network of army officers, the Tudeh had known in advance of the army plot against Mossadegh, and one of its leaders may have given him warning. After August 15 all the available intelligence suggested that Zahedi would retreat to the south of the country, and the party turned its attention back to politics. The communists believed that Iran was on the cusp of change and that they must not be left behind. If there was to be a republic, the Tudeh, not the nationalists, must bring it into being.

August 17 dawned, hot and torrid, and groups of Tudeh supporters came into the streets wearing their regulation white shirts and shouting for a 'democratic republic'. This was code for a Soviet client state of the kind that had been set up in Czechoslovakia and Bulgaria – the communists were showing their hand. Tudeh supporters gathered at the street corners and delivered passionate speeches. Then they rampaged through the city. Signs were torn down (Churchill Street was a predictable casualty), Reza Shah's mausoleum was attacked and his statue upended with a crane.[12] The evening papers were full of pictures of stricken royal bronzes.

No one was more delighted than Kim Roosevelt. It was 'the best thing we could have hoped for.' The next day there was more rioting and the nationalists and the communists were in violent competition to rid the city of all signs of the monarchy. Mossadegh gave the order that the surviving statues of Reza Shah be removed in an orderly fashion, a decision he later justified on the grounds that he could not oppose the will of the people. Goaded to a frenzy by Roosevelt's *agents provocateurs*, the Tudeh smashed the windows of mosques, ransacked the headquarters of a Mossadeghist party and bayed for the expulsion of US diplomats. The *New York Times* correspondent Kennett Love was nearly pulled from a taxi-cab and lynched by demonstrators fresh from toppling a statue of Reza Shah. Love was not the only American to be attacked, and it was all, of course, grist to Roosevelt's mill.

Through their actions on August 18, the Tudeh showed that they considered the ban on the party to be inoperative. State factories were paralysed by demonstrations to demand the release of communists from jail. The party's banned organ was being touted openly and cadres in Sepah Square, a short distance from Palace Street, unfurled a large banner which read, 'Long Live the Tudeh Party of Iran.'

The impression was of a rampant Tudeh on a collision course with all that traditional Iran held dear, and the coup-makers were egging the pudding. Pro-Shah newspapers played up the communist menace and mullahs received threatening letters in red ink, purportedly from the Tudeh. In fact, they had been forged in the house of Ayatollah Behbehani.[14]

After lunch, Mossadegh was alarmed enough to order the security forces to stop the demonstrations. He also gave instructions for anyone calling for a republic to be pursued judicially. With these decisions Mossadegh signalled that he would not become hostage to the Tudeh and its demands. But the Tudeh was the most disciplined force standing between him and defeat, and he was taking them out of the game.

For the royalist armed forces, Mossadegh's new attitude was an opportunity to expiate their hatred of the communist enemy. Trucks screeched around the capital disgorging armed men, who turned on the protesters with savage joy. In Kennett Love's telling, soldiers sent to quell fighting between the Tudeh and a group of Mossadeghists 'clubbed both factions impartially while shouting "Long Live the Shah, Death to Mossadegh". Carried away by excitement, the soldiers swarmed into Lalehzar Street and forced people emerging from movie theatres to repeat the same slogans on pain of a drubbing from a rifle butt or a jab from a bayonet.'[15]

According to Love, the soldiers were ordered back to barracks 'as hastily as possible', but the damage had been done. Hundreds of Tudeh supporters had been arrested and injured. Tear gas hung in the air. The communists licked their wounds and the coup-makers plotted for tomorrow.

Mossadegh was imperfectly aware that he presided over a situation of great peril. Few in his entourage had more than an inkling. He and his advisers were occupied with issues that now seem insignificant. The early morning of August 19 found Mossadegh discussing provisions for the widows of men who had been killed in the July uprising. Ghollamhossein was intending to view a potential site for the mental hospital he and his father had been planning. Sanjabi drove off to address cadets at the staff college and Shayegan brought his wife and infant child down to the city from his house in the mountains in order to have a bath. Muhammad-Ali Safari was bent over his desk in the offices of *Bakhtar-e Emrooz*. The first he would know of the sedition was the crash of breaking glass and the roar of a mob intent on killing him.

At 8 a.m. Ghollamhossein Sadiqi got to the interior ministry and busied himself with preparations for elections to the forthcoming regency council.[16] News came that groups of people, gathered in Sepah Square, were shouting for the Shah and that the police were urging them on. Sadiqi ordered a junior to take a ministry car and investigate, but the keys could not be found. He telephoned the chief of police, who professed complete ignorance of events. Then General Riyahi phoned to say that the chief of police had been sacked.

The situation in southern and central Tehran was getting worse. Several groups, two or three hundred strong, had been disgorged by military trucks and were on the move around the bazaar. There was a fight in Baharestan Square between royalists and government supporters, while the security forces sat and watched. Roosevelt's local agents led rioters to the offices of *Bakhtar-e Emrooz*, which were plundered and burned. (Muhammad-Ali Safari fled down a fire escape.) The premises of pro-Tudeh newspapers, a communist theatre and several Mossadeghist parties met the same fate.

At about 10 a.m. another group had set out from the fruit and vegetable wholesale market in south Tehran. Recruited from the 'houses of strength', traditional sports clubs with links to protection rackets, fired up with rumours that the Tudeh planned to fly their flag over the town hall, these muscle-bound wrestlers were led by the celebrated thick-neck Teyyeb Haj-Rezai, and carried knives, clubs and pictures of the Shah. Their numbers swollen by bystanders, many of them young boys or soldiers, they commandeered buses and trucks and forced passing drivers to turn on their headlights and honk in support of the monarch.

Another group of thick-necks, this one led by 'Icy' Ramazan, joined Teyyeb's. There was also a contingent of bare-foot slum-dwellers. 'Anyone they didn't like the look of,' recalled one Mossadegh supporter, 'they beat up.' The most picturesque column was organised by a celebrated madam, and was constituted of prostitutes with names like Sugar-lip Zeynab and Saucer-eyed Azam.[17] They shouted, 'Immortal Shah!'

In the administrative heart of the city, the marchers forced their way into official buildings, where they pinned the Shah's picture to the walls. Sadiqi saw them from his window in the interior ministry and phoned the martial-law rule administrator to ask why they were not being challenged. 'We don't trust our own men,' came the reply. The mayor of Tehran called Sadiqi and told him in French that the mayoralty had been overrun and the guards were doing nothing.

In Rome, Shah Muhammad-Reza Pahlavi was unaware of any of this. While he sipped his morning coffee at the Hotel Excelsior, the royalist tide rolled north.

Something extraordinary was happening. A centralised, modern government of men with French PhDs was being challenged by gangs of cut-throats while the army and police looked on. From the side of the road, students, civil servants and other citizens also watched, dumbfounded. Shopkeepers shuttered their shops and stood around protectively. Even so, it was hard to believe that this movement could amount to much. The crowds were not particularly big, and many streets were unaffected. The road from Tehran to Shemiran was quieter than usual – if only because the shops were closed.

Everyone with a radio tuned in. The 12.30 p.m. bulletin concentrated exclusively on foreign news. When would Mossadegh call his supporters onto the streets to sweep the trash away?

The picture we have of the prime minister on August 19 is not a flattering one. He oscillated between inertia and unfounded optimism. His judgement was fatally impaired. Ultimately, he tied himself up with his own principles. Then he lay down to die.

Several times before and during the events of that day, Mossadegh rejected offers of armed intervention in his favour. He recognised the danger of armies within armies and quashed the idea of a government militia. Offers came from the tribes: let us march on Tehran. Communists begged to form a 'national guard' under his command. Each time, he said no. Whether or not, as has been claimed, he received and rejected Tudeh offers of aid on the 19th, it is clear that Mossadegh neither hoped for nor solicited communist help as his government went under.

All this is in keeping with Mossadegh's character and politics. He was instinctively a pacifist. Also, he did not trust the Tudeh. He would not give guns to a group that would inevitably turn against him. But this does not explain why he refrained from using the popular support which remained at his disposal. Even now, without his intervening, his supporters in the bazaar had repulsed the royalists. The bazaar stood, a beacon of Mossadeghism! Why was there no declaration from 109 Palace Street, no word from the nationalist parties? Why did he stay transfixed as the sedition gained momentum and eventually overwhelmed him?

At least until late morning, Mossadegh seems not to have taken seriously the threat posed by the disturbances. Riot and affray had been features of Tehran for four days – why should this be any different? Mossadegh also had an exaggerated faith in the willingness of his security forces to quell the crowds. But the men who had pummelled the communists the previous night would not pummel citizens marching at the behest of a senior retired general and in the name of the Shah. And, as the morning wore on, the mobsters and servicemen were joined by ordinary, traditional-minded Iranians. Some of them had been supporters of Mossadegh, but Fatemi's radicalism had convinced them that the nationalists and the communists sought the same thing. The CIA's propaganda had encouraged them in that verdict. So, they joined the royalists.

Now Mossadegh made a terrible error of judgement. The police chief's chair lay vacant. A brigadier called Shahandeh was to fill it.

Then, around noon, Mossadegh phoned his interior minister to announce that he had had a change of heart. The new police chief would not be Shahandeh. It would be Mossadegh's own great-nephew, Brigadier Muhammad Daftary.

Daftary was in league with Zahedi. Everyone knew it. A warrant for his arrest had been drafted, but Mossadegh had suppressed it. The prime minister could not believe that a member of his own family would betray him. That morning, Daftary came to his uncle and wept. He beseeched him: 'What better time than now for me to perform a service for you?' Mossadegh was at his most vulnerable, and was swayed by the younger man. 'Go and take over the police,' he told Daftary. This is what Daftary did, and his first significant action was to order his men to desist from interfering with the marchers. Then he turned events decisively in the plotters' favour.

Just before noon, Brigadier Riyahi ordered a force of infantry and Sherman tanks to deal with the crowds heading north. The force was met by Daftary, who issued an emotional appeal. 'We are all comrades and brothers,' he declared. 'We all love the Shah.' For the members of this punitive force to be reminded of their sworn obligation to the Crown must have been excruciating. They wavered, dissolved. There was a love-in instead of a slaughter. The royalists commandeered the Shermans and went off to take the radio building.

The Shah's supporters would call the events of August 19 a popular uprising in favour of the monarchy. In fact it was a military coup, with the fate of a government decided by men in uniform. An account in the daily newspaper *Keyhan* makes this graphically clear: 'At 2pm the police headquarters and army headquarters were encircled by six tanks and several lorries carrying soldiers . . . Brigadier Daftary came to the police headquarters with several jeeps belonging to the customs police, and occupied it.' The *Keyhan* reporter also observed 'several lorries carrying soldiers and a number of policemen and a great many fully-equipped armoured cars, in addition to several trucks . . . all bearing pictures of the Shah and Reza Shah, front and back.'[18]

Brigadier Riyahi had instilled in Mossadegh a specious sense of optimism. Now the chain of command collapsed. Daftary was by no means the only traitor. Commanding officers kept their men out of the way or steered them towards benevolent neutrality. One major led a successful attack on the police jail to free the prisoners, who included General Nader Batmanghelich, Zahedi's choice as chief of the army staff. From noon onwards the crowds took their orders from the army and the police. A handful of treasonous officers were arrested. One Mossadegh supporter dismissed the arrests as 'an antidote administered after death'.

At 2.30 p.m. Ghollamhossein Sadiqi abandoned the interior ministry and drove north. He found the prime minister huddled on the first floor with his shell-shocked inner circle of allies and secretaries, and Palace Street defended by tanks and troops. The talk was no longer of summoning supporters onto the streets, but of a radio statement to reassure the mob that the government harboured no hostile designs on the Shah. Mossadegh refused: 'I have no issue with the Shah that I should put out such a statement.'

From around noon, hostile groups of civilians and soldiers, including members of the officially disbanded royal guard, had started arriving in the vicinity of Palace Street, but were scattered by the defenders. Gradually, more and more attackers arrived and the battle for the prime minister's house began in earnest with rifle and machine-gun fire. The prime-ministerial guard had taken over a four-storey building dominating the northern entrance to Palace Street, and there were machine-gun nests in the prime minister's own compound. From these positions, the guard responded with fusillades of their own.

Zahra and her female servants were among the last people to leave before the siege was complete. They were taken away by one of Mossadegh's nephews to Mansoureh and Ahmad Matine-Daftary's home nearby. Inside the besieged house there was an ominous calm. Hassibi was on a chair in the meeting room, lost in thought. Fatemi sat opposite him. Shayegan and Razavi were in an adjoining room, resting on the carpet. Sadiqi said he was hungry and a servant brought bread and jam and tea. 'I had just put in my second mouthful,' he recalled, 'when I heard the sound of a commotion and a struggle from the radio in the next room.' Everyone gathered around the set. There was more commotion, followed by a long silence. Then it was announced that the government had fallen and that the Shah was on his way home.

These were lies, of course, but who was to know? The radio had replaced the pulpit as the country's chief means of communication and propaganda, and Mossadegh had taken no special measures to protect it. The radio station had fallen with the loss of just three lives.

Mossadegh was sitting on his bed in his own room. Suddenly he let out a wail and the others rushed in and found him weeping bitterly. Mossadegh was not crying for himself or his government, but because the radio had announced that Fatemi and Sanjabi had been killed. This, too, was a lie. Fatemi was still in the building! Sadiqi calmed the prime minister 'with difficulty'. Then Brigadier Riyahi phoned. He was choking with emotion. He announced that all strategic locations in the capital had fallen and that there was no point continuing the struggle. At 5 p.m., Riyahi fled his post and went into hiding.

By then, the military equation at Palace Street had changed in favour of the putschists. The decisive event was the arrival of the Sherman tanks which had been standing outside the radio station. These had been sent by the *New York Times* correspondent Kennett Love, who later bragged about his role in 'speeding the final victory of the royalists'.* Shells fired by the Shermans destroyed first-floor rooms looking onto Palace Street, and disabled the tanks of the defenders.

In the heat of the battle, Colonel Ezzatullah Mumtaz, who had taken command of the defence force, came to Mossadegh and

---

* Love had gone to the radio exchange after it fell, where he found 'a half-dozen tanks swarming with cheering soldiers'. Love told the commanders that 'a lot of people were being killed trying to storm Dr Mossadegh's house and that they, the tank commanders, ought to go down there where they would be of some use instead of sitting idle at the radio station. They declared my suggestion to be a splendid idea. They took their machines in a body to [Palace Street].'[19]

explained the bleakness of the situation. Mumtaz's men had mounted a furious defence, inflicting severe casualties and fighting on even when badly wounded. Now they were outgunned, and ammunition was running low. Mumtaz promised Mossadegh that he would fight to the death. Mossadegh embraced him and sent him out again.

Mossadegh then received Brigadier Fouladvand, the commander of the attackers, who advised him to resign. He refused, but he did agree to the raising of a white flag. The shelling only intensified. The radio announced that Mossadegh had resigned: another lie. At 5.25 p.m., General Zahedi broadcast to the nation. He declared that he was the country's legal prime minister, named by the Shah.

The occupants of 109 Palace Street were now unable to communicate with the outside world. They were utterly alone.

Mossadegh waited to die. He sat on his bed in a pair of grey pyjamas. Around him were some of his closest allies. From the seventeenth majles, the cabinet and his own secretariat, they had gathered that morning to consult and aid their leader. Only Fatemi and Sanjabi had subsequently left.* The others sat in the prime minister's stifling little room with the iron door that Mossadegh had had installed shut against the corridor outside.

A few hours earlier, these same men had been giants striding into a new epoch. Now they were isolated and debased, sitting or slouching around the famous bed as the bullets slammed into the brickwork and ricocheted off the metal roof, and the dust from the ruined perimeter walls swirled around them. There was a hideous clang when a bullet smashed through the window of the prime minister's meeting room and into the iron door.

What did they think, as they looked into the abyss? Did they suffer for themselves and their families, or for the country they had served and failed? Each had reason to regret. Hassibi, who had set his face against the oil deal which might have saved the

---

* Fatemi's wife had become hysterical when she heard of his 'death', and he had rushed home to comfort her. Sanjabi had gone off to confer with allies and not returned.

government; Ahmad Zirakzadeh, the Iran Party stalwart who had only that morning led the charge for a republic; Shayegan, whose witticism – 'the delicacy that should have come to Tehran has gone to Baghdad' – would never be forgotten. Perhaps now, in the awful pause before oblivion, they found humility.

Mossadegh was . . . Mossadegh. He who had greatest cause for self-censure was thinking of how best to serve the moment. 'If I am murdered,' he declared, 'it will be more useful for the country and the people than if I stay alive.' Here was a manifesto for martyrdom. Even his thoughts of death were quintessentially Persian.

Suddenly the window behind Mossadegh's head shattered. The others dragged the bed away from it. They implored Mossadegh to move out of the bedroom and into another room, further from the line of fire. There might even be a chance of escaping over the wall – as Mossadegh had done on the previous occasion that his house had been attacked. These proposals seemed to irritate Mossadegh. Again, he insisted he would stay. He had no such expectations of his comrades. 'I implore you, gentlemen, go wherever you want to go.'

Mossadegh must have known they would not leave him. Mahmud Nariman, a nationalist member of the seventeenth majles, suggested mass suicide. 'Why are we sitting here waiting for those low-lifes to come and kill us?' Mossadegh angrily rejected the idea and his own and Nariman's revolvers were locked in the safe.

Over the next few minutes, Mossadegh had a change of heart. The defence was collapsing. It was only a matter of time before the attackers launched their final assault. Perhaps he did not want to die, after all. Perhaps he decided that the men around the bed should be saved so they could perpetuate his ideals. After another near-miss he agreed that they should all move to another room. His companions helped him out of the bedroom.

Now there was hope. With Mossadegh on his feet, everyone thought of escape. The eastern extremity of 109 Palace Street was adjacent to other houses set in gardens, and the attackers had been unable to approach it. The party came out into the garden by the eastern wall. They were twelve in all, and they were joined by six of Mumtaz's men, three of them covered in blood.

They leaned a ladder against the perimeter wall and some of them went over. Then it was Mossadegh's turn. He stood at the foot of the ladder and remembered Mumtaz. The colonel was summoned. The cause was lost and Mumtaz was encouraging those of his men who could, to get away. Mumtaz himself would not throw down his weapon until Mossadegh was out of danger. Mossadegh said, 'God bless your mother's milk.' Then he was helped up the ladder and over the wall.

The idea was to get as far away from 109 Palace Street as possible. In the next property, which was deserted, they found a wooden bed which they tipped onto its side and used to get over the next wall. And so it went on – inching eastwards, away from the chaos, through one house that contained women and children, where they were not welcome, and another whose inhabitants had spread a carpet on the flat roof and were watching the spectacle while drinking tea. They crawled along high walls and lowered themselves down tree trunks. Steadied by his comrades, Mossadegh survived intact. Zirakzadeh was less lucky. He fell and broke his leg.

The fourth property they entered belonged to a merchant who had gone away for the summer, leaving the house empty except for a caretaker to look after things. The merchant was contacted by phone, and graciously put his home at their disposal for the night.

Shortly after seven o'clock that evening, the sounds of battle ceased. The sky darkened and flames rose from the direction of 109 Palace Street. Mossadegh and Sadiqi stood and watched. Sadiqi recalled that 'a queer feeling came over us all, and dreadful visions and painful thoughts passed through us, which are difficult to describe.'*

* A few streets away Zahra was suffering agonies at the thought of what was happening to her husband. 'What are they doing to my house and my children's houses?' she demanded, and she prepared to go out and face the mob. Mossadegh's nephew offered to accompany her, and they got into his car, but it was a trick and he drove her far from the chaos.

They spent the night on the floors of the unfurnished house. There was nothing to eat save a few scraps of old bread. Zahedi's goons came knocking, looking for the fugitives, but the servant fobbed them off and they went away. Then it was the fire brigade asking for water to douse the flames in Palace Street.

They went their separate ways as soon as the curfew was lifted the following morning. Mossadegh, Sadiqi, Shayegan and Seifullah Muazzami, the minister of posts and telegraph, went to Muazzami's mother's house nearby. Mossadegh had been trying to work out the safest way of surrendering, but in the event a team of detectives found him first. One of them wandered into an upstairs room and saw the deposed prime minister, lying on a mattress. The detective called for a car and they all sped off to police headquarters.

That evening Mossadegh and his three colleagues were taken to the officers' club where General Zahedi had set up his new government. The coup-makers were there to greet them; Brigadier Fouladvand, commander of the force that had attacked Mossadegh's house; General Batmanghelich, the new head of the army; and Colonel (now Brigadier) Nassiri, who had delivered the Shah's edict to Mossadegh – an age ago, it must now have seemed.

The new prime minister received them magnanimously. Zahedi came forward to shake Mossadegh's hand.

'I am very sorry to see you here,' he said.

In the days that followed, a great number of people came and wandered around Palace Street, gawping at the annihilation of a neighbourhood. They saw the smouldering ruins of No. 109 and the blood and pieces of flesh on the road where the fighting had been most intense.

Among these visitors was a *Keyhan* reporter. He spoke to neighbours who had cowered with their terrified children during the fighting and seen the looting of their own houses – even though they had nothing to do with Mossadegh's government. Talking to them and other witnesses, this reporter was able to piece together what had happened after Mossadegh climbed over the wall.

As the defence crumbled, the tanks had rolled towards No. 109. One of them smashed through the door into the compound, drawing fire from inside the house and responding furiously. Eventually the last of the defenders were silenced and a second tank entered the compound. Two unidentified men were spotted among the ruins and shot. Then the few surviving defenders came out and surrendered.

From the first stirring of the crowds that morning, the putschists and their followers had been waiting for this moment. The tanks were followed by more tanks, and trucks loaded with soldiers. The mobs arrived; thick-necks like Teyyeb and Brainless Shaban (newly freed from jail); soldiers, some in uniform and some in civilian clothes; the prurient and the macabre. They came to gloat, steal and destroy. Photographs were taken of Teyyeb and the others, posing like conquering heroes.

The evening curfew was due to start shortly, but the people did not need much time. They annihilated the headquarters and spiritual home of Iran's national movement. They ransacked Mossadegh's offices and bedroom, taking or destroying tens of thousands of documents and letters – the record of the man. They broke tiles from the wall and wrenched electrical wires from the wainscots. Some of the booty was immediately auctioned to passers-by. A new electric fridge went for $36. The door of the prime minister's safe was wrenched off its hinges and the contents taken away. What they could not take, they trashed. As *Keyhan's* correspondent reported, 'Within minutes the house had been completely destroyed and levelled, and nothing that could be of the slightest use remained.'

In his new prison, Mossadegh was unexpectedly reunited with one item that had been looted from 109 Palace Street – a set of reading glasses he ordered during his trip to America. One of the guards at the officers' club told him, 'I know where your glasses are,' and a few minutes later they were in Mossadegh's hands.

The same diligence was applied to the houses of both Ghollamhossein and Ahmad Mossadegh, and a fourth house on the same plot, which – irony of ironies – Mossadegh had let out to the development arm of the United States government. It was not quite a free for all. The military did not let the mobs cart off some of the most valuable items, which were requisitioned and taken for safe-keeping. Once order had been restored to the streets and the mobs had gone, they were shared out among the valiant officers.

Ghollamhossein had lived in a fine family home with all the amenities. What he retained from this home was the set of clothes he put on that morning and the latchkey in his pocket. When he was captured a few weeks later and hauled before a military prosecutor, he could hardly believe his eyes. 'No doubt', he said, 'you are aware that my house and possessions and those of my father and brother were looted on August 19. It is a surprise to find one of the carpets from my own house here, under your feet!'[20]

According to the *Keyhan* reporter, some 35 people were killed in the battle for Palace Street, and 350 wounded. (Kennett Love put the dead at more than 300 across the capital, and 200 in the battle for the prime minister's home.) Over time, the ruination of Mossadegh's house would become a symbol of his fall and the wantonness of those who pushed him. His personal effects achieved a strange concatenation. Years later, Majid Bayat was contacted by an Iranian émigré in Australia, asking if he would like to buy some of his grandfather's personal papers. And Ghollamhossein's exercise bicycle, a new-fangled contraption, perplexing to the looters, achieved notoriety when it was presented as a transmitting device used by Mossadegh to contact his foreign masters.[21]

At the other end of the town, one of Mossadegh's supporters heard what had happened to his house, and was distraught. 'One day,' he said, 'they will do exactly the same thing to the house of the Shah.'

# 15

# Unperson

On August 20, the Shah started for home. He broke his journey in Iraq, where he visited the Shia holy places to thank God for his restoration. Photographs were taken of him with his hands on the grill around the tomb of Ali, the first Shia imam, and this image would be used by the propagandists in years to come. He touched down in Tehran, dressed in the uniform of the commander-in-chief of the air force (which had been flown to Baghdad specially), and was greeted by the new prime minister. Now a tsunami of sycophancy was unleashed. 'As soon as his feet were on the ground,' Kennett Love reported, 'high officials and old court retainers rushed forward to kiss his knees and shoes. His progress was impeded by these attentions, which visibly embarrassed him. At one point he was tripped by persons rushing at him and he barely saved himself from falling headlong.'[1]

The Shah's route to the palace was lined with the rowdies and royalists who had saved his throne. 'Flowers were strewn along the route,' wrote Love, 'over which there were triumphal arches built of wood and covered with rich Persian carpets.' That evening, in a radio broadcast, the sovereign thanked the people and told them that he had been prepared to sacrifice his life for them 'on numerous occasions' in the past, and would not shrink from doing so in future. How this accorded with his disgraceful flight from the country, he did not explain.* For a while, he was buoyed by the illusion that his subjects loved him after all.

---

* Later, the Shah would explain that he had left the country because he believed that 'it would force Mossadegh and his henchmen to show their real allegiances, and that thereby it would help to crystallize Persian public opinion.'[2]

In the days and weeks that followed the coup, he and Zahedi doled out rewards: cash, promotions and, in the case of Brainless Shaban, a convertible Cadillac. The toadies and editors changed their tune according to altered circumstances. Royal statues that had been treacherously uprooted were triumphantly re-erected. The tribes came to Tehran to affirm their loyalty. Anyone with an eye on preferment or promotion laid into Mossadegh without mercy. The radio called the former prime minister a liar weeping crocodile tears.

The monarch gathered up his discarded trappings. He meddled in the new government of General Zahedi, received Henderson and made plans for the bristling army which, he hoped, would dissuade anyone from challenging his authority in future. The distribution of Crown lands was resumed, and photos of the Shah giving out beribboned scrolls to sun-burned peasants became another feature of his publicity. In foreign policy, his goals were the same, only more so: to get the oil flowing and use the proceeds to save his country and himself.

In Washington, John Foster Dulles believed that the coup had given the United States a 'second chance' to save Iran, and emergency aid was pledged pending resolution of the oil crisis. The British could hardly protest: the Americans had pulled their chestnuts out of the fire. The world had pivoted perceptibly with the actions of Kim Roosevelt and his colleagues. From now on, the Americans would steer Anglo-US policy towards Iran, and their tone would be brisker than it had been, and less friendly to the so-called 'freedom-seekers'. Loy Henderson recommended to the Shah an 'undemocratic independent Iran', by which he meant an authoritarian regime pledged to the West.[3] The Shah thought this was a capital idea.

The new regime made up for the excessive toleration shown by its predecessor. Thousands of Mossadeghists and leftists were thrown behind bars. There were dozens of executions. The nationalist and pro-Tudeh newspapers whose premises had been torched on August 19 never reopened. Anti-government demonstrations were suppressed, and political detainees flung into dungeons in remote and sun-blasted parts of the country. With American and Israeli help, the ground was laid for a new secret police, called after its acronym, Savak, and soon it would be dangerous for intellectuals and writers even to meet in the cafés of central Tehran. There was a campaign of persecution against the Bahais – the Shah's concession to the mullahs, who had threatened to expose his philandering. The features of the last quarter century of Pahlavi rule were coming into focus: philistinism, intolerance and sops under pressure.

Mossadegh, the cause of all the problems, was behind bars. His prominent allies were too – or, as in the case of Hossein Fatemi, on the run. And yet, even now, cautionary notes were sounded. 'A revolution is in progress in Iran,' ran a State Department memo. 'The old pattern of rule has been irrevocably shattered and any leader must shape his programme on the basis of nationalist aspirations.'[4] In January 1954, after Britain reopened its embassy in Tehran, the new *chargé d'affaires* noted 'much latent support for Mossadegh'. It had taken three years and a coup for the British to acknowledge the bond that Mossadegh had with his people. The penny had dropped rather late in the day.

Even so, it would soon be impossible to mention Mossadegh except to deprecate him. The coup was given the grand title of a 'national resurrection' and a heroic statue was unveiled to mark its first anniversary. Under the surface, however, the events of August 19 were insinuating their way into the nation's psyche. Long before the extent of the foreign involvement became widely known, August 19 carried the odour of injustice and anomaly – 'that which should not have happened', in Muhammad-Ali Safari's plangent words. It could only be explained through religion. Mossadegh had gone willingly to heroic defeat like Imam Hossein, the 'prince of martyrs', when he and his seventy-two followers faced the caliph's army in 680. As with the imam, if there was any historical inevitability in all this, it was the inevitability of moral vindication.

The Shah gifted him a platform. Mossadegh was one of the world's most recognisable men. Executing him was out of the question; a canny dictator would have sent him to Ahmadabad and let him rot. But Henderson urged a prompt trial and the Shah agreed because he sought vindication of his own. The Court's line was that Mossadegh had become a rebel the moment he rejected the imperial edict dismissing him. He had presided over an orgy of republican *schadenfreude* and brought the Tudeh out of their lairs. The Shah hoped that the public, always so tolerant of the old lion, would see him for the snake he really was.

It was another of the Shah's miscalculations based on a false reading of his own virtues. With Mossadegh's fall from power, the old doubts over his political scruples also fell away. During his trials he was once again an old-fashioned hero, risking his life to speak what he believed to be the truth. Those whose faith in him had faltered on August 19, 1953, and who had been drawn onto the streets by a fear of communism and the unknown, were now hot with shame. They knew that the Shah and Zahedi had been marionettes twitched from Washington and London. Mossadegh's aura brightened with each insult and depredation.

On October 1, 1953, the indictment was issued charging Mossadegh with treason, and on October 13 the deposed prime minister received his first visit from Jalil Buzorgmehr, the staff colonel who had been assigned to represent him in court.[5] In the event, Mossadegh would conduct his own defence, but Buzorgmehr became his indispensable link with the outside world. Here, again, was an outsider forcing his way into Mossadegh's affections, and not without resistance from some other members of the family, who were now, more than ever, protective of the patriarch.

After being held at the officers' club following his arrest, Mossadegh had been transferred to the palace at Saltanatabad, a few miles north-east of Tehran. The complex had been a Qajar summer retreat. Now part of it had been turned over to a munitions factory, and another part to the corrupted machinery of military justice. Mossadegh was kept in an ornate room with barred windows in a polygonal tower which also contained a mirrored hall for use as a courtroom and cells occupied by other members of his cabinet. Saltanatabad was not a jolly prison, with the bark of the crows and the tatters of a bucolic past. Mossadegh complained about the light bulb that stayed on all night over his bed, and the snoring of the guards outside his window.

In these unpropitious circumstances, at life's nadir, Mossadegh might easily have abandoned himself to ill health and bitterness. But his sulks had never been deep or long-lasting. They had always been a preamble to renewed vigour. Moreover, no one with an ounce of poetic feeling could miss the fact that he was now a legend. He himself was quite aware of this, and he continued to be inspired by the same sense of responsibility he had felt while in power. The picture that Buzorgmehr has left us of Mossadegh in the weeks after his fall does not show a broken old man affected by doubt or self-pity. On the contrary, they show a younger person fizzing with the prospect of a new battle.

Bent over the table in his cell, his American spectacles on his nose and a copy of the military laws at his elbow, the ex-prime minister applied himself to his defence. He was capable of writing all day without tiring. (Reading, on the other hand, quickly wore him out.) He was attached to correct grammar and his attention to detail extended to strong views on the best place to pin together the pages of his defence. Old drafts were torn into tiny scraps and thrown in the lavatory to prevent government spies acquiring fore-knowledge of his defence. Buzorgmehr proposed amendments. Mossadegh would chew his finger thoughtfully and perhaps consult his dictionary, before they agreed on the correct formulation.

Far from the madman of his enemies' depiction, Mossadegh was in charge of all his faculties. He made haste slowly and he liked his drafts to sit around and 'moulder' a bit before he went back to them. He and Buzorgmehr took breaks for prison lunch (soup and chicken stew) or home-cooked rice dishes sent in by Zahra. At 4 p.m. Mossadegh drank weak tea with four spoons of sugar. And when, at the end of the day, Buzorgmehr left these eerie purlieus for the comforts of home, he was 'overcome with sadness and gloom that a man with such exalted human qualities should be fated to spend his days behind bars'.

One Friday, Zahra, Mansoureh, Mansoureh's son Ali, and Ahmad's wife, Qods Azam (who was also Mossadegh's niece) visited the prisoner, and there was a simple scene of a family united in adversity. Husband and wife kissed each other's hands and shoulders, and Mossadegh cried. Mansoureh said, 'Agha! Are you well, thanks to God? Dear Agha! Don't be sad!' The mob had destroyed Ahmad and Qods Azam's house on August 19, and Mossadegh kept repeating, 'What wrong did you do? You have all been caught up with me.' Wiping her eyes, Qods Azam said, 'Dear Uncle, everything [we have], we would sacrifice for you.' Then they spoke of banal matters and everyone except Mossadegh drank tea, and when the allotted hour was up he said, 'Off you go, now, and may God protect you.'

The trial started on November 8. The road to Saltanatabad was lined with troops and the mirrored hall was packed with barracking spectators and a big contingent of journalists. Mossadegh entered in his scruffy coat of barak wool and presented himself: 'Dr Muhammad Mossadegh, the lawful prime minister.' The flash bulbs popped. Mossadegh declared, 'Everyone around the world is waiting to see what sentence this court hands down.'

His instantly recognisable face was on the front pages and in the newsreels everywhere. Letters of support poured in. The president of the Iraqi bar association communicated his willingness to represent him. Some of the Shah's supporters had anticipated that Mossadegh, not the Court, would benefit from all the attention. 'What better vehicle can be conceived for publicising a crippled old man,' asked one senator, 'than for him to be tried by a group in jackboots?'[6]

Mossadegh did not expect fairness; he wanted to show that he had been the victim of an illegal coup and to bless the ideals that would outlast him and all his generation. The opening days of the trial were marked by strikes and demonstrations, and the cry went up, 'Mossadegh is victorious!' The army lay siege to the university and the bazaar was shuttered in protest. At least one person was killed in the ensuing crackdown.

Transparent justice had been promised. Tehran heaved with foreign reporters and the Iranian press also lavished attention on proceedings. There was massive demand for the latest news of the trial, with local evening paper print-runs rising to an unheard-off 50,000, and second and third editions also selling well. Mossadegh's defence was a typical mix of law, history and autobiography, and the president of the court countered his prolixity with a memorable putdown. 'For you,' he told the defendant, 'speaking is a medicine, and for others a poison.' But Mossadegh was undaunted. 'I am Dr Mossadegh,' he said, 'and it behoves me to point out what is anti-constitutional.'

A leisurely airing of secrets was the last thing the new regime wanted, and Buzorgmehr was pressured to take over the defence and put an end to it all. During the next session the president of the court threatened to hold the trial in camera; Mossadegh made for the door and a guard blocked his way. In the end the president of the court capitulated and the defendant was allowed to defend himself.

The man in charge of the prosecution, Brigadier Hossein Azmudeh, was a monarchist of the knuckle-headed type. He regarded Mossadegh as an insurgent and the men who had been killed while trying to storm 109 Palace Street as martyrs. His court-room manner was hectoring and abusive, and he brought Mossadegh to boiling point when he questioned his Muslim faith. But Mossadegh was even better at getting under the other man's skin. He refused to acknowledge Azmudeh's status in what he considered an illegal trial, referring to him as 'that man' and deriving innocent fun from correcting him when he mispronounced quite common words. When Azmudeh's wrath reached a zenith and he demanded that the 'hammer of the law' be brought down on the defendant, Mossadegh rested his head on his folded arms on the desk in front of him and shut his eyes. On the question of the upended statues, he neatly turned the accusation of irreligiosity on its head, hinting that the Shah was contravening Islam by erecting such icons. 'I am not in favour of statues,' he declared, 'nor do I think they are consonant with religious law.'

The main argument turned on whether the Shah had been within his rights to dismiss his prime minister without permission from the majles. 'If they take me to the gallows,' Mossadegh declared,

'I do not accept that in a constitutional country the Shah can sack the prime minister.' He claimed to have had doubts about the authenticity of the edict he had received on August 15 – even though he had signed a receipt for it. Why had it been delivered in the dead of night by an army officer defying the curfew? Why had the telephone wires been cut and Fatemi been abducted? 'Tell me, Brigadier Azmudeh, what more is required to stage a *coup d'état*?'

It was as much a performance as a defence. His entrance to the second hearing was vintage Mossadegh. 'Court officials', *The Times* reported, 'helped him to his seat when he entered the courtroom this morning, stumbling and staggering, and nodding his head from side to side. Photographers took his picture from all angles for several minutes, while he kept his head down on his chest, breathing heavily and sometimes moaning.' A stiff dose of Curamin perked him up and a few minutes later he was furiously disputing once more. In a later hearing, he challenged Brigadier Azmudeh to a wrestling match. 'I can assure you I will knock him down in no time, and if he beats me he can cut off my head.'[7] Even the most hostile observers were in stitches.

In the later hearings Azmudeh confronted him with members of his cabinet and other allies, some of whom were themselves in custody. There were moving recollections of the fall of 109 Palace Street, and, with the exception of General Riyahi, who buck-passed impenitently, no one betrayed his fallen leader. At one point Azmudeh demanded to know what telegraphs Hossein Fatemi had sent to Iran's overseas missions after the Shah's flight, and Seifullah Muazzami, Mossadegh's minister of posts and telegraph, replied with pained dignity that since he was opposed to censorship, he had no idea. 'It is not the job of the minister of posts and telegraph to read the people's telegraphs and letters!' Here, in a few words, was the humane credo that Iran had lost.

On the evening of December 21, the court rose to hear the verdict and the president announced that the Shah, in his 'infinite generosity', had foresworn his right to retribution. Mossadegh snapped, 'I never requested clemency, and will never seek it. I have done nothing wrong. You must give a verdict according to justice.'

Sentence was passed: three years' solitary imprisonment. It could have been much worse, but the authorities did not want to make him even more of a martyr. Mossadegh declared the conviction to be one of the honours of his career. He lodged his appeal there and then, apologised to the court secretaries for the trouble he had caused them, and walked back to his cell.

He could have opted for a quiet life, and the authorities enquired discreetly whether he would drop his appeal in return for banishment to Ahmadabad, but he refused to bargain. For the government, Mossadegh's appeal promised to be even more awkward than the original trial; it would be a chance to criticise the violence now being done to his legacy.

The Shah and Zahedi had wasted no time in unpicking Mossadegh's policies. Britain had reopened its embassy on the day Mossadegh was sentenced, and negotiations on an oil deal to undo nationalisation were under way. In December 1953, Eisenhower's vice-president, Richard Nixon, came to Tehran to bless the new dispensation, and protests against his visit were met with deadly machine-gun fire. Finally, preparations were underway for heavily supervised elections to the eighteenth majles, whose main job would be to rubber stamp the expected oil deal.

The authorities were determined to stop Mossadegh from using the appeal court as a soapbox from which to publicise his views. A culture of official intimidation was growing again in post-coup Iran, and, citing his own fear of assassination, the authorities had transferred him to a military barracks shortly before the end of the initial trial. Declaring the appeal proceedings closed to the public would have embarrassed the authorities; in the event, they were closed in all but name.

The military court of appeal convened on April 8, 1954, and Mossadegh's performance over a month of hearings was as spirited as it had been in his first trial. He made good use of articles, now starting to appear in the foreign press, which alleged that the US had funded the overthrow of his government. But much of what he said went unreported, for only a few dozen spectators were allowed into the courtroom and Colonel Azmudeh was telling the domestic press what to write. Gone from the evening papers were the old verbatim accounts of what had happened in the courtroom. Coverage was often reduced to a couple of insipid columns on an inside page.

Mossadegh responded to the new restrictions with typical pugnacity. He began a hunger strike in protest, but he weakened rapidly and was almost comatose when an old ally, Allahyar Saleh, rushed to his cell to plead with him. 'Is that you, Saleh?' he croaked, and Saleh reminded him that he was not a free agent but belonged to the whole country. 'At home,' Saleh went on, 'my wife and child are worried and expecting news and not eating and waiting for me to tell them the good news that you have ended your hunger strike.' Mossadegh's resolve broke and he breakfasted on water and rusk dipped in powdered milk. On May 12 the appeal court upheld the original verdict. He still had twenty-seven months of his sentence to run.

Solitary confinement is now recognised as a form of torture, and Mossadegh must have suffered horrendously in his cell in the prison of the Second Armoured Division in central Tehran. His request to be allowed to live under armed guard at home pending the result of a final appeal to the Supreme Court was rejected and Jalil Buzorgmehr was no longer allowed to visit him. During the seven months of their close association, Buzorgmehr had learned to coax Mossadegh out of his bleak moods with conversations about the prime minister's early life and experiences, which the colonel noted down for future publication. Now Mossadegh was denied regular access even to his three civilian counsels, although family visits were permitted to continue. He occupied himself with a furious correspondence with the judicial authorities and a volume of memoirs, but naturally there were moments of despair – and another abortive hunger strike. During the appeal proceedings, journalists allowed to visit his cell had witnessed the sight of the former prime minister in agonies on his bed. 'Better to live freely in a stable than locked in a palace!' he sobbed. 'Oh, freedom!'

Mossadegh's distress was compounded by the way things were

going on the outside. The 1954 elections were conducted in an atmosphere of violence and thuggery, with votes for Mossadeghist candidates not counted and Brainless Shaban and the others beating up anyone they suspected of anti-government sympathies. Pictures of the charred body of an opposition newspaper editor were published following his 'suicide' in jail, and Mossadegh's former justice minister died after being attacked by a gang.[8] Most disastrous of all, in October 1954 the new majles overwhelmingly ratified a deal whereby a consortium of western companies, including Anglo-Iranian, would take over the Iranian oil industry. In theory, the Iranian government remained the owner of its hydrocarbon resources. In effect, control once again lay with foreigners. Nationalisation was a dead letter.

Of all the personal losses he suffered during this period, none upset him more than the fate of the man who had first proposed oil nationalisation. Hossein Fatemi had made the suggestion in 1949, and he had ended up as Mossadegh's closest confidant. But Fatemi had done more than anyone to unleash a republican fervour after the failed coup of August 15, and his orders that Iran's missions in Baghdad and Rome should shun 'this boy', as he called the Shah, had aroused the sovereign's abiding hatred. So, there was much royalist jubilation when Fatemi was discovered in a safe house in Shemiran in February 1954, after a neighbour happened to observe him watering the plants. He was beaten and knifed savagely and taken to the martial-law governorate, where the top brass crowded round him for celebratory photographs.

The United States and Britain were at one in considering Fatemi to be the most dangerous of Mossadegh's associates. Sam Falle, who had served at the British Embassy in Tehran before the rupture in relations, thought he deserved to be executed. 'As long as these boys are alive and in Persia,' he wrote, 'there is always the danger of a counter-coup. Toughness is necessary.'[9] The Shah needed no persuading.

At 2 p.m. on the afternoon of Fatemi's arrest, as he was being led out of the martial-law governorate, he was set upon by Brainless Shaban and his cronies, who brandished knives and yelled, 'Kill him!' Fatemi's life was saved by his sister, who had rushed to the police headquarters upon hearing of his arrest, and who flung herself onto her brother as he was being attacked. Miraculously, she survived the ten stab wounds she sustained; she was treated, appropriately enough, in the Najmiyeh Hospital.

Fatemi himself had also been badly wounded, and his recovery was further imperilled by his subsequent hunger strike. Resigned to his fate, he conducted a remarkable clandestine correspondence with a Mossadeghist cleric who was being kept in the same jail as himself, declaring in one note that he wished to use up his last energies to the benefit of 'the movement and for the happiness of my compatriots'. Fatemi realised the propaganda value of standing trial, for even if what was said could not be printed, it could still be spread by word of mouth, and 'it will be on the historical record for ever.'[10]

The legal proceedings reeked of the Shah and his lust for revenge. Fatemi was tried in camera alongside Ali Shayegan and Ahmad Razavi – two others who had spoken venomously about the Shah after the first, failed coup. Fatemi was brought in on a stretcher after the press photographers had been shooed away and the doors were shut to observers. 'I don't want to threaten you,' the president of the court told the defendants' lawyers, 'but bear in mind that everything we have depends on the Shah and you lawyers must take into consideration the greatness of Iran's history when making your defence.' The trial lasted only a few days. Fatemi was sentenced to death, and the others to life imprisonment.

There was a sordid appeal, with Fatemi coughing up blood in the night and the military doctors declaring him as right as rain and his lawyer absconding after the morning session. Fatemi refused to mount a defence because the trial had been closed to the public, and the president of the court tossed notes made by another defence lawyer into the stove. In the event, Shayegan's and Razavi's sentences were reduced to ten years apiece, but Fatemi's death sentence was upheld. On November 10, 1954, he went before a firing squad.

\*   \*   \*

Mossadegh, now seventy-two, took a long time to die, and although he remained vitally alive for his family and other members of the nationalist movement, for the public at large the last eleven years of his life was the start of his posthumous legend: his statue in men's hearts. The judges of the Supreme Court, mortified by the miscarriage but under irresistible pressure from the government, shame-facedly upheld the sentence that had been passed against him. His three years were soon up and he was released from jail in August 1956 and sent to Ahmadabad, where he would remain under guard and be allowed contact only with his family and a few retainers, almost until his death.

Iran was on the move in the last decade of Mossadegh's life, with the Shah laying the foundations for a police state that would stiffen and bloat until the fatal seizure of 1979. Corruption and social imbalance grew as the country prospered from oil revenues and American loans, moving from boom to bust, and back to boom again, while elections were rigged, dissidents were tortured and, in 1963, protestors drilled with bullet holes. The Shah's programme of modernising reforms marked the end of the alliance between mullahs and monarch which had saved the throne in 1953. In its place came an oligarchic species of industrialisation, with the land-less poor becoming a new urban working class – fodder for Marxists and Islamists alike. The Shah ditched the barren Sorayya and was married for a third time, and in 1960 he obtained the heir he so craved. His influence rose until no decision of consequence could be taken without his say-so, and one prime minister introduced himself to parliament as the sovereign's 'slave'.

Mossadegh was out of all this, dangerous to mention, and yet he remained a painful, spectral presence. The Shah associated him with the Nasserite republicanism now stalking the region, and which spread to Iraq in 1958, where mobs carrying Nasser's picture beheaded King Faisal, and another friendly monarchy bit the dust. Three years later, in one of the Shah's spasmodic gestures towards liberalisation, the nationalists were allowed a rally at the race track and the applause lasted several minutes when Mossadegh's name was uttered. From Ahmadabad, using his family as a courier,

Mossadegh offered guidance to his former colleagues, but there were divisions in the nationalist camp and in 1962 he was obliged to issue a terse warning against those who showed signs of compromising with the Court. In 1965 the Shah decided once again to crush those who promoted the ideals of his old rival, and the latest manifestation of the National Front was obliterated with a wave of arrests.

In 1965 the Shah told a French journalist that Mossadegh had been confined to his estate for his own safety, for the people 'would lynch him if he returned to his home in Tehran . . . he is happy where he is. He eats well and, at eighty-six, engages in his favourite sport: riding donkeys. What more could he wish for?'[11] The Shah's uneasy bragadaccio confirmed the truth of the adage about two dervishes happily sharing the same rug and two kings who cannot share a continent.

The Shah swaggered and philandered; he assembled wealth; he dropped friends like Ernest Perron as brutally as he dropped his wives. And yet, he wanted to be known as a good man. How could he be? The country had had experience of a good man.

Mossadegh was three years younger than the Shah had made him out, and he did not ride donkeys – indeed, the Savakis crawling over his estate would probably not have let him do so. While the Shah strove to be loved and respected, growing only more feared and detested, Mossadegh had to do nothing for his reputation to grow. His actions as prime minister spoke for themselves. He had done his duty and played no part in his supporters' post-mortems of the coup and his government. He was not heard expressing regret for anything he had done. The Shah, by contrast, would buck-pass and fish for sympathy to his grave.

Mossadegh's existence had now been reduced to a few elements: family, correspondence and overseeing the Najmiyeh Hospital and bits of property. He was forever engaged in small acts of generosity. Hundreds of letters were smuggled into Ahmadabad from supporters and well-wishers, and none went unanswered. He was no longer performing, and the sobriety of his decline belied the old caricature of the bed-ridden maniac. There was no shrieking or writhing in pyjamas. That had been part of the performance, and now the performance was over. The tears, when they came, were real.

After the coup, his picture on exercise books was pasted over with that of the Shah, but schoolchildren found that by holding the books up to the light they could see Mossadegh's face looking straight through the sovereign. When Zahra went out to buy bread in Tehran, strangers would sidle up and request a signed photograph of her husband. 'They seem to think this ne'er do well is a prophet!' she joked, but she took to carrying around with her a wad of such photos.[12]

Once, permission was given for a handyman to come to Ahmadabad to fix a fault, without being told whose house he was entering, and he was bent to his task when the former prime minister appeared at the door. The man stared, his tools clattered to the floor, and he dropped to kiss Mossadegh's hand.

His legend shone all the brighter next to the growing irrelevancy of those erstwhile allies who had thrown their lot in with the Court. Ayatollah Kashani had revelled in the coup, but he soon fell out with the government he had helped bring to power, and his influence leaked away long before he died in 1962. Neither Hossein Makki nor Muzaffar Baghai achieved the high office both had coveted, and the latter died in 1987 in a revolutionary jail after falling foul of Khomeini's regime.

Former possessions arrived at Ahmadabad in the last years of Mossadegh's life, chattels surfacing from the wreck of 109 Palace Street. In the spring of 1958, for instance, Mossadegh received a book which had been looted and found its way into the hands of a bookseller in Baharestan Square. Mossadegh gave it away, as a 'keepsake', to the man who had returned it to him.[13]

Mossadegh continued to receive letters from the family of Hossein Fatemi, and they consoled each other on their shared loss. 'Whenever I think of the suffering that was inflicted on that brave man,' he wrote to Fatemi's nephew, 'I cannot help but be affected, and I am sure that his good name will forever remain on the pages of the history of Iran.'[14] In another letter, to one of the tribal leaders of Fars, Mossadegh recalled the man's offer on the day of the coup for him to flee to Shiraz and accept his protection. Mossadegh had rejected this offer for the same reason he had rejected all the others, because he hated bloodshed and would not be its cause.

Such a harmless old retiree – but the Shah would not leave him alone. No sooner had Mossadegh taken up residence at Ahmadabad than a crowd of hoodlums was dispatched to threaten him, and he was forced to ask for guards. They came in the form of a contingent of soldiers and two Savakis, and one of their first acts was to prevent him from walking around the estate and chatting with his tenants. With the overthrow of King Faisal, and the Shah once more shivering in the republican breeze, the guard around Mossadegh was supplemented.

To his jailers, he showed the same consideration he had shown during his incarceration at Birjand. In Ghollamhossein's recollection, the Savakis were treated as 'part of the household'. They appropriated two rooms that Mossadegh had had built as schoolrooms for the village, and were given their share of whatever Mossadegh ate. One winter Ghollamhossein bought ten woollen coats on his father's orders. Mossadegh took one, a few were distributed among the villagers, and two went to the Savakis.[15]

More than ever, he returned to the ascetic tradition, where simplicity is associated with virtue. He would rise early, dress in his *barak* costume, and drink a cup of tea with bread and cheese. Then he went out and sat in the small wooden hut he had had built in the garden, from where he could watch the farm workers come and go. Lunch and dinner were simple and repetitive. An earthquake caused cracks to appear in the walls; he stopped them with newspaper. When he learned how expensive oranges had become in Tehran, he told his children not to buy him oranges any more.

He was mostly subdued, and often depressed by the state of the country, but he livened up when the family came to visit. After sharing the first few months of his exile with him, Zahra had returned to her place in Heshmat ul-Dawleh Street, and after that she came on Fridays with the children or whoever else happened to be visiting – their grandson Hedayat Matine-Daftary, for instance, or Mossadegh's nephew Farhad Diba. The family treated him with that combination of affection and respect which gives texture and meaning to relations between the old and the young. A donkey might be saddled up for one of the great-grandchildren, and Ghollamhossein would dole out medicines to ailing villagers. Mossadegh studiously avoided the favouritism that mars many Iranian families, and he retained his old-world courtesy, on one occasion abstaining from breakfast until a thoughtless house-guest bestirred herself from bed several hours after he had risen.[16]

In 1960 the newspapers serialised the Shah's memoirs, complete with an account of Mossadegh's premiership and the events of August 1953. Mossadegh was amused by the Shah's egregious misrepresentations, but they spurred him to give his version of events and he began a second volume of memoirs dealing with his premiership and his dispute with the Shah, copies of which he gave Ghollamhossein and Ahmad for safekeeping. The Savakis got wind but did not manage to find the memoirs.

Zahra Zia al-Saltaneh died in 1965. She had caught pneumonia after taking a dip at her summerhouse in the hills. A woman of independent means and connections, she had kept her door open to all; she had been the centre of a huge extended family and was much loved. The couple ended their married life on terms of wry affection. Mossadegh would tease her for being so often at prayer, saying, 'Madam, I should like to know what it is that you want from this God of yours, that you should disturb him day and night.' And she would reply with her usual put-down, 'What would you know? Away with you!'[17] The Shah did not allow Mossadegh to go to her as she lay in the Najmiyeh Hospital, and she died without him by her side.

Mossadegh was devastated by the loss. Zahra had 'endured everything that befell me . . . and when she came to Ahmadabad she was a consolation and had a great effect on me. It was my desire to leave this world before her but now I have stayed and she has gone and there is nothing to be done but to ask God to take me as soon as possible and to release me from this pitiable existence.'[18]

Mossadegh had expressed similar sentiments periodically over the past quarter of a century, only for politics to scatter the morbid cloud. He had shown himself to be physically and mentally stronger than he had led anyone to believe. Now, he had had enough.

His mind remained alert until quite near the end, when a back-gammon partner caught him removing his pieces before he was allowed to. 'You can remove yours too, if you want,' he said, and the games stopped. At the end of 1966 visitors noticed a swelling on Mossadegh's left cheek and he was allowed to visit Tehran for tests. His minders came with him.

In Tehran, between tests, he was astonished by the number of cars on the streets, and saddened by the superficiality of modern life, referring to one of the magazines he never saw in Ahmadabad, and saying, 'Nowadays people are only interested in the surface and the appearance of things.'[19] Sometimes he was in good humour, teasing a young well-wisher by asking her what sort of husband she would like: 'Fat or thin? Bald or with a full head of hair?' But the test results were ominous. The swelling was cancerous.

Those who loved him wanted to save him but he was already thinking about his legacy. He was furious when he found out that Ghollamhossein had applied to the Shah for permission to take him out of the country. 'Why should I go to Europe? What good are you, who claim to be doctors and who studied abroad? If you really are doctors, then treat me here!' In the event, the Shah granted permission for foreign doctors to come and treat Mossadegh in situ. This made him even crosser. 'The curses of God be upon anyone who wants to spend the equivalent of several poor families' living expenses to bring in a foreign doctor to treat me!'

The cancer made it difficult for him to eat, and he got thinner. There was a successful operation to remove the tumour, followed by an ill-advised course of electrotherapy, which had a calamitous effect, bringing on a recurrence of the old internal bleeding that had troubled him since his youth. He was moved to the Najmiyeh Hospital, where the family mounted a vigil in the corridor outside his room, and he whispered to them his last words of love.

He died shortly before 7 a.m. on March 5 1967.

# Epilogue

## *A Movement in Men's Minds*

Mossadegh lived to see his ideals submerged under a tide of petro-dollars, and the tide would become a flood after the big oil-price rises of the early 1970s. Oil had turned the Middle East into the most coveted region on Earth, and it was increasingly the producers, not the companies, that called the shots. World demand followed a steep trajectory upwards, fuelling hitherto unimaginable booms in Iran, Saudi Arabia and the other monarchies of the Persian Gulf. Participation agreements, in which the producers acquired partial ownership of the oil they sold, superseded the old concessions, and in 1972 the Shah forced through a deal whereby the consortium companies became service contractors to the National Iranian Oil Company. On the face of things it was nationalisation redux, but it occasioned little jubilation for the Shah's Iran remained as tightly wedded to America as ever and could not absorb all the new money. Inflation, corruption and discontent rose to smite him.

The Shah had become a dictator and the most noticeable of his adversaries were radical Islamists and Leftists. Mossadegh's ideals were also being expressed as the national struggle reached its climax, but the 1979 revolution was only partially Mossadeghist, even if its nationalist tenor owed much to memories of 1953. In fact, as Ayatollah Khomeini quickly showed, he was no more sympathetic to Mossadegh's ideas than the Shah had been. 'We are not interested in oil,' he quickly announced after his triumphant return from exile. 'We want Islam.' As for western-style democracy, it amounted to 'the usurpation of God's authority to rule'.[1] Khomeini had worked out a way of reassuring people that republicanism would not be a danger to religion, and that was to make his republic an Islamic one.

Here was Khomeini's solution to the fissures created by rapid social change and the Cold War. His was not the only answer being proposed. Elsewhere in the Middle East, Nasser's pan-Arabism had evolved into despotic National Socialism, spawning such undistinguished offspring as Saddam Hussein and Hafez Assad. US-backed Turkey oscillated between military juntas and sclerotic civilian democracy, and Saudi Arabia and the other Gulf monarchies continued to prosper materially under American tutelage, while barely advancing towards democracy or an independent foreign policy. The United States and the Soviet Union both helped Saddam Hussein in his eight-year war with Khomeini's Iran, while the US promoted radical Islamism of the Saudi variety as a counterweight to communism in Soviet-occupied Afghanistan.

For as long as the Cold War was prosecuted with vigour in the historic lands of Islam, the rights of the individual and national independence were unlikely to prosper. And once it had finished, and the Soviet empire collapsed, the region's autocrats used various ruses to retain the support of the sole remaining superpower. They promised to be a bulwark against radical Islam, or Iran, or Saddam, and to tolerate Israel. In return, the United States forgave them a multitude of sins. No American president wished to 'lose' Saudi Arabia or Egypt, the way Jimmy Carter had 'lost' Iran in 1979.

Only with the passing of George W. Bush's presidency and America's declining appetite for overseas intervention did the US stop seeing foreign policy as a zero-sum game. Egypt was neither won nor lost when Hosni Mubarak fell at the beginning of 2011; rather, its people took a step towards autonomy that they should have been able to take decades before. The Arab spring has not only affected American clients, as Syria's upheavals have shown, nor has it been confined to Arabs – it was prefigured by Iran's Green Movement of 2009. On the contrary, it is connected to the 'wider movement in men's minds' that Mossadegh's friend George McGhee identified in the 1950s, and which later American governments very often disregarded in their pursuit of short-term US goals. The movement will take decades to spend itself and it is hard to predict how it will turn out. It is a hazardous and unruly exploration of new ways to live and to run society – modernity itself.

Few foreign interventions in the Middle East have been as ignoble as the coup of 1953, and few Middle Eastern leaders have less deserved our hostility than Muhammad Mossadegh. His understanding of independence and democracy was the result of a long immersion in the ideas of the West, and an even more profound identification with his own society and people. Nationalism had been a force for decades, but he was the first to try to build a modern Middle Eastern state on the basis of collective *and* individual liberty. The freedom of a person to speak or associate is a charade if the government representing him makes policy on the basis of outside pressure, or spirits criminal suspects away to foreign jurisdictions. This is why George W. Bush's promotion of democratic reform in the Arab world aroused such mistrust; it was accompanied by strong-arm tactics redolent of Britain's colonial administrators.

With Mossadegh's fall Iran was condemned to a quarter of a century of vulgar tyranny, and the explosion of 1979. This is not to postulate a heavenly outcome had there been no coup, for myriad other calamities might have befallen Mossadegh's government, but it is likely that Iran's history would have been much happier than it has been. Mossadegh's Iran might have become a positive example for other countries, and the region's human development accelerated, for his dream was substantially the same as the dream that became manifest with the Arab Spring of 2011 – and it anticipated those events by sixty years.

What can also be said, with as much confidence as the opacity of the Russian archives permit, is that in August 1953 Iran was not about to go communist.* For all their ability to disrupt, the Tudeh were nowhere near strong enough to take power on their own,

---

* The Iranian historian Kamal Parsi-Pour has established that, of the eleven Moscow archives with holdings that pertain to Russian-Iranian relations in this period, the majority are effectively off limits to foreign scholars. It may therefore be some years before the Soviet Union's intentions towards Mossadegh's Iran are known.[4]

and Mossadegh had no intention of being their cat's paw. With Soviet foreign policy in stasis following Stalin's death, Moscow was taken by surprise by the second coup, and its response was muted and confused; and the Tudeh, of course, had followed Mossadegh's orders not to take to the streets. Years later, American officials who had been responsible for monitoring the Tudeh admitted that the party had been 'really not very powerful', and that 'higher-level US officials routinely exaggerated its strength'.[2] In the end, Marxism would only have mass appeal in Iran when it accommodated elements of Islam – at which point, of course, it became something other than Marxism.

Mossadegh's overthrow was as much a British as an American action, and the jubilation was shared. In the jovial but not always reliable account he wrote of events, Kim Roosevelt described the meeting he had with a recumbent Churchill on his way back to the US through London. The prime minister was recovering from a stroke, and drifted in and out of sleep, but he was wide awake for the climax, which prompted him to declare, 'If I had been but a few years younger, I would have loved nothing better than to have served under your command in this great venture.'[3] Roosevelt dined out on that in his later life as a consultant with interests in Iran – as he did on everything else to do with the coup.

For all Churchill's pleasure, the writing was on the wall for Britain and its overseas mission. Mossadeghism struck again in 1956, when Nasser nationalised the Suez Canal, and Eden, Churchill's successor as prime minister, launched an invasion along with France and Israel. This time Eisenhower did not cooperate. He was furious at Eden's precipitate action, and US and Anglo-French vessels came within an ace of attacking each other on the high seas. There was a run on the pound and Eisenhower would only approve emergency financial aid if Eden withdrew his forces. Broken, embittered, Eden did as he was told, and it was a débâcle from every angle. The canal was lost and Anglo-American relations poisoned. Nasser's government lived on, more powerful than ever, and his pan-Arab ambitions became an instrument of Soviet penetration of the Middle East.

After that the British were in constant retreat. In the thirteen years following Suez, nearly all the African, Far Eastern and West Indian colonies gained independence. Huge sections of the armed forces were dismantled. Britain ceded its place to America under the Middle Eastern sun, and in 1968 the British withdrew militarily from the Persian Gulf. The Shah of Iran hoped to fill the gap and become the region's policeman. The Nixon administration agreed that he should, and by the mid-1970s Iran accounted for half America's total arms sales abroad.

Along with Gandhi in his loincloth, Mossadegh in his pyjamas would be associated with the humbling of an empire, even if his adventure, unlike Gandhi's, was stopped in its tracks. On the face of it, the British were the winners in August 1953, but there could be no return to the status quo ante. When Anglo-Iranian (by now renamed British Petroleum) returned to Iran, it was as a minority stakeholder in a consortium which contained five US majors. Clinging to the mystique of British power, some Iranians were reluctant to accept that Britain's imperial decline amounted to more than a cunning delegation of heavy lifting to the United States, but it was true and unstoppable. Over time, in Iran as elsewhere, Britain fell in with American strategy and methods, sometimes grumpily, sometimes with relief. It was worth it for Britain, if only to avoid the fate that Eden had foreseen – of becoming 'no more than some millions of people living on an island off the coast of Europe, in which nobody wants to take any particular interest'.[5]

Coups make few friends and many enemies. America and its officials denied involvement in the drama of August 1953, and the Shah was suave and equivocal, but for the majority of Iranians it was an axiom that Eisenhower had taken down Mossadegh and stuck a despot in his place. Almost overnight, the US had gone from being a force for good to the Shah's accomplice in injustice and oppression. In 1960, a chastened Kennett Love wrote that 'Iranians are well aware of the American role [in the coup] although the American public is not. Thus it is that many Iranians hold the United States responsible for creating and supporting a regime that they believe has become an increasingly malign influence.'[6]

Love's warning went unheeded, and Iran's affairs became ever harder to disentangle from those of the United States. By 1979, the US Embassy in Tehran had a staff of nearly 1,000 and there was bilateral cooperation in virtually every field: military and commercial, strategic and cultural. The US had a particularly close relationship with the intelligence organisation, Savak.

In the aftermath of the Shah's flight in January 1979, and Khomeini's return from exile, the revolutionaries naturally assumed that the Americans would try to bring back their friend, the Shah. Had they not done so in 1953? Carter's humanitarian gesture of admitting the Shah for cancer treatment was all the confirmation they needed. On November 4, 1979, radical students went over the walls of the US Embassy and the Iranian hostage crisis began.

For the United States and much of the world, the detention of dozens of people enjoying diplomatic immunity was a rank offence against honour and decency. But history had taught Iranians that foreign missions were fronts for spying and plotting, and some of the documents they found inside the US Embassy supported this view. The hostage-takers regarded their actions as pre-emptive but they were also actuated by a sense of historic injustice. In the course of the interrogations they conducted of their captives, the students were tougher on the CIA agents they managed to unmask than they were on the regular diplomats. In the view of one agent, the hostage-takers regarded him and his colleagues as 'surrogates for the CIA of 1953; unable to punish those involved in the 1953 coup, the Iranians took out their anger on us'.

At the beginning of the revolution, it had looked as though the Mossadeghists might end up with the lion's share of political power. Mehdi Bazargan, the man who had implemented oil nationalisation for Mossadegh, was Khomeini's provisional prime minister, and Karim Sanjabi was foreign minister. But Khomeini wanted a distilled, purer revolutionary spirit, and the hostage crisis was an opportunity. The radicals around him used it to humiliate Bazargan, who resigned after failing to have the students evicted. The hostages would only go free in January 1981 – after President Jimmy Carter had been ejected by the US electorate for failing to end the hostages' ordeal. For years to come, the poison of the hostage crisis would stay in the United States, just as the poison of August 19, 1953 carried on circulating in Iran.

After the revolution, people made up for the decade and a half they had been unable to say Mossadegh's name. They renamed Pahlavi Street, the capital's main north–south artery, after him, and Mossadegh kebab houses opened for business. Stamps and bills were issued with his head on them, and his memoirs were published. The historian Iraj Afshar called for a centre for Mossadegh studies to be set up, and for Ahmadabad to be turned into a museum.

Mossadegh had left the estate to his children and, while none had gone to live there, they had kept it in good repair. Crumbling perimeter walls were mended and his bedroom was preserved as it had been when he left, with a thin mattress in one corner (the Russian bed no longer suited him), a rope bolted to the wall which had allowed him to haul himself to his feet, and a table laid out with pills and pens.[7] The bits of newspaper he had stuffed in the cracks of the walls had been taken out and the cracks plastered in. Then the scraps of newspaper had been glued onto the plaster. It looked as if nothing had changed.

Mossadegh had been buried at Ahmadabad because the Shah refused to let him lie alongside the martyrs who had fallen in the 1952 uprising against Qavam. He was lowered into the floor of the dining room – to which henceforward attached the reverence and sanctity of a shrine.

The twelfth anniversary of Mossadegh's death came six weeks after Iran gained its freedom from the Shah. It would be the first opportunity for the public to come together and remember him. The bus operators announced that they would put dozens of vehicles at the mourners' disposal, and a fast-food outlet offered to move its operations to Ahmadabad. The door into the dining room would be opened, and people invited to file in and read the *fateheh*, the prayer for the dead, while touching his raised gravestone.

The great caravan stirred on March 5, 1979, with the buses gunning and moving off from Tehran University, but as ever Mossadegh surprised everyone. The family had made provision for

20,000 or 30,000 people, not for the several hundred thousand who made the pilgrimage. They came in cars, trucks, on motorbikes and on foot, and preparations went by the board. The road approaching Ahmadabad became impassable, the bus for reporters was bogged down and abandoned, and elderly veterans of the nationalisation movement were forced to trudge miles through the mud. There could be no graveside *fateheh*; the doors to the house were shut to prevent a stampede. Of lunch, there was no sign.

And yet, everyone seemed happy, people who had met or seen him, alongside people who knew only the empty space he had left behind, standing in the cold around the house at Ahmadabad and in the fields either side, straining to hear speeches from a scaffold that had been erected in Mossadegh's garden. Thus, at last, he was remembered.[8]

And the years passed, and the war with Iraq ground on, and the Islamic Republic grew purer and more isolated. It became harder to commemorate him. Books and articles appeared trashing his memory, and the followers of Kashani claimed that the nationalisation of oil had been the ayatollah's achievement and that Mossadegh had been a British agent all along. I arrived in Iran during the thaw, when the restrictions were relaxed and it was possible to love him again. I was there, also, to watch the thaw end, and with it the government's toleration of the dead, secular hero.

His name is no longer on the street sign, or his face on the stamps, but his memory is safe in the hearts of Iranians, because his ideals are universal and mock the ephemera of power. 'Good days and bad days go past,' he once told the Shah. 'What stays is a good name or a bad name.'

# Notes

FRUS (unless otherwise indicated): Foreign Relations of the United States 1952–54, Vol. X: Iran, 1951–1954, United States Government Printing Office, 1989

### One: The Unchanging East

1. Feuvrier, Preface • 2. Bell, p. 27 • 3. Hourani, p. 257 • 4. Dabashi, p. 69

### Two: A Silver Spoon

1. Farmanfarmaian, Manucher and Roxane, p. 96. Najm al-Saltaneh's language could be very fruity indeed. In this book, her nephew recalls her telling another member of the family, a public figure who had been pilloried in the press, 'I'd prefer to be sexually abused than to be fucked [as] you have been by the papers.' • 2. Lambton, *Qajar Persia*, p. 76 • 3. Mossadegh, *Khaterat va Ta'limat*, p. 55 • 4. Bani-Jamali, p. 35 • 5. Mossadegh, ibid., p. 50 • 6. National Documents Organisation, doc. no. 2983001690. cit. Bani-Jamali, p. 49 • 7. National Documents Organisation, doc. nos 298004470, 298005408, cit. Bani-Jamali, p. 48. Also see Mossadegh, *Khaterat va Ta'limat*, p. 53 • 8. Ettehadieh, *Zanani ke zir-e Maghnaeh Kolahdari Nemudeand; Zendegi-ye Malek Taj Khanom Najm al-Saltaneh*, p. 72 • 9. Makki, *Doktor Mossadegh*, p. 39 • 10. Ettehadieh and Sa'advandian, p. 83 • 11. Foreign Ministry Archives, Tehran: carton 20, file 6 (1901); carton 60, file 9 (1900); carton 15, file 23 (1899), carton 20, file 20 (1899), cit. Bani-Jamali,

pp. 72–3 • 12. Ettehadieh, and Sa'advandian, pp. 441, 447, and Bani-Jamali, p. 75 • 13. Farmanfarmaian, Manucher and Roxane, p. 37 • 14. Mossadegh, *Khaterat va Ta'limat*, p. 52 • 15. Afshar and Salour (vol. 2), p. 1196 • 16. Ettehadieh, *Zanani ke zir-e Maghna'eh Kolahdari Nemudeand*, p. 74 • 17. Bayat, pp. 24–6 • 18. Sami'i, pp. 124–5 • 19. Bayat, p. 26 • 20. Author's conversation with Abdolmajid Bayat, Geneva, 2010 • 21. Bani-Jamali, p. 78 • 22. Mossadegh, *Khaterat va Ta'limat*, p. 55 • 23. Ibid. • 24. Schuster, p. 21–22 • 25. Browne, pp. 207–8 • 26. Mossadegh, *Khaterat va Ta'limat*, p. 93

## Three: Fokoli

1. *Rooznameh-ye Majles*, February 27, 1910 • 2. For Renée Vieillard's impressions of Mossadegh, I have drawn on Abdolmajid Bayat's unpublished *Pages d'histoires de L'Iran: Mossadegh*, which contains extracts from her own unpublished memoir. • 3. *Les Nouvelles*, August 22, 1909 • 4. Mossadegh, *Khaterat va Ta'limat*, p. 68 • 5. Matine-Daftary, Hedayat, *Mossadegh dar Paris: Dowran-e Tahsil*, from *Azadi*, summer and autumn editions, 2001, p. 95. Speculation that Mossadegh may have destroyed evidence for the interview in question is my own. • 6. Mossadegh, *Khaterat va Ta'limat*, p. 74 • 7. Sami'i, p. 122 • 8. Mossadegh, Ghollamhossein, p. 16 • 9. Walters, p. 253 • 10. Mossadegh, *Le Testament en droit musulman (Secte Chyite)*, p. 84

## Four: Razing Caesarea

1. Churchill, p. 131 • 2. *Kapitulasyon va Iran* (published privately, 1914), cit. Afshar, *Mossadegh va Masael-e Huquq va Siyasat*, p. 72 • 3. Katouzian, Homa, *Musaddiq and the Struggle for Power in Iran*, p. 11 • 4. *Ra'ad*, February 13, 1918 • 5. Ibid., January 5, 1918 • 6. Buzorg Omid, p. 280 • 7. Ibid., p. 277 • 8. Mossadegh, *Khaterat va Ta'limat*, p. 106 • 9. Afrasiyabi, p. 49 • 10. Amini, p. 85 • 11. Moradi-Nia, p. 643 • 12. Waterfield, p. 63 • 13. Memo by Armitage-Smith, November 22, 1920, FO 371/4909 • 14. Norman to Curzon, December 5, 1920, FO 371/4909 • 15. Memo by Curzon, FO 371/4927 • 16. Afshar, *Mossadegh va Masa'el-e Huquq va Siyasat*,

p. 66 • **17**. Borhan, p. 143 • **18**. Author interview with Abdolmajid Bayat, Geneva, 2010 • **19**. Bayat, Abdolmajid, Appendix. The Mossadeghs travelled under the name Habib. • **20**. Norman to India Office, September 22, 1920; FO 371/4927 • **21**. Farahmand, p. 195 • **22**. Torkaman, vol. 1, p. 346 • **23**. Bani-Jamali, p. 164 • **24**. Memo by Churchill, November 2, 1919; FO 371/4929 • **25**. Memo by Oliphant, July 6, 1921; FO 371/6404

## Five: Eclipse of the Qajars

**1**. Loraine to Curzon, May 21, 1923, FO 248/1369 • **2**. Bahar, vol. 1, p. 139 • **3**. Mossadegh, *Khaterat va Ta'limat*, p. 148 • **4**. Farahmand, *Valigari-ye Mossadegh (2)*, p. 230 • **5**. Bahar, Vol. 2, p. 262 • **6**. Torkaman, Vol. 2, p. 88 • **7**. Makki, *Tarikh-e Bist Sal-e Iran* (Vol. 3), p. 323 • **8**. Mostowfi, p. 604 • **9**. Wilber, p. 88 • **10**. Makki, *Tarikh-e Bist Sal-e Iran* (Vol. 3), p. 184 • **11**. Afshar, *Taqrirat-e Mossadegh dar Zendan*, p. 102 • **12**. Makki, *Tarikh-e Bist Sal-e Iran* (Vol. 3), p. 423 • **13**. Ibid. Mossadegh's speech can be found on pp. 442–50. • **14**. Author conversation with Abdolmajid Bayat, Geneva, 2010 • **15**. Golban, p. 45, cit. Bani-Jamali, p. 217 • **16**. Lees-Milne, pp. 258–9 • **17**. Makki, *Doktor Mossadegh*, p. 392 • **18**. Ibid., p. 367 • **19**. Ibid., p. 313 • **20**. Ibid., p. 346 • **21**. Avery, p. 283 • **22**. Afshar, *Mossadegh va Masa'el-e Huquq va Siyasat*, p. 196

## Six: Isolation

**1**. Bayat, Abdolmajid, p. 74 • **2**. Moradi-Nia, p. 590 • **3**. Author interview with Abdolmajid Bayat, Geneva, 2010 • **4**. Ibid. • **5**. Bayat, Abdolmajid, *Hekayati Sade az Dowran-e Kudaki*, from *Azadi*, combined summer and autumn issue, 2001 • **6**. Author interview with Abdolmajid Bayat, Geneva, 2010 • **7**. Torkaman, Vol. 1, p. 113 • **8**. Mossadegh, Ghollamhossein, p. 19 • **9**. Author interview with Abdolmajid Bayat, Geneva, 2010 • **10**. Torkaman, Vol. 2, p. 68 • **11**. Author interview with Abdolmajid Bayat, Geneva, 2010 • **12**. Torkaman, Vol. 2, p. 69 • **13**. Ibid., p. 71 • **14**. Ibid., p. 72 • **15**. Bani-Jamali, p. 237 • **16**. Mossadegh, Ghollamhossein, p. 49

## Seven: The Tragedy of Khadijeh

1. Unless otherwise indicated, the information for this chapter has been drawn from the following sources: Ghollamhossein Mossadegh and Abdolmajid Bayat; the author's conversations with Abdolmajid Bayat in Geneva in 2010; Ahmad Mossadegh's interview with his father's cook, Javad Hajji Tehrani, published in Afshar, *Mossadegh va Masa'el-e Huquq va Siyasat*; and Hossein Makki's introduction to his book, *Doktor Mossadegh va Notghha-ye Tarikhi-ye vey dar Dowre-ye Panjom va Shishom-e Taghniniye*. • 2. Katouzian, *Musaddiq and the Struggle for Power*, p. 33 • 3. Mossadegh, Ghollamhossein, p. 30 • 4. Pahlavi, Muhammad-Reza, p. 65 • 5. Author interview with Hedayat Matine-Daftary, London, 2010

## Eight: The Prize

1. Wilbur, p. 191 • 2. Katouzian, *Musaddiq and the Struggle for Power in Iran*, p. 48 • 3. Farmanfarmaian, Manucher and Roxane, p. 168 • 4. Bullard, p. 154 • 5. Katouzian, ibid., p. 55 • 6. Kay-Ustuvan, p. 289 • 7. Makki, *Doktor Mossadegh*, p. 13 • 8. I gleaned much of the information in this chapter regarding the Anglo-Iranian Oil Company from J. H. Bamberg's *The History of the British Petroleum Company*, Vol. 2, and L. P. Elwell-Sutton's *Persian Oil*. • 9. Jeffrey, p. 436 • 10. Kay-Ustuvan, Vol. 1, p. 181 • 11. *Omid-e Iran*, Vol. 11, April 16, 1979, cit. Nejati, p. 65 • 12. Kay-Ustuvan (Vol. 1), p. 191 • 13. Ibid., p. 224 • 14. Elwell-Sutton, pp. 114–115 • 15. Bamberg, p. 256 • 16. Le Rougetel to Bevin, February 9, 1949; FO 371/75464 • 17. Torkaman, Vol. 1, p. 101

## Nine: Victory or Death

1. Makki, *Khaterat-e Siyasi*, p. 184 • 2. Borhan, p. 94 • 3. Barnett to the British Embassy, FO 371 75468; Le Rougetel to the Foreign Office, November 18, 1949, FO 371 75468 • 4. Safari, Vol. 1, p. 296 • 5. Rahnama, p. 112 • 6. For this account of elections to the fifteenth majlis, I am indebted to Rahnama, pp. 114–116, and Makki, *Ketab-e Siyah* (Vol. III: *Khal'e-yad*), pp. 9–23 • 7. Le Rougetel to Bevin, November 11, 1949, FO 371/75467 • 8. Shepherd to Younger,

June 9, 1950, FO 371/82330 • **9**. FRUS 1950, Vol. V, p. 516 • **10**. *The Times*, Tuesday November 22, 1949 • **11**. Shepherd to Strang, April 6, 1950, FO 371/82311 • **12**. Memo by Fry, February 6, 1951, FO 371/91522 • **13**. Safari, Vol. 1, p. 329. Much of my information about parliament's activities before and during Mossadegh's premiership was drawn from this invaluable book. • **14**. Rahnama, p. 155 • **15**. Ibid., p. 158 • **16**. Ibid., p. 167. Northcroft's excellent information about the commission's deliberations probably came from his subordinate Geoffrey Keating, who, according to one Foreign Office note, 'did a good deal of lobbying among the majles deputies, and, in particular, among members of the oil commission.' See FO 371/91522. • **17**. Rountree to McGhee, FRUS 1950, Vol. V, p. 634 • **18**. Shepherd to Foreign Office, January 5, 1951, FO 371/91452 • **19**. Rahnama, p. 198 • **20**. *Khaterat-e Iraj Eskandari*, Mu'assesseh-ye Mutale'at va Pazhoheshha-ye Siyasi, 1993, p. 191 • **21**. Mossadegh, *Khaterat va Ta'limat*, p. 246 • **22**. Shepherd to Furlonge, May 6, 1951, FO 248/1514

## Ten: Mossadeghism

**1**. *Daily Express*, May 30, 1951, cit. Enayat, p. 99. I draw below from this useful study for other reactions to nationalisation in the British press. • **2**. Shepherd to Furlonge, May 6, 1951, FO 248/1514 • **3**. Shepherd to Bowker, May 28, 1951, FO 371/91542 • **4**. Avon, p. 36 • **5**. *Time*, January 7, 1952 • **6**. Mehdi Bazargan, *Khal' e-Yad az Este'mar-e Ingilis va Esteghrar-e Hakemiyat-e Mellat*, from Basteh-Negar, p. 139 • **7**. Bamberg, p. 430 • **8**. Kinzer, p. 115 • **9**. Mehdi Bazargan, ibid., from Basteh-Negar, p. 141 • **10**. Malcom Byrne, *The Road to Intervention: Factors Influencing US Policy Toward Iran, 1945–53*, from Gasiorowski and Byrne, p. 201 • **11**. Fateh, p. 517 • **12**. *The Economist*, November 17, 1951, cit. Enayat, p. 139 • **13**. Minutes of a meeting between the AIOC and Iranian government officials on June 17, 1951, FO 371/91575 • **14**. Harriman to Truman, August 22, 1951, FRUS, p. 145 • **15**. Sanjabi, p. 125 • **16**. Elm, Mostafa, Oil, *Power and Principle*, Syracuse University Press, 1992 • **17**. Memo by Stutesman, May 31, 1951, FRUS, p. 59 • **18**. Henderson to State Department, September 30, 1951, FRUS p. 186 • **19**. Esfandiary Bakhtiari, p. 127 • **20**. Milani, p. 51 • **21**. Walters, p. 247 • **22**. Abramson, p. 472 • **23**. Acheson, p. 503 • **24**. Walters, p. 247 • **25**. *New York Herald*, July 15, 1951, cit. Elm, p. 122

## Eleven: Winning America

1. *Security Council Official Records, 559th Meeting*, cit. Kinzer, p. 121
• **2**. Mossadegh, Ghollamhossein, p. 80 • **3**. Walters, p. 261 • **4**. *The Times*, October 16, 1951 • **5**. For more details of the proposed deal, see McGhee, pp. 397–99 • **6**. The Associated Press, October 28, 1951 • **7**. Mossadegh, Ghollamhossein, p. 91 • **8**. McGhee, p. 385 • **9**. FRUS • **10**. *The Times*, November 20, 1951

## Twelve: Riding Satan's Donkey

1. Nejati, *Mossadegh: Salha-ye Mobarezeh va Moqavemat*, p. 265 • **2**. Buzorgmehr, *Khaterat az Doktor Muhammad Mossadegh*, p. 144 • **3**. Makki, *Ketab-e Siyah* (Vol. III, *Khal' e-Yad*) p. 241, and Nejati, *Mossadegh* (Vol. 1), p. 264. • **4**. For these and other insights into Mossadegh's prime ministerial style, I have drawn on Morteza Rasoolipour. • **5**. Henderson to State Department, January 15, 1951, FRUS p. 324 • **6**. Penfield to State Department, January 18, 1951, FRUS p. 331 • **7**. Muvahed, pp 388–89 • **8**. Safari, Vol. 1, p. 582 • **9**. An excellent English-language account of relations between the Shah, the British and the political elite between 1941 and 1953 can be found in Fakhreddin Azimi's *Iran: The Crisis of Democracy*. • **10**. For my account of Mossadegh's meeting with the Shah, I have drawn from Makki, *Vaghayeh-e Si-ye Tir-e*. My telling of the subsequent uprising owes much to this book and to Hassan Arsanjani's *Yaddashtha-ye Siyasi dar Vaghayeh-e Si-ye Tir-e 1320*. • **11**. Khamei, p. 950 • **12**. Author interview with Hedayat Matine-Daftary, London, 2011 • **13**. Wm. Roger Louis, *Britain and the Overthrow of Mossadegh*, from Gasiorowski and Byrne, p. 166 • **14**. Rahnama, p. 685 • **15**. Nejati, *Mossadegh*, p. 484 • **16**. MacLean, p. 274 • **17**. *Harvard Iranian Oral History Project*, see transcript of Habib Ladjevardi's interview with Sir George Middleton in November 1985 • **18**. Rahnama, Ali, *Nirooha-ye Mazhabi bar Bastar-e Harekat-e Nehzat-e Melli*, Gam-e No, 2005, p.815 • **19**. *Harvard Iranian Oral History Project*, transcript of Habib Ladjevardi's interview with Sir George Middleton in November 1985 • **20**. Ibid. • **21**. Henderson to State Department, February 22, 1953, FRUS p. 676 • **22**. Safari, Vol. 1, p. 746 • **23**. Mossadegh, Ghollamhossein, p. 65

## Thirteen: A Coup of his Own

1. *Ettela'at*, May 11, 1953 • 2. Rahnama, p. 940 • 3. Malcom Byrne, 'The Road to Intervention: Factors Influencing US Policy Toward Iran, 1945–1953', from Gasiorowski and Byrne, p. 223 •4. Woodhouse, p. 117 • 5. Dorril, p. 583 • 6. Love, p. 24 • 7. Sanjabi, *Omidha va Na-omidha*, p. 138 • 8. Editorial note regarding Dulles's press conference of July 28, 1953, FRUS, p. 740 • 9. In 1954, Wilber was commissioned to write a CIA internal history of the coup, 'Clandestine Service History, Overthrow of Premier Mossadeq of Iran, November 1952–August 1953', which the *New York Times* acquired and posted on its website in 2000, with some names omitted. This internal history, along with Kim Roosevelt's account of the operation, *Countercoup*, are the two main first-hand accounts of the American side of the operation, subsequently amplified by the interviews and research of Mark Gasiorowski. The internal history can be seen at: http://www.nytimes.com/library/world/mideast/041600iran-cia-index.html. My own efforts to gain access to MI6 records of events before and during the coup were rebuffed by the British authorities. • 10. Mark J. Gasiorowski, 'The 1953 Coup d'Etat Against Mosaddeq', from Gasiorowski and Byrne, p. 245 • 11. Record of a telephone conversation between Allen and Foster Dulles, July 24, 1953, FRUS, p. 738 • 12. Dorril, p. 588 • 13. Roosevelt, Kermit, *Countercoup*, McGraw, 1979, p. 146 •14. Roosevelt, *Arabs, Oil and History: The Story of the Middle East*, p. 103 • 15. Roosevelt, *Countercoup*, p. 110 • 16. Roosevelt, *Countercoup*, p. 154 • 17. *Harvard Iranian Oral History Project*, cit. Katouzian, *Musaddiq and the Struggle for Power in Iran*, p. 187 • 18. Katouzian, Introduction to Maleki, p. 104 • 19. *Be Revayat-e Asnad, Rohani-ye Mobarez, Ayatollah Seyyed Abolqassem Kashani* (Vol. 2) Markaz-e Barrassi-ye Asnad-e Tarikhi-ye Vezarat-e Ettela'at, 2000, p. 589 • 20. Rahnama, p. 972 • 21. Wilber, internal history, p. 38

## Fourteen: Mussy Duck Shoot

1. Safari, Vol. 1, p. 831 • 2. *Ettela'at*, August 16, 1953 • 3. Roosevelt, *Countercoup*, p. 173 • 4. Safari, Vol. 1, p. 833 • 5. Ibid., p. 834 • 6. *Bakhtar-e Emrooz*, August 16, 1953 • 7. Ghollamreza Nejati's interview with Ghollamhossein Sadiqi, from Nejati's *Jonbesh-e Melli*, p. 535

• **8**. *Ettela'at*, August 17, 1953 • **9**. Ibid. • **10**. Safari, Vol. 1, p. 859
• **11**. Henderson to State Department, August 18, 1953, FRUS, p. 752
• **12**. *Ettela'at*, August 17, 1953 • **13**. Mark J. Gasiorowski, 'Coup d'Etat
Against Mosaddeq', from Gasiorowski, and Byrne, p. 254 • **14**.
Rahnama, p. 1008 • **15**. Love, Kennett, *The American Role in the Pahlavi
Restoration on August 19, 1953*, n.p. • **16**. We will probably never have
a flawless account of the events of August 19, 1953. There are too
many competing testimonies, and there was a great deal of confu-
sion on the day. For my account, in addition to the different
American versions by Gasiorowski, Wilber, Roosevelt and Love,
I am indebted to various editions of the newspaper *Ettela'at*,
Ghollamreza Nejati's *Jonbesh-e Melli Shodan-e San'at-e Naft-e Iran va
Kudeta-ye 28 Mordad, 1332*, with its important eye-witness testimonies,
Nejati's interview with Ghollamhossein Sadiqi in the same book,
Ali Shayegan's telling of events in his son Ahmad's book *Seyyed Ali
Shayegan; Zendeginameh-ye Siyasi, Neveshtehha va Sokhanraniha*,
Muhammad-Ali Muvahed's magisterial *Khab-e Ashufteh-e Naft*, with
its extracts from Kazem Hassibi's unpublished diary, the reporter
Muhammad-Ali Safari's recollections in *Qalam va Siyasat*, as well
as my own conversations with Dr Hossein Fatemi's nephew Said
Fatemi and the political activist Nasser Takmil-Homayun in Tehran,
as well as Mossadegh's grandson Hedayat Matine-Daftary. • **17**.
Shahri, Vol. III, p. 411 • **18**. *Keyhan*, August 20, 1953 • **19**. Love, p. 39
• **20**. Mossadegh, Ghollamhossein, p. 121 • **21**. Ibid., p. 122

## Fifteen: Unperson

**1**. *New York Times*, August 22, 1953 • **2**. Pahlavi, Muhammad-Reza,
• **3**. Henderson to State Department, September 18, 1953, FRUS,
p. 799 • **4**. Memo by Byroade, August 21, 1953, FRUS, p. 760 • **5**.
For my account of Mossadegh's trials I have drawn heavily on
Buzorgmehr's three books about the proceedings (see Bibliography)
• **6**. *Khandaniha*, November 7, 1953 • **7**. *The Times*, Wednesday
December 2, 1953 • **8**. Diba, p. 190 • **9**. Memo by Falle, September
3, 1953, FO 371/104584 • **10**. Nejati, *Mossadegh*, Vol. 2, p. 301 • **11**.
*Le Monde*, December 9, 1965 • **12**. Sami'i, p. 125 • **13**. Torkaman,
Vol. 1, p. 274 • **14**. Ibid., p. 290 • **15**. Mossadegh, Ghollamhossein,
p. 147 • **16**. Sami'i, p. 100 • **17**. Ibid., p. 124 • **18**. Ibid., p. 347 • **19**.
Sami'i, p. 175

## Epilogue: A Movement in Men's Minds

1. Hiro, p. 106 • 2. Kinzer, p. 206. In the words of Maziar Behrooz, an Iranian scholar of the Tudeh, 'The Tudeh neither had the intention nor the power to oust Mosaddeq.' (Maziar Behrooz, 'Legacy of the Tudeh', from Gasiorowski and Byrne, p. 124) • 3. Roosevelt, *Countercoup*, p. 207 • 4. Parsi-Pour, unpublished article • 5. Avon, p. 36 • 6. Love, p. 41 • 7. *New York Times*, March 5, 1979 • 8. Author interview with Hedayat Matine-Daftary, London, 2011

# Bibliography

Abrahamian, Ervand, *Iran Between Two Revolutions*, Princeton University Press, 1982

Abramson, Rudy, *Spanning the Century: The Life of W. Averell Harriman, 1891–1986*, William Morrow, 1992

Acheson, Dean, *Present at the Creation*, Hamish Hamilton, 1970

Afrasiyabi, Bahram, *Khaterat va Mobarezat-e Doktor Hossein Fatemi*, Entesharat-e Sokhan, 1987

Afshar, Iraj (ed.) *Taqrirat-e Mossadegh dar Zendan*, compiled by Jalil Buzorgmehr, Entesharat-e Farhang-e Iranzamin, 1980

—— and Salour, Massoud (eds), *Rooznameh-ye Khaterat-e Ayn al-Saltaneh*, Entesharat-e Ferdowsi, 2001

—— (ed.) *Mossadegh va Masael-e Huquq va Siyasat*, Entesharat-e Sokhan, 2003

—— *Zendegi-ye Tufani: Khaterat-e Seyyed Hassan Taqizadeh*, Elmi, 2003

Agheli, Baqer (ed.), *Khaterat-e yek Nakhost Vazir, Doktor Ahmad Matine-Daftary*, Elmi, 1991

Amini, Iraj, *Bar Bal-a Bohran: Zendegi-ye Siyasi-ye Ali Amini*, Nashr–e Mahi, 2007

Arsanjani, Hassan, *Yaddashtha-ye Siyasi dar Vaghaye-ye Si-ye Tir-e, 1320*, Hirmand, 1987

Avery, Peter, *Modern Iran*, Ernest Benn, 1967

—— Gavin Hambly and Charles Melville (eds), *Cambridge History of Iran* (Vol. 7), Cambridge University Press, 1991

Avon, Earl of, *Memoirs of Sir Anthony Eden: Full Circle*, Cassell, 1960

*Azadi* (periodical, London)

Azimi, Fakhreddin, *Iran: The Crisis of Democracy*, I. B. Tauris, 1989

Bahar, Muhammad Taqi, *Tarikh-e Mokhtasar-e Ahzab-e Siyasi-ye Iran*, Mu'assesseh-ye Entesharat-e Amir Kabir, 1984

*Bakhtar-e Emrooz* (newspaper, Tehran)

Bamberg, J. H., *The History of the British Petroleum Company: The Anglo-Iranian Years* (Vol. 2), Cambridge University Press, 1994

Bamdad, Mehdi, *Sharh-e Hal-e Rejal-e Iran dar Gharn-e Davazdah, Sizdah va Chahardah-e Hejri*, Entesharat-e Zavar, 1978

Bani-Jamali, Ahmad, *Ashoub*, Nashrani, 2007

Basteh-Negar, *Muhammad Mossadegh va Hakemiyat-e Mellat*, Entesharat-e Qalam, 2002

Bayat, Abdolmajid, *Pages d'histoires de L'Iran: Mossadegh*, unpublished

Bayat, Mangol, *Iran's First Revolution: Shi'ism and the Constitutional Revolution of 1905–1909*, Oxford University Press, 1999

Behbudi, Soleiman, *Khaterat*, Tarh-e No, 1993

Bell, Gertrude, *Persian Pictures*, Ernest Benn, 1928

Bonakdarian, Mansour, *Britain and the Iranian Constitutional Revolution of 1906–1911*, Syracuse University Press, 2006

Borhan, Abdullah (ed.), *Ranjha-ye Siyasi-ye Doktor Muhammad Mossadegh*, compiled by Jalil Buzorgmehr, Saless, 1998

Browne, E. G., *The Persian Revolution of 1905–1909*, Cambridge University Press, 1910

Bullard, Reader, *Letters from Tehran*, I. B. Tauris, 1991

Buzorgmehr, Jalil, *Doktor Muhammad Mossadegh dar Dadgah-e Tajdid-e Nazar-e Nezami*, Sherkat-e Sahami-ye Enteshar, 1986

—— *Muhammad Mossadegh dar Mahkame-ye Nezami*, Entesharat-e Nilufar, 1990

—— *Mossadegh dar Mahkameh-ye Nezami*, Entesharat-e Doostan, 1990

—— *Khaterat az Doktor Muhammad Mossadegh*, Entesharat-e Nahid, 1994

—— *Doktor Muhammad Mossadegh va Residegi-ye Farjami dar Divan-e Keshvar*, Sherkat-e Sahami-ye Enteshar, 1998

—— *Na-Goftehha va Kam Goftehha az Doktor Muhammad Mossadegh va Nehzat-e Melli-ye Iran*, Nashr-e Ketab-e Nader, 2000

Buzorg Omid, Abolhassan, *Az Mast ke Bar Mast*, Tehran, 1956

Byron, Robert, *The Road to Oxiana*, Macmillan, 1937

Churchill, Winston S., *The World Crisis, 1911–1914*, Thornton Butterworth Ltd, 1923

Copeland, Miles, *The Real Spy World*, Weidenfeld & Nicolson, 1974

Costello, Francis J., *Enduring the Most*, Brandon, 1995

Cottam, Richard W., *Iran and the United States: A Cold War Case Study*, University of Pittsburgh Press, 1988

Curzon, George N., *Persia and the Persian Question*, Frank Cass and Co. Ltd, 1966

Dabashi, Hamid, *Iran: A People Interrupted*, The New Press, 2007

Destree, Annette, *Les Fonctionnaires Belges au service de la Perse (1898–1915)*, Acta Iranica, Series III, Volume VI, Bibliotheque Pahlavi, 1976

Diba, Farhad, *Mossadegh: A Political Biography*, Croom Helm, 1986

Dorril, Stephen, *MI6: Fifty Years of Special Operations*, Fourth Estate, 2000

Elm, Mostafa, *Oil, Power and Principle*, Syracuse University Press, 1992

Elwell-Sutton, L.P., *Persian Oil: A Study in Power Politics*, Lawrence & Wishart, 1955

Enayat, Hamid, *British Public Opinion and the Persian Oil Crisis, 1951–54*, unpublished thesis submitted to the University of London, May 1958

Esfandiari Bakhtiari, Sorayya, *Le Palais des solitudes*, Michel Lafon, 1991

Eshraghi, F., *Anglo-Soviet Occupation of Iran in August 1941*, Middle Eastern Studies, XX, 1, January 1984

Ettehadieh (Nezam-Mafi), Mansoureh, *Inja Tehran ast*, Nashr-e Tarikh-e Iran, 1998

—— *Abdolhossein Mirza Farmanfarma, Zaman va Karnameh-ye Siyasi va Ejtema'i*, Ketab-e Siyamak and Nashr-e Tarikh-e Iran, 2004

—— *Zanani ke zir-e Maghnaeh Kolahdari Nemudeand; Zendegi-ye Malek Taj Khanom Najm al-Saltaneh*, Nashr-e Tarikh-e Iran, 2009

—— and Bahman Farman (eds), *Farmanfarmaian, Muhammad Vali Mirza, Az Roozegar Rafteh Hekayat*, Ketab-e Siyamak, 2003

—— and Siroos Sa'advandian (eds), *Afzal al-Tavarikh*, Nashr-e Tarikh-e Iran, 1982

—— *Amar-e Dar-ul Khalafeh-ye Tehran*, Nashr-e Tarikh-e Iran, 1989

*Ettela'at newspaper*, Tehran)

Farahmand, Jalal, *Valigari-ye Mossadegh (1): Fars, Tarikh-e Mu'asser-e Iran*, autumn 2007; (2): *Azerbaijan*, winter 2007.

Farmanfarmaian, Manucher, *Az Tehran Ta Karakas: Naft va Siyasat da Iran*, Nashr-e Tarikh-e Iran, 1994

Farmanfarmaian, Manucher and Roxane, *Blood and Oil: Memoirs of a Persian Prince*, Random House, 1997

Fateh, Mustafa, *Panjah Sal-e Naft-e Iran*, Payam, 1979

Ferrier, R.W., *History of the British Petroleum Company* (Vol. 1): *The Developing Years, 1901–1932*, Cambridge University Press, 1982

Feuvrier, Dr, *Trois ans à la cour de Perse*, F. Juven (no date)

Ford, Alan W., *The Anglo-Iranian Oil Dispute of 1951–52: A Study of the Role of Law in the Relations of States*, University of California Press, 1954

Foreign Ministry Archives, Tehran

Gasiorowski, Mark J., and Malcolm Byrne (eds), *Muhammad Mosaddeq and the 1953 Coup in Iran*, Syracuse University Press, 2004

Ghani, Cyrus, *Iran and the Rise of Reza Shah: From Qajar Collapse to Pahlavi Power*, I. B. Tauris, 1998

Golban, Muhammad, *Dar Ayeneh-ye Tarikh: Khaterat-e Siyasi-ye Abbas Khalili, Modir-e Rooznameh-ye Eqdam*, Entesharat-e Anousheh, 2001

Graves, Philip, *Life of Sir Percy Cox*, Hutchinson, 1941

Harvard Iranian Oral History Project

Hedayat, Mehdi-Gholi (Mokhbar al-Saltaneh), *Khaterat va Khatarat*, Entesharat-e Ketabforoushi-ye Zarrat, 1965

Hiro, Dilip, *Iran Under the Ayatollahs*, Routledge, 1987

Hobsbawm, E. J., *The Age of Empire (1875–1914)*, Weidenfeld & Nicolson, 1987

Hourani, Albert, *A History of the Arab Peoples*, Faber and Faber, 1991

Jefferey, Keith, *MI6: The History of the Secret Intelligence Service, 1909–1949*, Bloomsbury, 2010

Kashani, Seyyed Abolqassem, *Be Revayat-e Asnad, Rohani-ye Mobarez, Ayatollah Seyyed Abolqassem Kashani* (Vol. 2), Markaz-e Barrassi-ye Asnad-e Tarikhi-ye Vezarat-e Ettela'at, 2000

Katouzian, Homa, *Musaddiq and the Struggle for Power in Iran*, I. B. Tauris, 1999

—— *State and Society in Iran*, I. B. Tauris, 2000

Katouzian, Homa (ed.), *Khaterat-e Siyasi-ye Khalil Maleki*, Entesharat-e Ravaq, 1981

Kay-Ustuvan, Hossein, *Siyaset-e Muvazeneh-e Manfi dar Majles-e Chahardahom*, Entesharat-e Rooznameh-e Muzaffar, 1948

*Khandaniha*, periodical, Tehran

Khamei, Anvar, *Khaterat-e Siyasi*, Guftar, 1993

Kianuri, Nur al-Din, *Khaterat*, Entesharat-e Ettela'at, 1993

Kinzer, Stephen, *All the Shah's Men*, John Wiley, 2003

Lambton, Ann K. S., *Landlord and Peasant in Persia*, Oxford University Press, 1953

—— *Qajar Persia*, I. B. Tauris, 1987

Lapping, Brian, *End of Empire*, Granada, 1985

Lees-Milne, James, *Harold Nicolson: A Biography* (Vol. I), 1886–1929, Chatto & Windus, 1980

Lenczowski, George, *Russia and the West in Iran*, Greenwood, 1968

*Les Nouvelles* (periodical, Paris)

Lorimer, J.G., *Gazetteer of the Persian Gulf, Oman and Central Arabia*, Government of India, 1908

Love, Kennett, *The American Role in the Pahlavi Restoration on 19 August 1953* (unpublished), 1960

MacLean, Fitzroy, *Eastern Approaches*, Jonathan Cape, 1949

Makki, Hossein, *Tarikh-e Bist Sal-e Iran*, Nashr-e Ketabforoushi-ye Muhammad-Ali Elmi, 1944

—— *Doktor Mossadegh va Notghha-ye Tarikhi-ye vey dar Dowre-ye Panjom va Shishom-e Taghniniyeh*, Sazman-e Entesharat-e Javidan, 1979

—— *Ketab-e Siyah*, Bongah-e Tarjomeh va Nashr-e Ketab, 1981

—— *Vaghayeh-ye Si-ye Tir*, Bongah-e Tarjomeh va Nashr-e Ketab, 1981

—— *Khaterat-e Siyasi*, Elmi, 1989

Maleki, Khalil, *Khaterat-e Siyasi*, Entesharat-e Raraq, 1981

Matine-Daftary, Hedayat (ed.), *Azadi*, Vol. 2, issues 26 and 27, 2001

McGhee, George, *Envoy to the Middle World: Adventures in Diplomacy*, Harper & Row, 1983

Milani, Abbas, *The Shah*, Palgrave Macmillan, 2011

Moradi-Nia, Muhammad-Javad (ed.), *Khaterat-e Seyyed Muhammad Kamare'i* (Vol. 1), Nashr va Pazohesh-e Shirazeh, 2003

Morgan, David, *Ann K. S. Lambton (1912–2008) and Persian Studies*, Journal of the Royal Asiatic Society, Series 3, 21, 1, 2011

Mossadegh, Ghollamhossein, *Dar Kenar-e Pedaram*, Mossadegh, Mu'assesseh-ye Khadamat-e Farhangi-ye Rassa, 1990

Mossadegh, Muhammad, *Le Testament en droit musulman (Secte Chyite)*, Georges Cres, 1914

—— *Khaterat va Ta'limat*, Entesharat-e Elmi, 1986

—— *Notghha va Maktubat-e Doktor Mossadegh dar Dowreh-ye Shanzdahom*, Entesharat-e Mossadegh (no date)

Mostowfi, Abdullah, *Sharh-e Zendegani-ye Man*, Entesharat-e Zavvar, 2005

Muvahed, Muhammad-Ali, *Khab-e Ashufteh-e Naft: Doktor Mossadegh va Nehzat-e Melli-ye Iran*, Nashr-e Karnameh, 2005


Najmi, Nasser, *Mossadegh: Mobarez-e Buzorg*, Tehran, 1980

National Documents Organisation, (Sazman-e Asnad-e Melli)

Nejati, Ghollamreza, *Jonbesh-e Melli Shudan-e San'at-e Naft-e Iran va Kudeta-ye 28 Mordad, 1332*, Sherkat-e Sahami-ye Enteshar, 1989

—— *Mossadegh: Salha-ye Mobarezeh va Moghavemat*, Mu'assesseh-ye Khadamat va Farhangi-ye Rassa, 1998

Pahlavi, Ashraf, *Faces in a Mirror*, Prentice-Hall, 1980

Pahlavi, Muhammad-Reza, *Mission for My Country*, Hutchinson, 1960

Parsi–Pour, Kamal, *The Soviet Union and Iran (1941–1954): A Survey of Archival Repositories in the Russian Federation* (unpublished)

*Ra'ad* (periodical)

Rahnama, Ali, *Nirooha-ye Mazhabi bar Bastar-e Harekat-e Nehzat-e Melli*, Gam-e No, 2005

Ramazani, R.K., *Iran's Foreign Policy, 1941–1973*, Charlottesville, Virginia, 1975

Rasoolipour, Morteza (ed.), *Na-Gofteh-ha az Dowlat-e Doktor Mossadegh, Dastneveshtehha-ye Muhammad Ebrahim Amir-Teimur (Kalali)*, Mu'assesseh-ye Mutale'at-e Tarikh-e Mu'asser-e Iran, 2001

Richard, Yann, *L'Iran: Naissance d'une république islamique*, Éditions de La Martinière, 2006

Ronaldshay, Earl of, *Life of Lord Curzon*, Ernest Benn, 1928

Roosevelt, Kermit, *Arabs, Oil and History: The Story of the Middle East*, Harper and Bros, 1949

—— *Countercoup*, McGraw, 1979

*Rooznameh-ye Majles* (periodical, Tehran)

Sackville-West, Vita, *Passenger to Tehran*, Hogarth Press, 1926

Safari, Muhammad-Ali, *Ghalam va Siyasat: Az Estefa-ye Reza Shah ta Soghut-e Mossadegh*, Namak, 1992

Sanjabi, Karim, *Omidha va Na-omidha: Khaterat-e Siyasi-ye Doktor Karim Sanjabi*, Entesharat-e Jephe, 1989

—— *Khaterat-e Siyasi*, Seda-ye Mu'asser, 2002

Sami'i, Shireen, *Dar Khalvat-e Mossadegh*, Nashr-e Saless, 2007

Shahri, Jafar, *Tehran-e Qadim*, Moin, 2004

Shayegan, Ali, *Zendeginameh-ye Siyasi, Neveshteha va Sokhanraniha*, Agah, 2006

Shuster, Morgan, *The Strangling of Persia*, T. Fisher Unwin, 1912

Skrine, Claremont, *World War in Iran*, London, 1962

Tabrizi, Javad, *Asrar-e Tarikhi-ye Komiteh-ye Mojazat*, Iran va Eslam, 1983

Torkaman, Muhammad, *Namehha-ye Doktor Mossadegh* (Vols 1 & 2), Nashr-e Hezaran, 1995, 1998

Walters, Vernon, *Silent Missions*, Doubleday, 1978

Wilber, Donald, *Riza Shah Pahlavi: The Resurrection and Reconstruction of Iran, 1878–1944*, Exposition Press, 1975

—— 'Clandestine Service History, Overthrow of Premier Mossadeq of Iran, November 1952 – August 1953, CIA internal history, 1954

Waterfield, Gordon, *Professional Diplomat: Sir Percy Loraine of Kirkharle Bt, 1880–1961*, John Murray, 1973

Woodhouse, C.M., *Something Ventured*, Granada, 1982

Wright, Denis, *The English Amongst the Persians*, Heinemann, 1977

—— *The Persians Amongst the English*, I.B. Tauris, 1985

—— *Britain and Iran (1790–1980): The Collected Essays of Sir Denis Wright*, The Iran Society, 2003

Wynn, Antony, *Persia in the Great Game*, John Murray, 2003

# Illustrations

13. An anti-Mossadegh crowd. Courtesy of the Institute for Iranian Contemporary Historical Studies.

14. Ayatollah Abolqassem Kashani © Dmitri Kessel/Time & Life Pictures/Getty Images.

15. General Fazlollah Zahedi © Carl Mydans/Time & Life Pictures/Getty Images.

16. Shah Muhammad-Reza Pahlavi and Queen Sorayya © Keystone-France/Gamma-Keystone via Getty Images.

17. Shah-loyalists celebrate the success of the coup atop a tank © Bettmann/CORBIS.

18. Winston Churchill, Anthony Eden, Foster Dulles and Dwight D. Eisenhower © National Park Service/Dwight D. Eisenhower Library.

19. Mossadegh in his aba. Courtesy of the Institute for Iranian Contemporary Historical Studies.

# Index